*The Mitchell Beazley pocket guide to*

# Butterflies

Paul Whalley

Mitchell Beazley

# Nomenclature

The common names of butterflies differ not only between countries but often within the same country. For example, the Camberwell beauty is also known as Le Morio, Antiope and Mourning cloak, but its scientific name (*Nymphalis antiopa*) is the same all over the world. There are strict international rules governing the formation of scientific names, which consist of two parts for each species: the first part is the *genus* name, and the second is the *specific* name. The Large tortoiseshell, *Nymphalis polychloros*, shares the same genus name as the Camberwell beauty, indicating a closer relationship than to the Small tortoiseshell, *Aglais urticae*, although all three species are in the same family, Nymphalidae.

Sometimes local populations of the same species differ slightly, giving rise to a third, *subspecific*, name. The Small tortoiseshell in Corsica and Sardinia (*A. urticae ichnusa*) is brighter than the nominate subspecies (*A. urticae urticae*). Individual variation may also occur in the same population, and this is marked by form, variety or aberration names.

# Abbreviations

For abbreviated place names, see explanation under Distribution (p 4).

| | | | | | |
|---|---|---|---|---|---|
| D | distribution | Gen | generation (number of broods in a year) | mts | mountains |
| esp | especially | | | sp(p) | species (plural) |
| f. | form | | | subsp | subspecies |
| FP | Foodplant (of caterpillar) | hwing | hindwing | var. | variety |
| | | incl | including | WS | wingspan* |
| fwing | forewing | m | metre | ♂ | male |
| | | mm | millimetre | ♀ | female |

*The wingspans given in the text are based on twice the length of one forewing, measured along the costa (front margin) from the base to the apex, plus the width across the body.

# Symbols

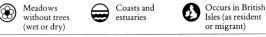

| | | |
|---|---|---|
| Coniferous woods | Mountains | Heathland |
| Broadleafed woods | Hills and slopes | Moorland |
| Meadows without trees (wet or dry) | Coasts and estuaries | Occurs in British Isles (as resident or migrant) |
| Parkland, meadows with trees | Agricultural land and hedgerows | Protected by law in some countries |
| Marshland, including rivers and lakes | Chalk and limestone areas | |

**Editor** Michele Staple **Designers** Hazel West and Jacquie Gulliver
**Illustrator** Richard Lewington / The Garden Studio

Edited and designed by Mitchell Beazley Publishers
part of Reed International Books Ltd, Michelin House,
81 Fulham Road, London SW3 6RB

Reprinted 1982, 1983, 1984, 1987, 1988, 1990, 1991, 1992

ISBN 0 85533 348 0

Colour reproduction by Gilchrist Brothers Ltd, Leeds
Produced by Mandarin Offset
Printed in Malaysia

# Contents



# Introduction

Should a reason be needed for another book on butterflies, then surely it is the butterflies themselves that provide it. Their beautiful colours add richness to the countryside and offer hours of fascination to the butterfly watcher. There are about 16,000 species of butterflies in the world (contrast with about 150,000 moths), of which about 400 occur in Europe. This book aims to cover all those European species, and includes some new species which have not previously appeared in a field guide.

All the illustrations are painted life-size (with the exception of the Monarch) from actual specimens and are technically accurate. Most species are illustrated by showing an upperside and underside view, and where possible both sexes are depicted if they differ appreciably. Some subspecies are also illustrated if the species is known to form distinct local populations.

# How to use this book

How to use this book is for the most part self-evident: the important thing is that you use it in the field to identify living butterflies, and not at home on dead specimens. The book has been specially designed for ease of reference, so that similar butterflies are grouped together for comparison, and the text for each species appears on the same page as the illustration—this can prove invaluable if your butterfly is moving restlessly about!

All the upperside views of the butterflies are in the "set" position (with the hind margin of the forewing at right angles to the body) to show maximum detail. In the field the butterfly rarely sits like this, and often the pattern is partially obscured by overlapping wings. Diagnostic characters are pointed out in the captions, and the text enlarges on the habitat (indicated by symbols), behaviour and any peculiarities of that species. The information summarized at the end gives the wingspan (*WS*), flight period (*Flight*), number of generations or broods in a year (*Gen*), the foodplant of the caterpillar (*FP*—which differs from the foodplant of the adult) and distribution (*D*—see p 4). Wingspan measurements should only be used as an approximate guide to size and are often slightly larger than the wingspans of the illustrated specimens to allow for the different angles at which the wings may be held. The flight period gives the earliest month that the butterfly may be seen; in the north it usually emerges later and has fewer generations than those which breed in warmer, southern parts. Often only principal foodplants are mentioned under *FP* as lack of space precludes giving a fuller list.

# Distribution

The countries and mountain ranges that are listed under the distribution of each species are featured on this map of Europe. All the butterflies that occur in this region, from the northern limits of the Arctic Circle to the Mediterranean coastline (including the main islands but not North Africa) and eastwards to the Russian frontier, are included in this book. Many of these species occur further east in Asia and/or have ranges which vary from year to year, especially at the extreme edges; others may be confined strictly to mountains. For these reasons, and also through lack of information in many cases, the distribution given for each species should only be used as a broad guide. Where possible, a complete list of all the countries is provided, but sometimes a more general area, such as SE Europe, is given. It is unlikely that a butterfly will be equally common over the whole of this area; instead it is often described as "locally common", i.e. common in a number of small, restricted areas.

If distribution is marked simply as Europe, then the butterfly is common throughout. Where Britain is specifically excluded from a range, it is safe to assume that Ireland is also, unless otherwise stated.

**Abbreviated countries**
**Czech** Czechoslovakia
**Scand** Scandinavia; this includes Denmark, Norway, Sweden, Finland
**Scot** Scotland
**Switz** Switzerland

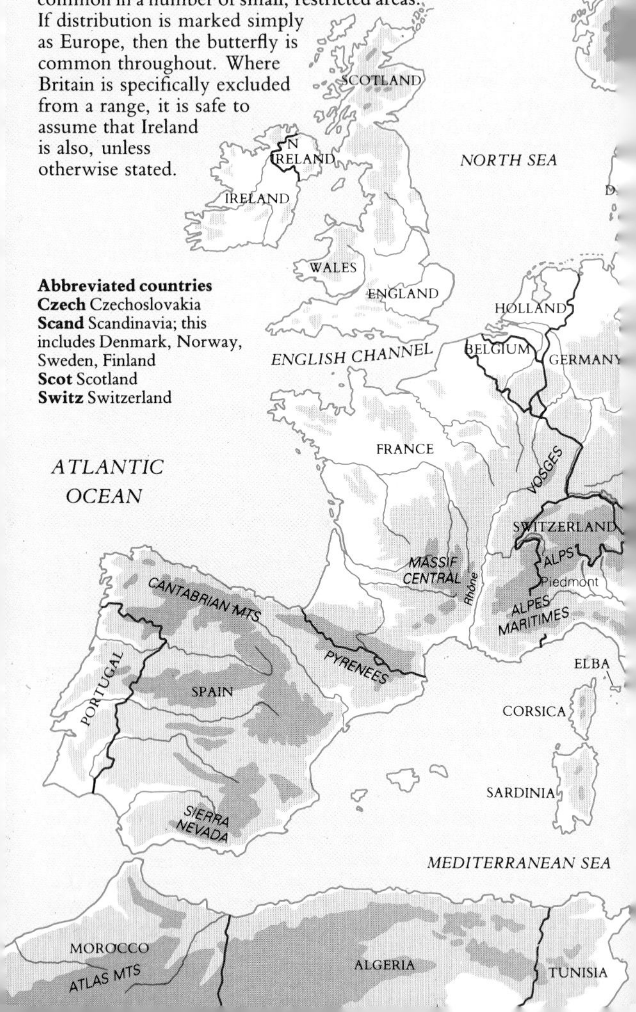
SCOTLAND
N IRELAND
IRELAND
NORTH SEA
WALES
ENGLAND
HOLLAND
ENGLISH CHANNEL
BELGIUM
GERMANY
FRANCE
ATLANTIC OCEAN
VOSGES
SWITZERLAND
MASSIF CENTRAL
Rhône
ALPS
Piedmont
ALPES MARITIMES
CANTABRIAN MTS
PYRENEES
PORTUGAL
SPAIN
ELBA
CORSICA
SARDINIA
SIERRA NEVADA
MEDITERRANEAN SEA
MOROCCO
ATLAS MTS
ALGERIA
TUNISIA

VEGIAN
SEA
Arctic Circle
1000m
200m
FINLAND
RWAY
SWEDEN
BALTIC
SEA
RK
RUSSIA (USSR)
POLAND
SUDETEN
MTS
TATRA
MTS
CZECHOSLOVAKIA
CARPATHIANS
AUSTRIA
HUNGARY
ROMANIA
Danube
BLACK
SEA
YUGOSLAVIA
Dalmatia
APENNINES
ADRIATIC SEA
BALKANS
BULGARIA
ITALY
ALBANIA
GREECE
TURKEY
SICILY
CRETE

# The structure of a butterfly

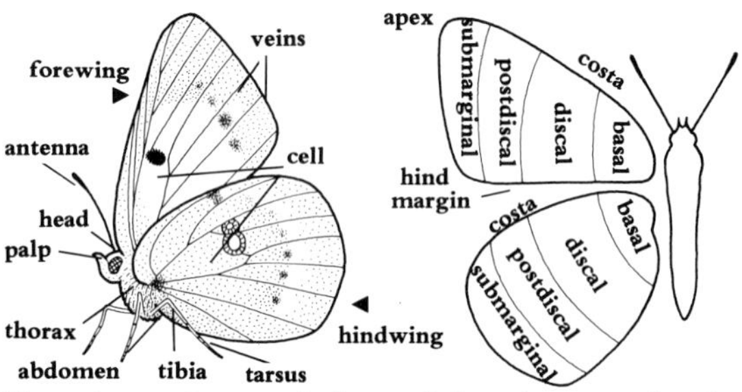
forewing
veins
antenna
cell
head
palp
thorax
abdomen
tibia
tarsus
hindwing
apex
submarginal
postdiscal
discal
costa
basal
hind margin
costa
basal
discal
postdiscal
submarginal

The colour, pattern and shape of the wings are of major importance in identification, and in order to draw attention to diagnostic features it is convenient to divide the wing into various areas as shown in the figure. The body to which the wings are attached has a hard outer covering (chitin) and consists of three parts: the head, thorax and abdomen. The head bears the major sense organs and a specially adapted feeding structure (the proboscis) characteristic of butterflies. The proboscis is a long curled tongue which, unlike other insects, coils up underneath the head like a spring. Through this the butterflies suck up liquids such as nectar, sap, juice from rotting fruit and also less salubrious substances like the liquid which exudes from decomposing animal corpses.

The thorax is the broadest and most muscular part of the body, and this bears the wings (two pairs) and three pairs of jointed legs. Each wing has a series of veins, the arrangement of which is typical for the species. The central area of the wing is vein-free, and is known as the cell.

Covering the whole of the wings and body are fine scales which give the butterfly its colour and pattern. The colours are produced either by pigments in the scales (as in the whites and reds) or by the structural surface of the scales reflecting certain wavelengths of light. The blues and metallic hues are produced in this way. The arrangement of the scales gives rise to the intricate patterns which may camouflage the butterfly when at rest (like the underside of the Comma) or frighten off small predators (like the startling eye-spots on the upperside of the Peacock).

Colour and pattern are also important in the recognition of one sex by the other. Certain scales (androconia) on male butterflies are specially modified to release a scent attractive to females, and these scales may by grouped together to form a sex brand. Where the sexes are similar in appearance, and sex brands are not obvious, females are generally distinguished from males by their slightly larger size and fatter abdomens.

# Life history

Most people know that there are four stages to a butterfly's life—the egg, caterpillar, chrysalis or pupa and adult—but information on the first three stages is incomplete for many species. The following account should be regarded as a broad outline only; for advice on eggs and rearing caterpillars, you should consult some of the references on p 164.

Butterflies lay eggs that are variable in shape and may be delicately patterned or ribbed. Often the eggs are stuck on to the foodplant of the caterpillar, but a few species scatter their eggs in the grass. When the caterpillar hatches from the egg, it consumes the shell and then proceeds to feed almost continuously on the leaves or flowers of the plant. To enlarge, it moults its skin, increasing its size after each moult. A caterpillar will usually moult four times, after which it stops feeding and looks for a suitable place to fix itself before pupation. The caterpillar then sheds its skin for a fifth time, only on this occasion a relatively immobile structure, the chrysalis, is produced. Although called the resting stage, inside the chrysalis there is tremendous activity as the caterpillar changes (by a process called metamorphosis) into the butterfly. Eventually the chrysalis splits and the crumpled insect emerges. After a short rest period to allow its wings to expand and dry, the fully formed butterfly flies off to feed and find a mate, thereby restarting the whole cycle.

## Caterpillars

You will find examples of caterpillars given with the introductions to each family. Basically there are two main types: the cylindrical, worm-like ones and the woodlouse or slug-like ones. All produce silk from special glands below the head, and this silk may be used in different ways according to the species. Some caterpillars are gregarious and spin a large web from this silk, in which they live for the greater part of their lives. Others may draw the ends of leaves or blades of grass together with silk, so forming an effective shelter. Caterpillars may take anything from two weeks to two years to develop into a butterfly, during which time they are vulnerable to attack by both predators and parasites. Caterpillars of the Large white, a pest of cabbages, are parasitized by tiny wasps, and these wasps probably provide the best form of control of this prolific species. Each species has its own method of survival: some are extremely well camouflaged, while others are colourful but distasteful, and may even utilize toxins in the foodplant to make themselves poisonous to predators.

## Migration

It is now widely accepted that butterflies are capable of long-distance migration, although for a long time it was thought that these insects were far too frail. The best-known European migrants are the Painted lady, Red admiral, Clouded yellow and Large white, and large-scale invasions of Britain by these butterflies take place every year. Their main breeding grounds are in the Mediterranean, and in the spring they move north, breeding en route, so that individuals appearing in northern Europe are often the offspring of those that initially started out. The Red admiral is thought to be unable to survive the harsh northern winter, and each year the northern population is replaced by fresh migrations from the south. Unlike birds, migration of butterflies is one-way, although there is some evidence to support a partial return migration. Many more observations on migration are needed before we can make any more definite statements.

## Butterfly behaviour

Only in recent years have we discovered that the apparent aimless fluttering of the butterfly may in fact be far more purposeful than we realized. Careful observation and experimentation have shown that many species have a complex daily life with display flights, territorial disputes and feeding habits that follow very definite patterns. In courtship display, not only are the colours and patterns significant in attracting the opposite sex, but the butterflies also release scents called pheromones to stimulate their mates. The encounter leading up to mating may be brief or involve a complicated display flight, with the male fluttering around the female until she responds. Pairing takes place with the tips of the abdomens linked as shown in the figure. This position has given rise to many accounts of two-headed butterflies! Territorial behaviour has been demonstrated in the male Speckled wood, which will patrol an area of sunlight in a wood and chase out any intruding males. How males recognize intruders, and how they mark out their territory (by scent-marking?) are areas of behaviour which are still not fully understood.

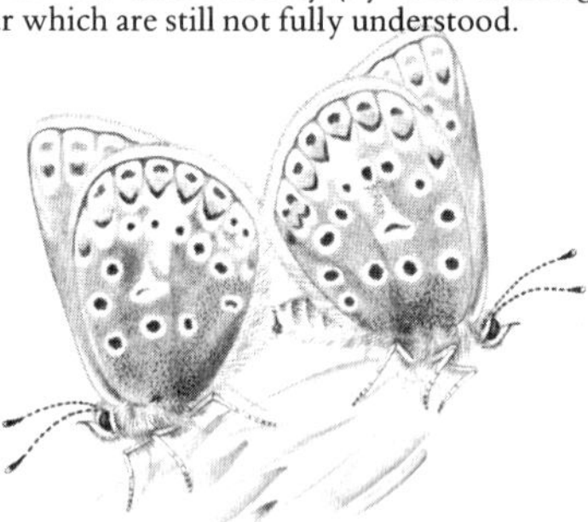

Mating position of the Common blue (*Polyommatus icarus*)

The reason why butterflies prefer some flowers to others may be determined by the length of their proboscis, which has to be able to probe far enough into the flower to obtain the nectar. Females also need to be able to recognize the correct plants on which to lay their eggs, and recent studies indicate that the female probably responds to a chemical stimulus in the plant. It is clear from the many gaps in our knowledge of butterfly behaviour that much more research needs to be done.

## Butterfly watching

Like birdwatching, butterfly watching requires patience and plenty of practice. Do not expect to identify all the butterflies you see on your first serious attempt, although in Britain this will not be too difficult as there are only some 50 to 60 species. Familiarize yourself with the main characteristics of each family, so that you will know to which section of the book you should refer. Wherever you are watching them, it is always a good idea to make a note of the date, time, locality and any nearby plants, as these may give you clues to their identity and be useful later.

To get close to the butterfly, you will have to adopt a stealthy approach, taking care not to let your shadow fall on it. Examine its markings closely, and try to match them against the illustrated specimens in the book. Binoculars or a short-focus optical telescope will enable you to see its pattern in much greater detail, which can be important when the difference between two species depends on the presence or absence of a particular spot! Remember too that the species you see is far more likely to be a common one than a very rare one. Certain closely allied species will prove almost impossible to identify in the field, and may only be distinguished with certainty by dissection. Leave these to the entomologists. If you want to pursue the classification of butterflies in more depth, then you should consult the guide by Dr Higgins (see p 164).

Photography is an ideal way of "collecting" butterflies. Try to take a photograph of both wing surfaces and estimate its wing-span by measuring the plant on which it was resting. If your butterfly refuses to keep still long enough for you to identify it, then it may be possible to catch it with a fine net (*not* the type used for shrimping) without harming it. Place it in a covered jar with a twig for it to rest on, and hopefully it will sit still. Don't forget to release your butterfly as soon as you have examined it. Unfortunately some species are so active that they will not settle, and these are better set free before they seriously damage themselves. If too many scales are rubbed off the wings, then the butterfly may lose its ability to fly.

The study of butterfly behaviour is still at an early stage, and there is a great deal of opportunity for the amateur to make new and useful observations. Get to know the butterflies in your area: find out when the adults emerge, at what time during the day they appear, how they are affected by weather, and whether they always feed on the same type or colour of flower. (You can tell if a butterfly is feeding by watching its proboscis unfurl and delve into the flower-head.) We do not know where butterflies roost at night, how they "defend" their territories, or how often they change their feeding habits. Butterflies can be encouraged to visit your garden by planting flowers such as buddleia and Michaelmas daisies, and here you can watch them at your leisure.

Distribution maps of most British and European butterflies have been published by the Institute of Terrestrial Ecology (Monks Wood Experimental Station, Abbots Ripton, Huntingdon, PE17 2LS), but these are subject to change as populations disappear from one area and colonize another. If you are keen to conserve the butterflies in your area, then you might like to assist in the habitat surveys being conducted by the British Butterfly Conservation Society (Tudor House, Quorn, Nr Loughborough, Leics LE12 8AD). On a wider basis, the Societas Europaea Lepidopterologica (℅ Landessammlungen für Naturkunde, Erbprinzenstrasse 13, D–7500 Karlsruhe 1, West Germany) has members all over Europe who are actively interested in the study of butterflies and moths.

## Conservation

Most of the landscape we see today has been altered, whether by major geological events or by human activities. Destruction of natural habitats has been accelerated over the last century with the expansion of industry and the introduction of modern farming methods, and there has been a consequent disappearance of many forms of wildlife. Butterflies are particularly sensitive to environmental change, and the extinction of certain species in Britain such as the Large copper and the Black-veined white must be partly attributed to loss of habitat.

While we cannot halt progress, we should at least try to temper it so that some parts of our environment are preserved. Human needs should be carefully weighed against those of the environment, and with sensible planning it should not be too difficult to arrive at a natural compromise. For example, farmers could leave a small area of land unploughed, and instead of developing marginal land, the farmer should be paid by the community for it to be left in a wild state. Excessive use of fertilizers and insecticides should also be discouraged. Very few butterflies are harmful and yet they are often the victims of chemical sprays intended for crop pests.

Some countries protect endangered species or their subspecies, and these are denoted by a symbol in the book. Protection of a species from over-enthusiastic collectors is to be commended, but in practical terms it is often insufficient to save the species unless its habitat also receives some measure of protection.

# **Skippers** Hesperiidae

There are about 40 species of skippers in Europe, eight of which occur in Britain. They have a rapid whirring or skipping flight and are especially active on warm, sunny days. Structurally they are very primitive butterflies with short, broad bodies and even broader heads bearing two widely separated pointed antennae. At rest they hold their wings like a moth—either spread out flat or the fore- and hindwings at separate angles to each other.

***Grizzled skipper caterpillar***

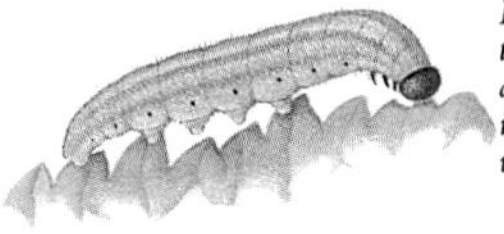

*Feeds on leaves, pulling them together to form a tube of silk in which it later pupates. Overwinters as a pupa.*

## Large grizzled skipper

## *Pyrgus alveus*

♂

***Hindwing*** *has faint white spots*

***Underside hindwing*** *olive-brown to green with white marks*

♂

A variable-patterned butterfly with many subspecies. It is often confused with the Safflower skipper (p 13), but may be distinguished by the more widely spaced white spots in the cell of the forewing. Widespread and found on flowery slopes between 900 and 1,800 m. *WS:* 22–32 mm; *Flight:* June–Aug; *Gen:* 1–2; *FP:* Cinquefoil (*Potentilla*), Rock rose (*Helianthemum*), Blackberry (*Rubus*); *D:* Europe (not Britain, Denmark, Holland, N Scand). ***P. warrenensis*** (Warren's skipper) is similar but smaller with tiny white markings. *WS:* 18–24 mm; *D:* Alps (France, Switz).

## Grizzled skipper

## *P. malvae*

♂

*White markings well defined on both wings; margins alternately marked light and dark*

***Hindwing*** *has clear row of small postdiscal spots*

***Underside*** *green-brown varying to yellowish*

♂

In Britain the range of the Grizzled skipper is chiefly confined to central and southern England, with a few scattered colonies in Wales. It flies rapidly and close to the ground over bogs and flowery meadows up to 2,000 m, pausing to rest on bare soil rather than flowers with its wings held erect over its back. A second generation usually occurs in the warmer parts of southern Europe, but rarely further north. The Grizzled skipper is one of the few British species to overwinter as a pupa. *WS:* 22–26 mm; *Flight:* Apr–June, July–Aug; *Gen:* 2; *FP:* Wild strawberry (*Fragaria vesca*), Cinquefoil (*Potentilla*), Mallow (*Malva*); *D:* Europe (but not N Scand, Ireland, Scotland).

## Oberthur's grizzled skipper

### *P. armoricanus*

♂
Uppers resemble P. alveus; darker when first emerged
Hindwing markings pale but distinct
Underside hindwing has large central spot

Widespread throughout Europe but commoner in the south, Oberthur's grizzled skipper feeds on flowers of dry, hilly scrubland up to 1,200 m. The second generation, found only in southern parts, has a smaller wingspan. *WS:* 24–28 mm; *Flight:* May–June, Aug–Sept; *Gen:* 2; *FP:* Wild strawberry (*Fragaria vesca*), Cinquefoil (*Potentilla*); *D:* Europe (not Britain, Holland, most of Scandinavia except for few records in Denmark).

## Foulquier's grizzled skipper

### *P. foulquieri*

♂
♂
Underside hindwing more white on wing than in P. alveus
Hindwing pale marks form band across wing

The female often has a pale yellow suffusion over the upperside and smaller white markings. As with other grizzled skippers, Foulquier's grizzled skipper is extremely difficult to identify in the field, and a closer examination is nearly always required. It is locally common in southern Europe on mountain slopes up to 2,000 m. A smaller, yellower subspecies occurs in Italy. *WS:* 26–30 mm; *Flight:* July–Aug; *Gen:* 1; *FP:* Cinquefoil (*Potentilla*); *D:* S and C France, N Spain, Italy.

## Olive skipper

### *P. serratulae*

♂
♂
Forewing spots generally small
Hindwing almost unmarked, spots indistinct
Underside hindwing olive-green to grey-green

Rarely seen in lowland areas, the Olive skipper is locally common in mountainous districts up to 2,500 m, especially in southeastern Europe. It has a rapid flight and tends to settle on bare patches of ground. A larger subspecies, *P. serratulae major*, has a darker underside and clearer white markings. *WS:* 24–28 mm; *Flight:* July–Aug; *Gen:* 1; *FP:* Cinquefoil (*Potentilla*); *D:* S and C Europe (but not Britain, NW France, Holland, Scand).

# Carline skipper

## *Pyrgus carlinae*

♂

***Forewing*** *white mark in cell curved outwards like a C*

***Hindwing*** *marks pale and obscure*

***Underside hwing*** *pale red-brown with large white mark near margin*

♂

In the wetter areas of the southwestern Alps, up to 2,500 m, the Carline skipper may often be seen assembling in large numbers. It has the typical rapid flight of skippers, and when at rest the reddish tinge to the underside hindwing distinguishes it from the Olive skipper (p 11). It has smaller, less distinct markings on its upperside than the Cinquefoil skipper. *WS:* 26–28 mm; *Flight:* late June–Aug; *Gen:* 1; *FP:* Spring cinquefoil (*Potentilla verna*); *D:* Alps (S France, Austria, Switz, Italy).

# Cinquefoil skipper

## *P. cirsii*

♂

***Fwing*** *has squarish white spot in cell*

***Underside hwing*** *olive-yellow to reddish brown*

♂

A local species with a quick, darting flight, the Cinquefoil skipper may be found in flowery meadows up to 1,500 m. Some authorities list this skipper as a subspecies of the Carline skipper, for it is known that they breed together where their territories overlap. *WS:* 26–28 mm; *Flight:* July–Aug; *Gen:* 1; *FP:* Spring cinquefoil (*Potentilla verna*); *D:* Spain, Portugal, C France (incl Pyrenees), Germany, Switz, Austria, Corsica.

# Rosy grizzled skipper

## *P. onopordi*

♂

*Pale yellow suffusion over dark brown ground colour. Pattern on forewing well defined*

***Underside hindwing*** *has anvil-shaped mark near centre*

♂

The Rosy grizzled skipper has a preference for the same kind of habitat as the Cinquefoil skipper and may be distinguished by the generally larger white patches on the underside hindwing and the paler, yellower upperside. The female is often slightly larger than the male and has fewer yellow scales. *WS:* 22–28 mm; *Flight:* Apr–June, July–Sept; *Gen:* 2; *FP:* Cinquefoil (*Potentilla*); *D:* Spain, Portugal, S France, Italy (records from the Mediterranean islands need confirmation).

# Yellow-banded skipper

## *P. sidae*

**Sandy grizzled skipper, P. cinarae** ▶

♂

**Underside hindwing** *olive-brown with white markings* ▼

♂

♂

***Uppers** covered in grey hair near wing base. **Underside hwing** 2 yellow bands diagnostic* ♂

***P. sidae*** flies over flowery meadows up to 1,500 m. There is a smaller Italian subspecies with paler bands underneath. *WS:* 32–38 mm; *Flight:* June–July; *Gen:* 1; *FP: Abutilon avicennae*; *D:* S France, Italy, Greece, Yugoslavia, Bulgaria, Romania.
***P. cinarae*** prefers dry stony hills up to 1,000 m. The female has smaller spots on the uppers. *WS:* 30–32 mm; *Flight:* June; *FP:* unknown; *D:* Yugoslavia, Albania, Bulgaria, C Spain.

# Safflower skipper

## *P. carthami*

♂

*♀ is larger and less hairy*

***Hindwing** has regular row of postdiscal spots*

***Underside hindwing** strongly mottled, white markings edged in grey*

♂

The Safflower skipper is a widely distributed and often locally common butterfly of meadows and hillsides up to 1,500 m. The Spanish form has larger white markings. *WS:* 30–34 mm; *Flight:* June–Sept; *Gen:* 1; *FP:* Hollyhock (*Althaea*), Mallow (*Malva*); *D:* S and C Europe (but not N France, Britain, Holland, Scand).

# Alpine grizzled skipper

## *P. andromedae*

♂

*Pattern well defined on forewing, but not on hindwing*

***Underside hwing** has white streak and round spot near lower edge*

♂

Preferring the damp habitat offered by mountain lakes, the Alpine grizzled skipper may be found flying up to 1,500 m in the Pyrenees and Alps, although further north in Scandinavia it is considered to be a lowland species. It commonly occurs within the Arctic Circle. *WS:* 26–30 mm; *Flight:* June–July; *Gen:* 1; *FP:* unknown; *D:* N Scandinavia, France (Pyrenees, Alps), N Spain, Austria, Switzerland, Yugoslavia, Bulgaria.

# Dusky grizzled skipper

## *Pyrgus cacaliae*

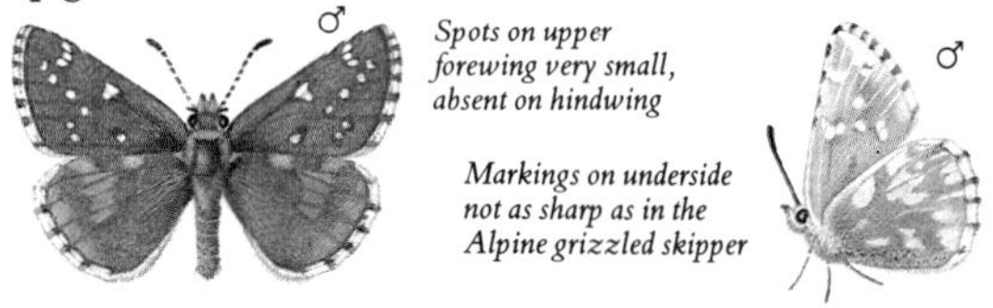
♂
Spots on upper forewing very small, absent on hindwing
Markings on underside not as sharp as in the Alpine grizzled skipper
♂

Similar to the Alpine grizzled skipper (p 13) but with less white on its forewings, the Dusky grizzled skipper has a rapid, whirring flight and lives in mountainous regions above 2,000 m. *WS:* 26–30 mm; *Flight:* June–Aug; *Gen:* 1; *FP:* Coltsfoot (*Tussilago farfara*); *D:* Austria, Switzerland, France (Alps), the Pyrenees (needs confirmation), Romania, Bulgaria.

# Northern grizzled skipper

## *P. centaureae*

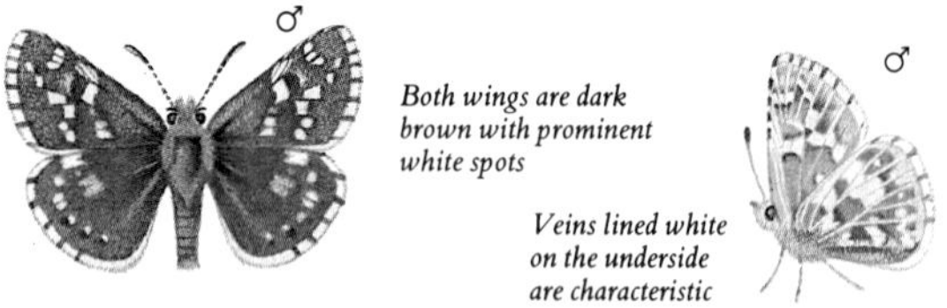
♂
Both wings are dark brown with prominent white spots
Veins lined white on the underside are characteristic
♂

This rather grey-brown species may be seen rapidly flying over bogs, moorlands and tundra up to 1,000 m. It is locally common throughout the mountainous regions of Scandinavia, but noticeably absent from the cultivated southern part. *WS:* 26–30 mm; *Flight:* June–July; *Gen:* 1; *FP:* Cloudberry (*Rubus chamaemorus*); *D:* Scandinavia.

# Red underwing skipper

## *Spialia sertorius*

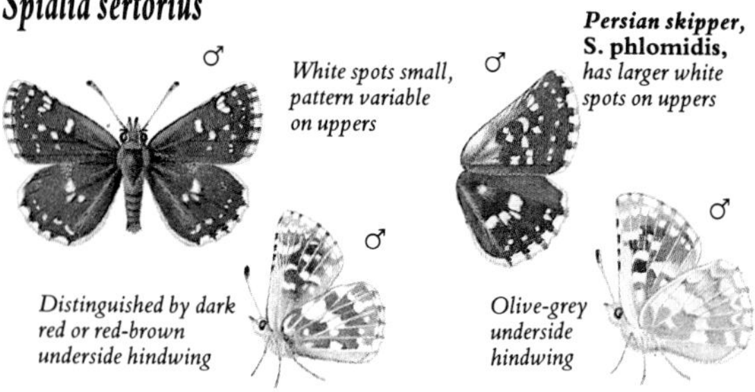
♂
White spots small, pattern variable on uppers
♂
**Persian skipper, S. phlomidis,** *has larger white spots on uppers*
♂
Distinguished by dark red or red-brown underside hindwing
♂
Olive-grey underside hindwing

***S. sertorius***, a small skipper with many subspecies, is locally common on mountains up to 1,400 m. The second generation is smaller. *WS:* 22–26 mm; *Flight:* Apr–Aug; *Gen:* 2; *FP:* Great burnet (*Sanguisorba*), Raspberry (*Rubus*), Cinquefoil (*Potentilla*); *D:* Spain, Portugal, France, Italy, S Germany, Switz, Austria.
***S. phlomidis*** flies at lower altitudes. *WS:* 28–30 mm; *Flight:* June–July; *FP:*unknown; *D:* Greece, Albania, SE Yugoslavia.

## Hungarian skipper

### *S. orbifer*

***Forewing*** *has regular row of submarginal spots*

***Underside hindwing*** *has round costal spot*

Once regarded as a subspecies of *S. sertorius* (p 14), this species is separated by its olive-green underside hindwing. Flies over rough ground up to 1,600 m. *WS:* 22–28 mm; *Flight:* Apr–Aug; *Gen:* 2; *FP:* Cinquefoil (*Potentilla*), Burnet (*Sanguisorba*); *D:* E Europe.

## Tessellated skipper

### *Syrichtus tessellum*

***Uppers*** *well marked.* ***Underside*** *more olive-brown than* S. cribrellum

***Spinose skipper,*** **S. cribrellum** ▶

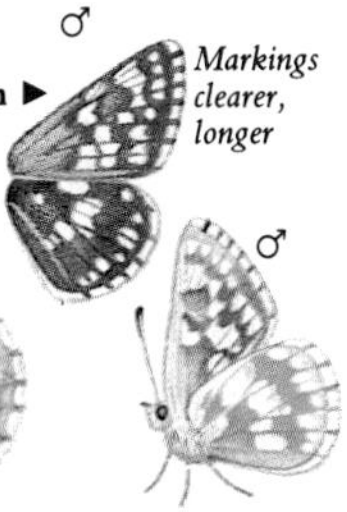

*Markings clearer, longer*

**S. tessellum**, not a well-known skipper, occurs in flowery grassland up to 1,000 m. *WS:* 32–36 mm; *Flight:* May–June; *Gen:* 1; *FP: Phlomis tuberosa*; *D:* Greece, SE Yugoslavia.
**S. cribrellum** is also little-known. Found in dry, treeless countryside, it may be distinguished by the clear white marks, especially near the wing margin, the yellowish underside hindwing and its smaller size. *WS:* 26–32 mm; *Flight:* late May–June; *Gen:* 1; *FP:* Cinquefoil (*Potentilla*); *D:* Romania.

## Sage skipper

### *S. proto*

***Forewing*** *has white, well-marked central spot*

***Underside*** *yellow-grey to reddish with pale markings*

◀ *Submarginal spots obscure on both wings*

A rapid flier, prone to variation in wing pattern, the Sage skipper is locally common on lowland grassland and mountain slopes up to 1,700 m. The female is similar but has less hair near the wing base. In late summer the species is often smaller with a more reddish brown underside hindwing. *WS:* 28–30 mm; *Flight:* Apr–Sept; *Gen:* 1; *FP:* Jerusalem sage (*Phlomis fruticosa*); *D:* S France, Spain, Portugal, Italy, Sicily, Greece, Yugoslavia.

# Mallow skipper

## *Carcharodus alceae*

♂ *Uppers brown with darker marbling*

***Hindwing** markings indistinct*

***Underside fwing** ♂ lacks tuft*

♂

The first generation is darker than the second. Flies over flowery slopes up to 1,500 m. *WS:* 26–34 mm; *Flight:* Apr–Aug; *Gen:* 2 (1 at high altitudes); *FP:* Mallow (*Malva*), Hollyhock (*Althaea*); *D:* S and C Europe (but not Britain, Holland, N Germany, Scand).

# Marbled skipper

## *C. lavatherae*

♂ ***Fwing** olive-brown with darker marbling and white spots*

***Hwing** darker with large central spots and arrow-shaped postdiscal spots*

*Fwing not tufted; hwing pale green*

♂

Local on dry chalky slopes up to 1,800 m. *WS:* 28–34 mm; *Flight:* May–Aug; *Gen:* 1, possibly 2; *FP:* Woundwort (*Stachys*); *D:* S and C Europe (not Corsica, Sardinia, Sicily), rare north of the Alps.

# Tufted marbled skipper

## *C. flocciferus*

♂

***Uppers** grey-brown with darker marbling and large spots on forewing. **Underside fwing** has hair tuft*

♂

***Southern marbled skipper, C. boeticus***

♂ ▼

♂ *Banded pattern on hwing*

***Oriental skipper, C. orientalis** underside hwing marks regular; fwing tufted* ▶

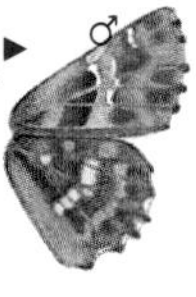

♂

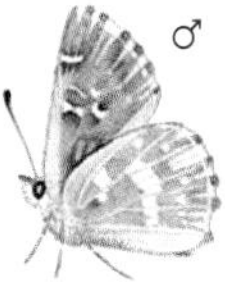

♂

**C. *flocciferus*.** *WS:* 28–32 mm; *Flight:* May–Sept; *Gen:* 2–3; *FP:* White horehound (*Marrubium vulgare*); *D:* S and C Europe.
**C. *boeticus*.** *WS:* 26–28 mm; *Flight:* May–Oct; *Gen, FP:* as for *C. flocciferus*; *D:* Spain, Portugal, S France, Italy, Switz.
**C. *orientalis*.** *WS:* 28–30 mm; *Flight:* Apr–Sept; *Gen:* 2–3; *FP:* unknown; *D:* Albania, Greece, Yugoslavia, Bulgaria.

# Large chequered skipper

## *Heteropterus morpheus*

♂

**Uppers** *dark brown, unmarked, but for pale yellow patches near front edge of forewing*

***Underside hwing** has large, ringed spots*

♂

Scattered colonies occur throughout Europe in damp meadows. Recognized by its underside pattern. *WS:* 32–38 mm; *Flight:* June–Aug; *Gen:* 1; *FP:* grasses, esp Brome (*Bromus*); *D:* N Spain, France, Germany, Holland, S Scand, Italy, Switz, E Europe.

# Dingy skipper

## *Erynnis tages*

♂

***Inky skipper,* E. marloyi,** *has dark brown uppers and unders, unmarked but for spot on forewing*

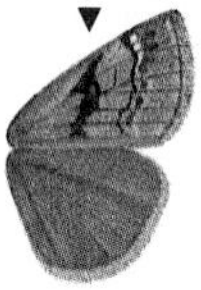

♂

♂

**Uppers** *dark grey-brown, with complete row of white marginal dots on forewing.* **Underside** *paler, sparsely marked*

***E. tages*** is widespread in a variety of open habitats up to 1,800 m. *WS:* 26–28 mm; *Flight:* May–June; *Gen:* 1 (2 in south); *FP:* Birdsfoot trefoil (*Lotus corniculatus*); *D:* Europe (not N Scand).
***E. marloyi*** is a mountain species. *WS:* 28–30 mm; *Flight:* May–June; *Gen:* 1; *FP:* unknown; *D:* Greece, Albania, S Yugoslavia.

# Chequered skipper

## *Carterocephalus palaemon*

♂

*Patches on wings may vary in size*

*♀ slightly larger, usually with less distinct markings*

♀

**Uppers** *dark brown, chequered with deep yellow patches.* **Underside hwing** *brown, tinged yellow, with pale yellow spots*

♂

♀

**Underside** *similar to ♂, but more heavily dusted with yellow scales*

This species is now thought to be extinct in England, surviving only very locally in Scotland. It is found in open woodland. *WS:* 26–29 mm; *Flight:* June–July; *Gen:* 1; *FP:* grasses, esp Brome (*Bromus*); *D:* Europe (not Spain, Portugal, Italy, Ireland, Holland).

# Northern chequered skipper

## *Carterocephalus silvicolus*

♂

***Forewing*** *yellow with brown spots*

***Hindwing*** *similar to* C. palaemon, *but has extra spot near costa*

*♀ has more extensive dark areas*

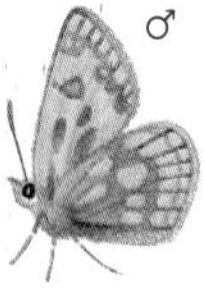

♂

Even heavily marked examples of this species are never as dark as the Chequered skipper (p 17). Locally common in wooded valleys. *WS:* 24–26 mm; *Flight:* June–July; *Gen:* 1; *FP:* grasses, esp Dog's-tail (*Cynosurus*); *D:* N Germany, Poland, Scand (not Denmark).

# Lulworth skipper

## *Thymelicus acteon*

♂

***Uppers*** *golden brown.* ***Forewing*** *pale marks in semi-circle; sex brand (dark line) prominent*

***Underside*** *relatively unmarked*

♂

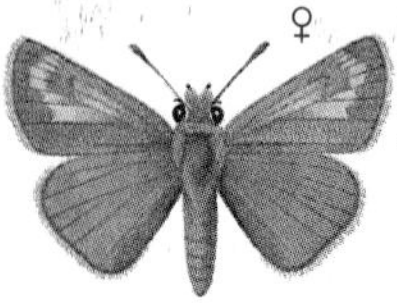

♀

***Uppers*** *darker brown.* ***Forewing*** *yellow spots more conspicuous; sex brand absent*

***Palps*** *white in both sexes*

♀

The Lulworth skipper is locally common at altitudes of up to 1,600 m in the south, but is rarer further north. In Britain it is restricted to the coast of Devon and Dorset. There are several subspecies which vary in size and colour. *WS:* 22–26 mm; *Flight:* May–Aug; *Gen:* 1; *FP:* grasses, esp Brome (*Bromus*); *D:* Europe (but not Scand, Ireland, Holland, Corsica, Sardinia).

# Essex skipper

## *T. lineola*

♂

***Uppers*** *tawny brown.* ***Forewing*** *(♂ only) has thin black interrupted line (sex brand) parallel to wing edge*

*Antennal tips black underneath*

♂

The key distinguishing feature between this species and the Small skipper (p 19) is the coloration of the underside of the tips of the antennae. The southeastern counties form the main breeding ground in England, but in the rest of Europe it is widespread in flowery meadows up to 1,800 m. *WS:* 24–28 mm; *Flight:* May–Aug; *Gen:* 1; *FP:* grasses; *D:* Europe (but not Ireland, N Scand).

# Small skipper

## *T. flavus*

♂

***Uppers*** *tawny brown as in Essex skipper, but sex brand is long, curving*

*Antennal tips orange underneath*

***Underside forewing*** *orange-red*

♂

The Small skipper is more abundant than the very similar Essex skipper (p 18), its range in Britain covering most of Wales and southern and central England as far north as Yorkshire. It has the typical rapid flight of skippers, often pausing to rest on the ground with its hindwings spread out flat and its forewings raised. It is common in flowery fields and hills up to 1,800 m. *WS:* 26–30 mm; *Flight:* June–Aug; *Gen:* 1; *FP:* grasses; *D:* Europe, incl Denmark (but not rest of Scand, Ireland, Scotland).

# Silver-spotted skipper

## *Hesperia comma*

♂

***Uppers*** *orange-brown with paler spots.* ***Forewing*** *(♂ only) has prominent ridged sex brand*

***Underside hindwing*** *olive-green with silver spots*

♂

The habitat of the Silver-spotted skipper is mainly the rough grassy fields of chalky and limestone areas up to 2,500 m. Numbers have drastically declined in Britain so that only a few scattered colonies remain in southern England. The female lacks a sex brand and is both larger and darker with more extensive spots. *WS:* 28–30 mm; *Flight:* July–Aug; *Gen:* 1; *FP:* grasses; *D:* Europe (but not Ireland, S Italy, Corsica, Sardinia).

# Large skipper

## *Ochlodes venatus*

♂

***Forewing*** *sex brand conspicuous (not in ♀)*

*Dark veins on orange-brown background*

***Underside*** *yellowish, faint marks on hindwing*

♂

A common and widespread species of meadows, chalk downs and woodland edges, the Large skipper may also occur in coastal areas. The plain underside makes it easy to distinguish from the more local Silver-spotted skipper. It is a very active butterfly, rarely staying long at any one flower. *WS:* 28–34 mm; *Flight:* June–Aug; *Gen:* 1 (2 in south); *FP:* various grasses; *D:* Europe (but not Scotland, Ireland, N Scand, Corsica, Sardinia).

# Mediterranean skipper

## *Gegenes nostrodamus*

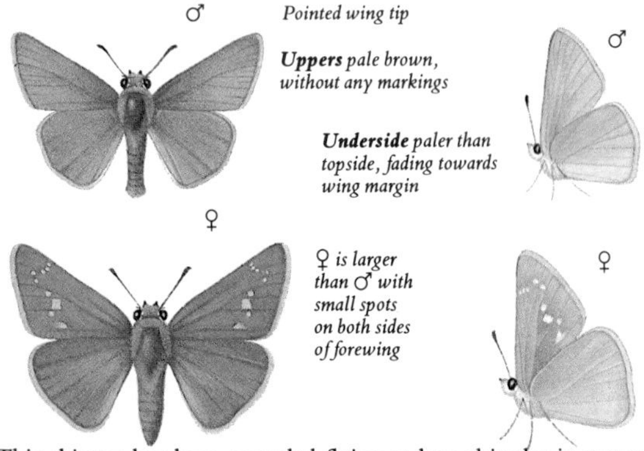
♂
Pointed wing tip
Uppers pale brown, without any markings
♂
Underside paler than topside, fading towards wing margin
♀
♀ is larger than ♂ with small spots on both sides of forewing
♀

This skipper has been recorded flying at low altitudes in many locations around the Mediterranean coast, but especially near dry river beds. Has paler, more sandy brown uppersides than the Pigmy skipper. *WS:* 30–32 mm; *Flight:* May–Oct; *Gen:* 2; *FP:* grasses; *D:* Spain, Portugal, Italy, Sicily, Greece, Yugoslavia.

# Pigmy skipper

## *G. pumilio*

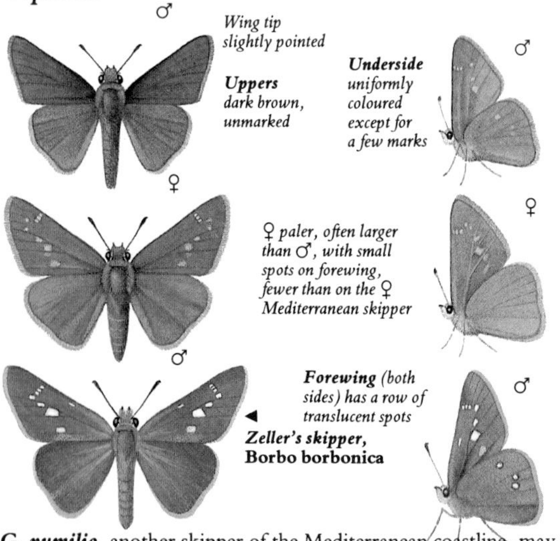
♂
Wing tip slightly pointed
Uppers dark brown, unmarked
Underside uniformly coloured except for a few marks
♂
♀
♀ paler, often larger than ♂, with small spots on forewing, fewer than on the ♀ Mediterranean skipper
♀
♂
Forewing (both sides) has a row of translucent spots
Zeller's skipper, Borbo borbonica
♂

***G. pumilio***, another skipper of the Mediterranean coastline, may often be seen resting on the ground in full glare of the sun. *WS:* 26–28 mm; *Flight:* Apr–Oct; *Gen:* 2 or more; *FP:* grasses; *D:* S Spain, S France, Italy, Sicily, Yugoslavia, Greece.

***Borbo borbonica*** has been seen in various coastal areas of the Mediterranean, but these reports need confirmation. *WS:* 28–30 mm; *Flight:* Sept–Oct; *Gen:* 1–2; *FP:* unknown; *D:* Gibraltar.

# Swallowtails Papilionidae

Swallowtails are generally large, well-patterned butterflies with slow, flapping flight which can be considerably quickened if pursued. All have three pairs of legs, each of which ends in a single apical claw but, contrary to popular belief, not all species have "tails" on the posterior margin of the hindwing. There are over 600 species of swallowtails in the world, but only 11 are European, and of these, *Papilio machaon* is the sole British representative. The caterpillars, by way of a defensive mechanism, have a brightly coloured, eversible gland, or osmeterium, just behind the head, which can be extruded to produce a pungent smell if they are threatened.

***Swallowtail caterpillar***

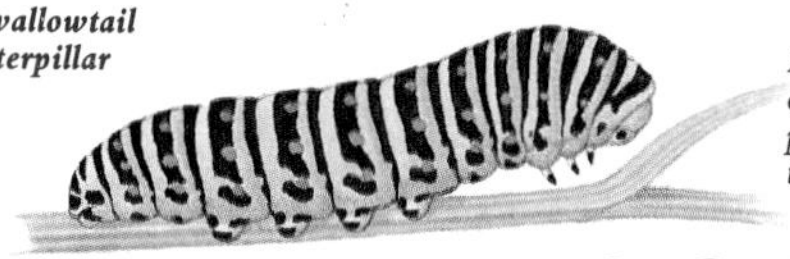
*Bright colour warns off predators. Food-plant may contain toxins*

## Swallowtail

## *Papilio machaon*

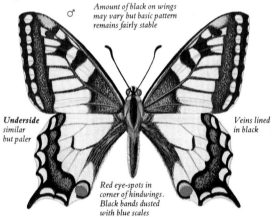

♂
*Amount of black on wings may vary but basic pattern remains fairly stable*
***Underside*** *similar but paler*
*Veins lined in black*
*Red eye-spots in corner of hindwings. Black bands dusted with blue scales*

The Swallowtail, easily recognized by its striking appearance, is a fast and agile flier, likely only to be confused with the very local Corsican swallowtail or the Southern swallowtail (p 22). Problems of identification should not occur in Britain, therefore, as this is the only resident swallowtail, with a range restricted to the low-lying fens of East Anglia. The more widely distributed continental subspecies, which flies over flowery meadows up to 2,000 m, occasionally occurs as a migrant in southern England. Differing slightly in wing pattern, it is paler yellow than the British Swallowtail, and the black band on the forewing has straighter edges. The first generation is generally darker than the second, although in more northerly areas the appearance of a second brood largely depends on the warmth of the summer. Sex differences are small; the female tends to be larger with less angular wings. *WS:* 64–100 mm; *Flight:* Apr–Aug; *Gen:* 2–3; *FP:* Milk parsley (*Peucedanum palustre*), Wild carrot (*Daucus carota*), Fennel (*Foeniculum vulgare*); *D:* Europe (not Ireland, Scotland).

# Corsican swallowtail

## *Papilio hospiton*

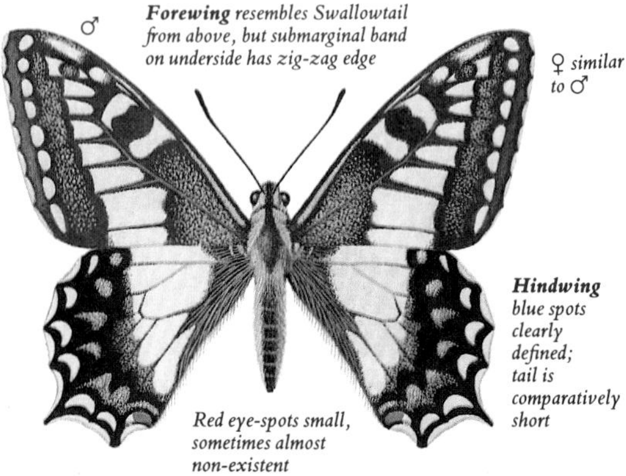
♂
**Forewing** resembles Swallowtail from above, but submarginal band on underside has zig-zag edge
♀ similar to ♂
**Hindwing** blue spots clearly defined; tail is comparatively short
Red eye-spots small, sometimes almost non-existent

The Corsican swallowtail, very similar in appearance to the Swallowtail (p 21), may be distinguished by the wavy submarginal band on the underside of its forewing. A local species, it is found only in the mountainous regions of Corsica and Sardinia between 600 and 1,500 m. *WS:* 72–76 mm; *Flight:* May–July; *Gen:* probably only 1; *FP:* Giant fennel (*Ferula communis*) and other Umbelliferae; *D:* Corsica, Sardinia.

# Southern swallowtail

## *P. alexanor*

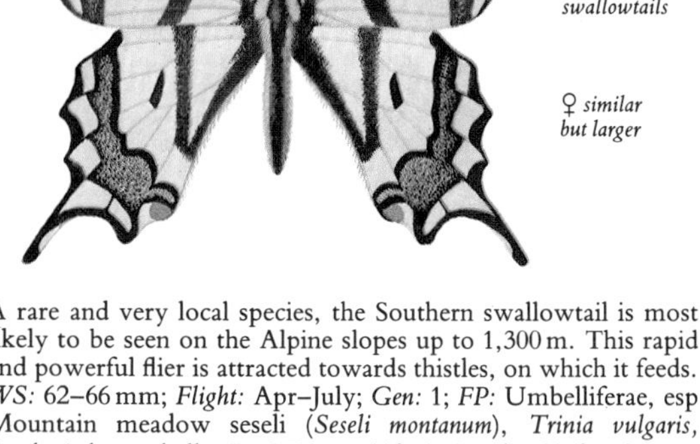
♂
**Forewing** yellow basal area diagnostic; submarginal band generally paler than in the related swallowtails
♀ similar but larger

A rare and very local species, the Southern swallowtail is most likely to be seen on the Alpine slopes up to 1,300 m. This rapid and powerful flier is attracted towards thistles, on which it feeds. *WS:* 62–66 mm; *Flight:* Apr–July; *Gen:* 1; *FP:* Umbelliferae, esp Mountain meadow seseli (*Seseli montanum*), *Trinia vulgaris*, *Ptychotis heterophylla*; *D:* S France (Alps), S Italy, Sicily, Greece, Albania, Yugoslavia.

# Scarce swallowtail

## *Iphiclides podalirius*

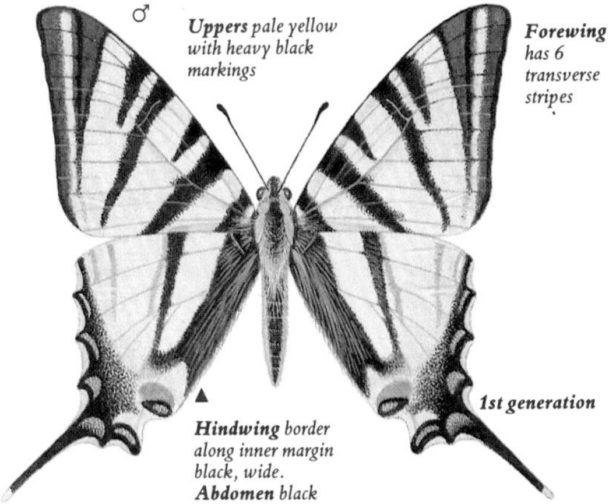
♂
**Uppers** pale yellow with heavy black markings
**Forewing** has 6 transverse stripes
1st generation
**Hindwing** border along inner margin black, wide.
**Abdomen** black

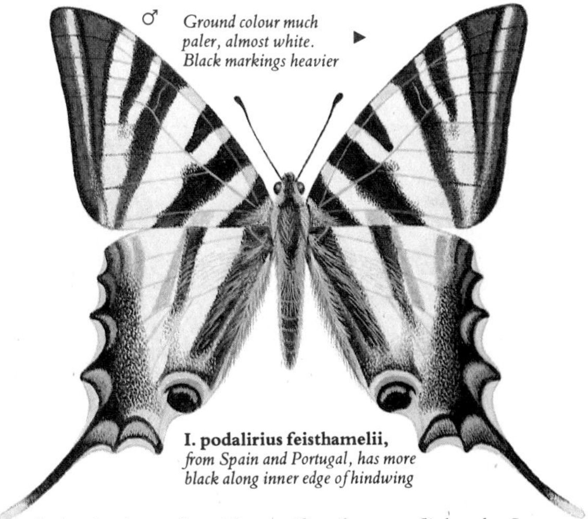
♂
Ground colour much paler, almost white. Black markings heavier
**I. podalirius feisthamelii,** from Spain and Portugal, has more black along inner edge of hindwing

A distinctive butterfly with a swift and strong flight, the Scarce swallowtail has been recorded in Britain, although it is doubtful if it was ever established here, despite authentic early reports. Within the Scarce swallowtail's range, it is not "scarce", although recently it has become less common. In the spring it may congregate in hilly areas up to 1,600 m but during the summer it prefers the orchards and light woodlands of moister lowlands. A second generation, found only in the south, differs slightly in colour, having creamy white uppers with less heavy markings and a white-tipped abdomen. *WS:* 64–90 mm; *Flight:* Mar–Sept; *Gen:* 1 or 2; *FP:* Sloe (*Prunus*), Cherry (*Cerasus*), Hawthorn (*Crataegus*), and other cultivated fruit trees; *D:* Europe (but not Britain, N Scand; migrant to Holland, Denmark, S Sweden).

# Southern festoon

## *Zerynthia polyxena*

♂

*Small red spot present near forewing apex. Marginal marks pronounced*

♂

*The red patches on the underside vary in size*

This species is easily confused with the Spanish festoon where their ranges overlap in southeast France. Identified by the absence of extensive red areas in the upper forewing, the Southern festoon is local in rocky regions up to 1,000 m. *WS:* 46–52 mm; *Flight:* Apr–May; *Gen:* 1; *FP:* Birthwort (*Aristolochia*); *D:* Italy, Austria, SE France, Hungary, Romania, Yugoslavia, Bulgaria, Greece.

# Spanish festoon

## *Z. rumina*

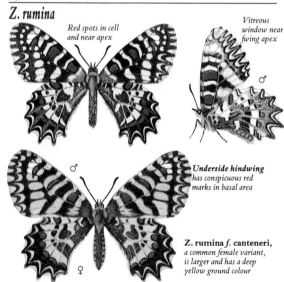

*Red spots in cell and near apex*

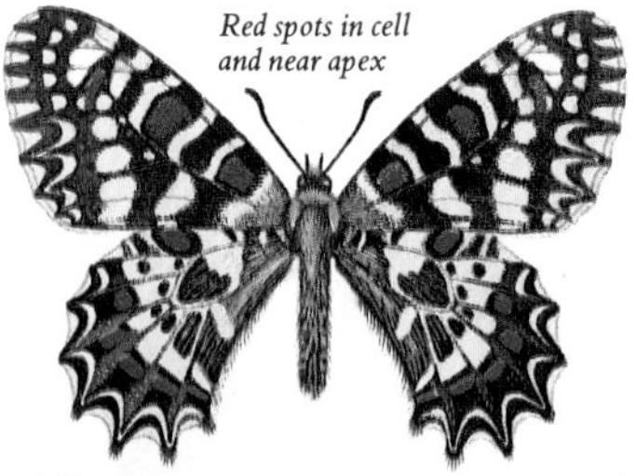

*Vitreous window near fwing apex*

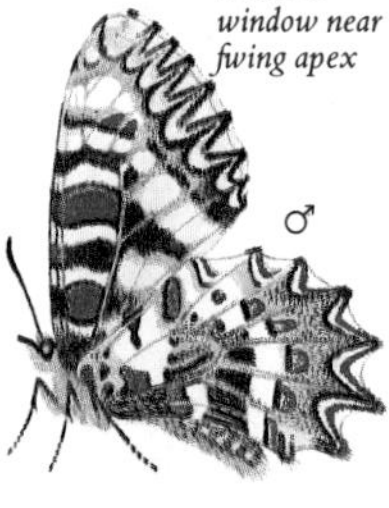
♂

♂
♀

***Underside hindwing** has conspicuous red marks in basal area*

**Z. rumina *f.* canteneri,** *a common female variant, is larger and has a deep yellow ground colour*

Early to appear, the Spanish festoon is a variable-patterned butterfly, locally common on rough slopes up to 1,500 m. Many subspecies are listed. *WS:* 44–46 mm; *Flight:* Feb–May; *Gen:* 1; *FP:* Birthwort (*Aristolochia*); *D:* SE France, Spain, Portugal.

# Eastern festoon

## *Z. cerisyi*

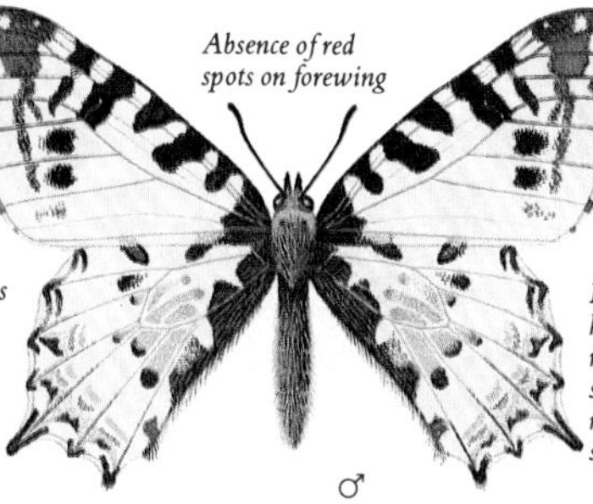
Absence of red spots on forewing
Black markings scarce on both wings; more extensive in ♀
Hindwing has scanty red marks, scalloped margin and short tail
♂

Flying over rough ground up to 1,400 m, the Eastern festoon can be distinguished from other festoons by the lack of any red on the forewings and its scalloped hindwings. In Crete it is paler and smaller. *WS:* 52–62 mm; *Flight:* Apr–June; *Gen:* 1; *FP:* Birthwort (*Aristolochia*); *D:* Albania, Yugoslavia, Bulgaria, Greece, Crete.

# False apollo

## *Archon apollinus*

Forewing grey, almost translucent, with 2 large black spots in cell
♂
Hindwing characterized by 6 black, red and blue submarginal marks

Ground colour and degree of speckling vary in both sexes
♀
♀ usually larger, more heavily marked and yellower in colour
Hindwing has brighter, more complete submarginal marks

In flight, the False apollo looks yellower than most other festoons. Found in isolated colonies in rocky areas up to 1,500 m, this species, which is widespread in Asia, occurs only in the extreme southeast of Europe. *WS:* 54–60 mm; *Flight:* Mar–Apr; *Gen:* 1; *FP:* Birthwort (*Aristolochia*); *D:* Bulgaria, Greece.

# Apollo

## *Parnassius apollo*

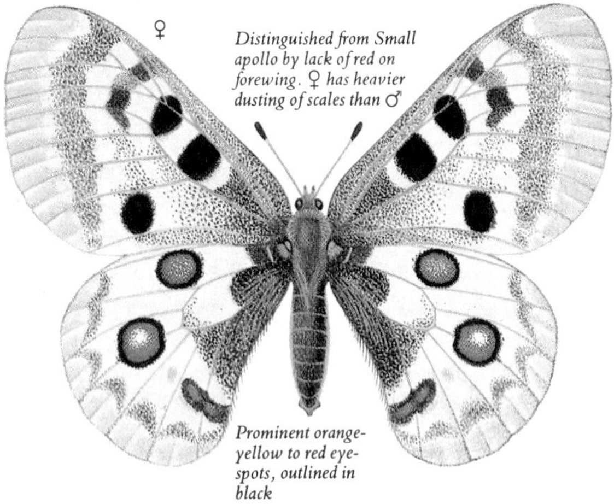
♀
Distinguished from Small apollo by lack of red on forewing. ♀ has heavier dusting of scales than ♂
Prominent orange-yellow to red eye-spots, outlined in black

♂
Antennae pale grey, ringed darker grey in both sexes
Eye-spots often smaller and darker red in ♂

The very distinctive pattern of the Apollo is prone to variation and consequently many subspecies from different localities have been listed which all differ slightly in colour and markings. This large butterfly has a rather heavy, flapping flight which makes it easy prey for collectors. Due to its increasing rarity over recent years, there are now laws prohibiting the collection of the Apollo in several countries, as well as restrictions on trading in specimens. In Europe the Apollo is widely distributed, occurring in isolated colonies on mountainous regions from 700 to 2,000 m. It may be distinguished from the related Small apollo (p 27) by the absence of red spots on the forewings and the much lighter dusting of dark scales which give it a whiter appearance. *WS:* 70–85 mm; *Flight:* June–Sept; *Gen:* usually 1; *FP:* Stonecrop (*Sedum*); *D:* Europe (but not Britain, NW France, Denmark, N Scand, C Germany, Czechoslovakia, Corsica, Sardinia).

# Small apollo

## *P. phoebus*

**Fwing** spotted red; black spot near hind margin much smaller than corresponding mark on Apollo
**Antennae** white, conspicuously ringed black
Ground colour yellow-white rather than pure white
♂


At first glance the pattern of the Small apollo resembles that of the Apollo (p 26), but closer study reveals that it has more red on its forewings. Localized and comparatively rare, it occurs in small colonies on mountains over 2,000 m, often by streams. The female is greyer with heavier markings. *WS:* 60–80 mm; *Flight:* July–Aug; *Gen:* 1; *FP:* Yellow saxifrage (*Saxifraga aizoides*), Mountain houseleek (*Sempervivum montanum*); *D:* Alps.

# Clouded apollo

## *P. mnemosyne*

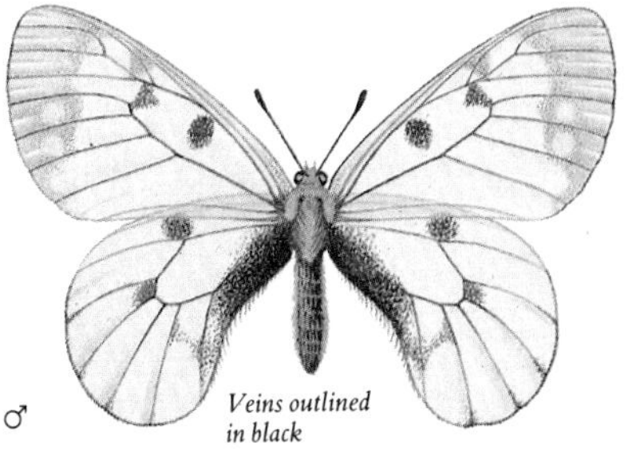

**Forewing** poorly marked with only 2 black spots
**Uppers** lack any red spots and are dusted with black scales, often giving a very grey appearance
♂
Veins outlined in black


The absence of any red marks on both wings separates this species from other apollos. The female is similar to the male but for a heavier dusting of black scales. Clouded apollo prefers wooded hills up to 1,500 m in central Europe, but further north it is considered to be a lowland species of damp meadows. There is some variation in pattern over its range; specimens from Greece, *P. mnemosyne athene*, are both paler and smaller, while the female, f. *melaina*, found in more mountainous terrain, has more extensive black markings on its upperside. The butterfly has a flapping flight and is locally common in central Europe, but in Norway it is very rare and occurs in only a few localities. *WS:* 52–62 mm; *Flight:* May–July; *Gen:* 1; *FP:* Corydalis (*Corydalis*); *D:* the Pyrenees, C and S France, Italy, Sicily, the Alps, C and S Germany, Scandinavia, Yugoslavia, Romania, Bulgaria, Greece (but not Britain, Denmark, Spain, Portugal).

# Whites and Yellows Pieridae

Some of the commonest European butterflies belong to this large family, including those whose caterpillars are pests of cabbages and related plants. The species are easily recognized by their white or yellow black-spotted wings, and the caterpillars are generally green and smooth. The adults have six legs of equal size, each of which ends in four claws instead of the normal two. Although they seem fluttery in flight, many are strongly migratory and travel long distances. The sexes and various generations usually differ.

***Clouded yellow caterpillar***

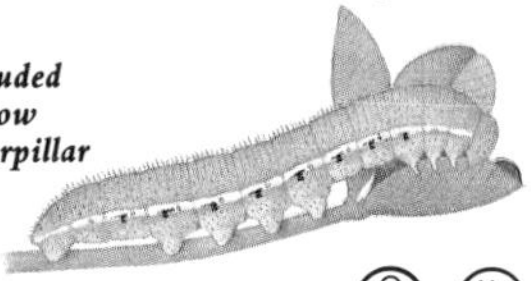

*Usually feeds on clover or lucerne. Green body has a pale, red-spotted line down the side*

## Large white

## *Pieris brassicae*

♀ ***1st generation***

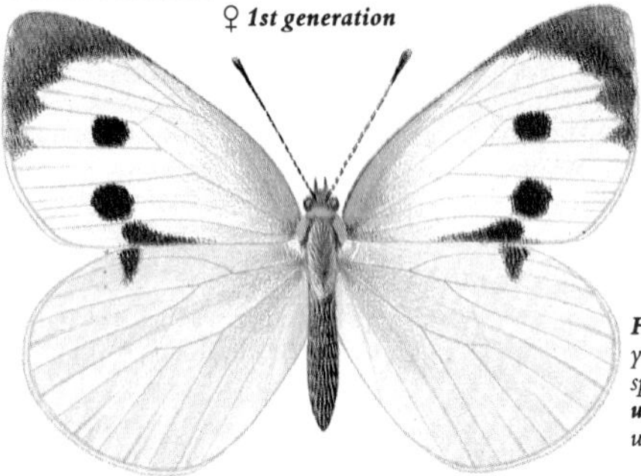

*Black or grey-black apex*

***Forewing** marked by 2 black spots and a black bar near hind margin*

***Hindwing** pale yellow with single spot near front edge; **underside** dusted with grey scales*

♂ ***1st generation***

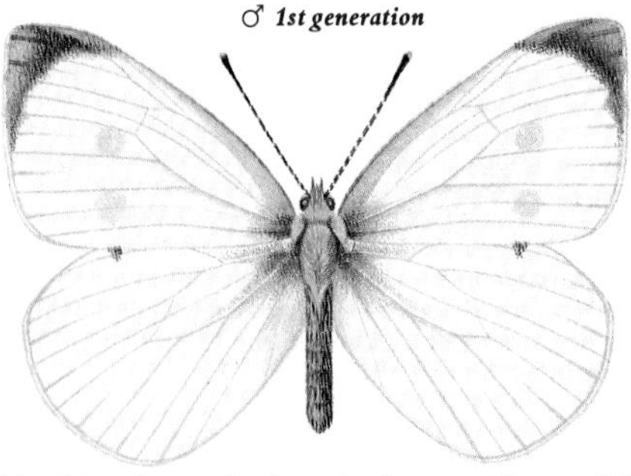

***Forewing** unmarked but for black apex; **underside** has 2 black spots*

***Hindwing** whiter, with less prominent spot near front edge than in ♀*

Capable of completely stripping a cabbage of its leaves, the caterpillars of the Large or Cabbage white can be a serious garden pest. Surprisingly, the resident population in Britain is fairly small, the numbers being increased each year by the influx of migrants from across the Channel. Specimens from the summer generation are larger with more black on the wing tips than those seen in spring and autumn. *WS:* 57–66 mm; *Flight:* Apr–Oct; *Gen:* 2–3; *FP:* Cruciferae, esp Cabbage (*Brassica*); *D:* Europe.

# Small white

## *Artogeia rapae*

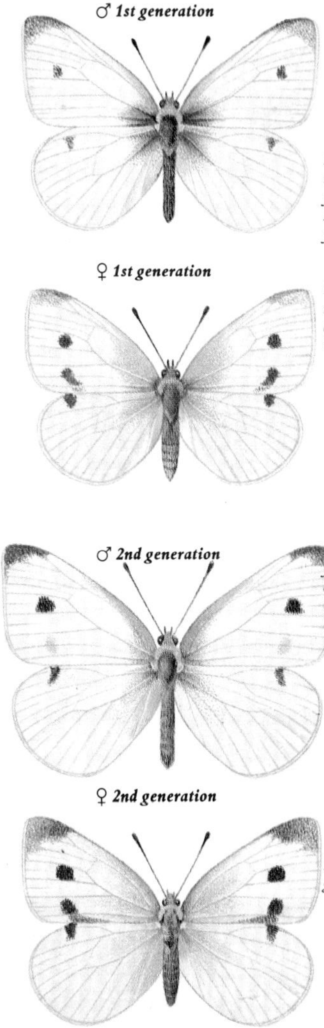
♂ 1st generation
**Forewing** has small, greyish marks, poorly defined; more distinct on underside
**Hindwing** unmarked but for small black spot towards front edge
♀ 1st generation
Ground colour pale yellow with extensive dusting of grey scales in basal area
Spots are more clearly defined than in 1st gen ♂
♂ 2nd generation
Border around forewing apex and spots on both wings are blacker than in 1st gen ♂
**Underside hindwing** yellow in both sexes, but 2nd gen has fewer grey scales than 1st gen
♀ 2nd generation
Black spots are heavy, well-defined on both sides
Richer, yellower ground colour

The favourite haunt of the Small white, one of the commonest British butterflies, is likely to be the cabbage rows of market gardens, although it may be found in a variety of habitats, from urban parks to open countryside. It is noticeably smaller but more numerous than the Large white, and feeds on a greater variety of plants. The resident British population is augmented each year by large numbers from abroad. *WS:* 46–55 mm; *Flight:* Mar–Sept; *Gen:* 2–3; *FP:* Cruciferae, esp Wild mignonette (*Reseda lutea*), Cabbage (*Brassica*); *D:* Europe (less common in N Scand).

## Southern small white

### *Artogeia mannii*

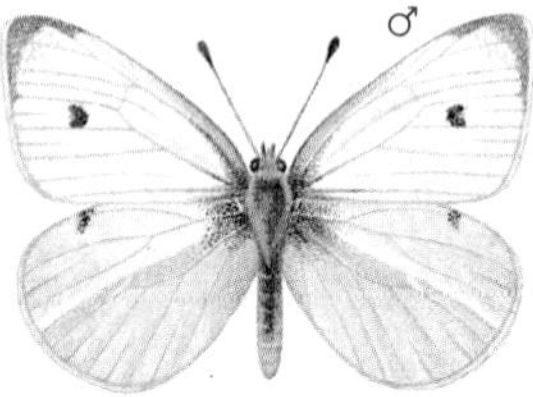

♂

***Forewing*** *apical spot usually extends further down wing margin than in Small white*

***Underside hindwing*** *yellow, dusted with black scales*

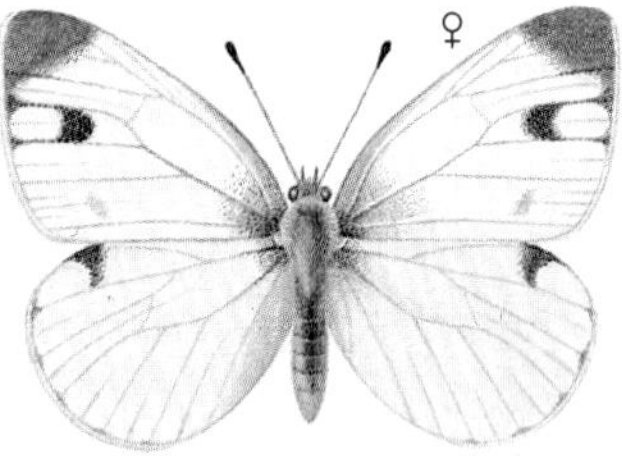

♀

***Forewing*** *apical spot broader, blacker than in ♂; crescent-shaped spot linked to margin by dark scales along the veins*

***Hindwing*** *costal spot outwardly concave*

Smaller than the Small white (p 29). Flies over cultivated land, but fortunately the caterpillars feed only on wild Cruciferae. Later generations are larger and darker. *WS:* 40–46 mm; *Flight:* Mar–Sept; *Gen:* 3–4; *FP:* Evergreen candytuft (*Iberis sempervirens*); *D:* Spain, France, Switz, Austria, Italy, SE Europe.

## Mountain small white

### *A. ergane*

♂

***Forewing*** *dark apical spot rather square*

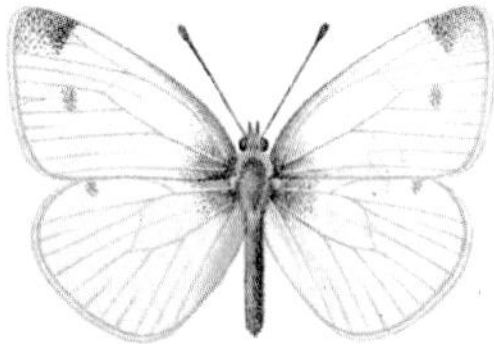

***Underside fwing*** *unmarked except for yellow apex*

***Hindwing*** *small grey costal mark often absent*

♀

***Forewing*** *has additional black spot in ♀*

***Hindwing*** *pale yellow with larger costal spot than ♂*

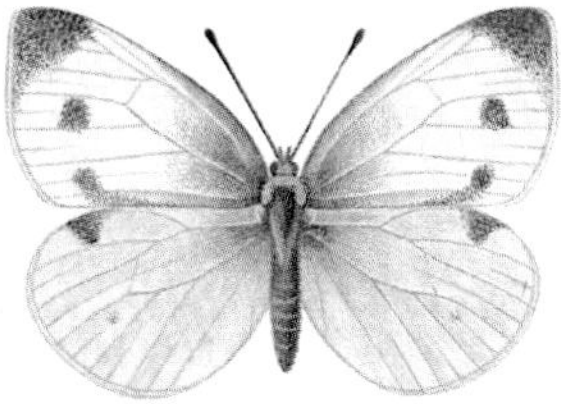

*Dark spots on uppers may show through on the underside*

*Later generations are darker*

One of the smaller, less common whites in Europe, found on grassy mountain slopes up to 1,800 m. *WS:* 36–48 mm; *Flight:* Mar–Sept; *Gen:* 2 or more; *FP:* Cruciferae, esp Burnt candytuft (*Aethionema saxatile*); *D:* NE Spain, S France, Italy (Apennines), Romania, Hungary, Yugoslavia, Albania, Bulgaria, Greece.

# Green-veined white

## *A. napi*

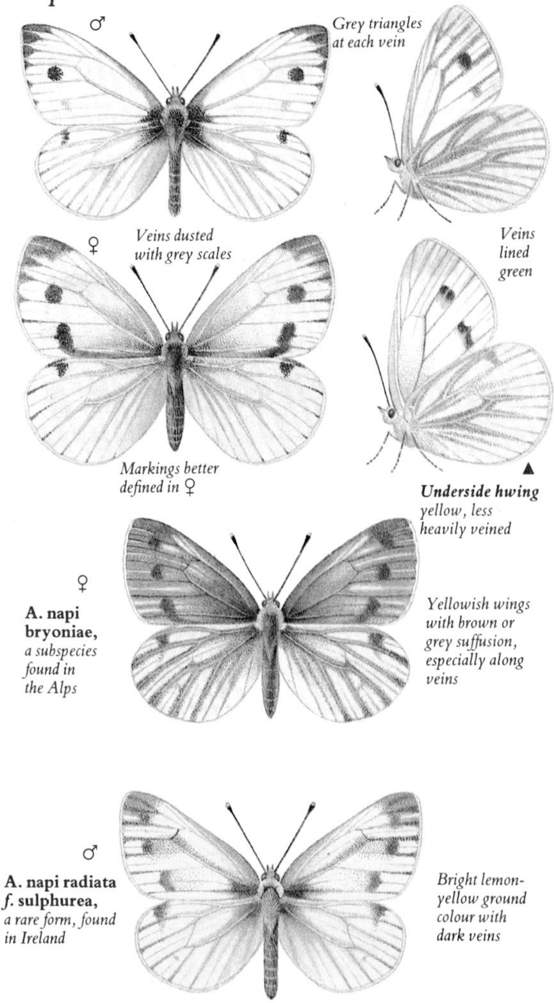
♂
Grey triangles at each vein
♀
Veins dusted with grey scales
Veins lined green
Markings better defined in ♀
▲
**Underside hwing** yellow, less heavily veined
♀
**A. napi bryoniae,** *a subspecies found in the Alps*
Yellowish wings with brown or grey suffusion, especially along veins
♂
**A. napi radiata *f.* sulphurea,** *a rare form, found in Ireland*
Bright lemon-yellow ground colour with dark veins

There are many named forms of the Green-veined white based on variation in colour and spotting, but they all share a common feature in their green-veined undersides, which are especially conspicuous at rest. Distinct differences also occur between spring and summer generations, the latter being larger with paler veins. Unfortunately this species, which is not a garden pest, may be mistaken for the harmful Small white, as they both fly over similar terrain. The Green-veined white prefers damp meadows up to 1,500 m. *WS:* 36–50 mm; *Flight:* May–Sept; *Gen:* 2 or more; *FP:* Cruciferae, esp Wild mignonette (*Reseda lutea*), Hedge mustard (*Sisymbrium officinale*); *D:* Europe (rare in N Scand).

# Krueper's small white

## *Artogeia krueperi*

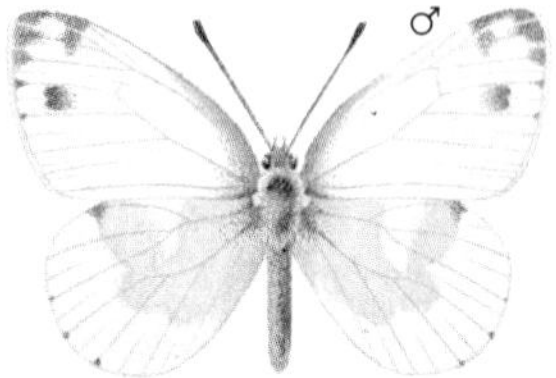
♂

***Forewing*** *dark costal bar immediately before apex; apical border of small triangles at vein ends*

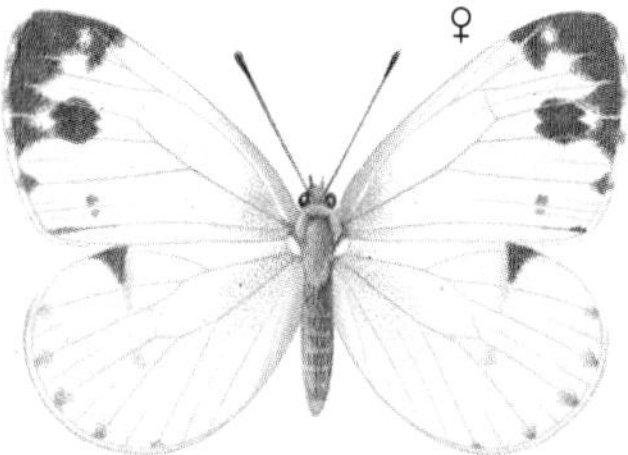
♀

***Forewing*** *markings larger, more extensive than in ♂*

***Underside hindwing*** *has greenish basal area which is pale yellow in 2nd generation*

Krueper's small white is widespread in rocky areas up to 2,000 m and may be separated from the Mountain small white (p 30) by its distinctive apical forewing marks and the greenish basal area underneath the hindwing. Closer inspection of the upper hindwing margin will also reveal a row of small grey marks, but these are barely visible in some specimens. *WS:* 42–50 mm; *Flight:* Mar–Sept; *Gen:* 2 or more; *FP:* Mountain alison (*Alyssum montanum*); *D:* Greece, Bulgaria, Albania, Yugoslavia.

# Black-veined white

## *Aporia crataegi*

♂

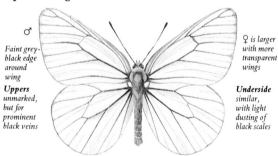

*Faint grey-black edge around wing*

***Uppers*** *unmarked, but for prominent black veins*

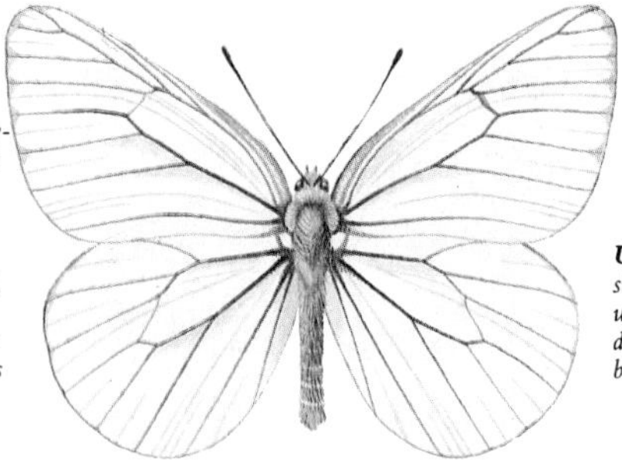

*♀ is larger with more transparent wings*

***Underside*** *similar, with light dusting of black scales*

This distinctive butterfly is usually seen flying in its rather laboured fashion over clover fields and in orchards, where it can be a pest if numerous. The population fluctuates drastically from year to year, and a good year may see an occasional migrant to Britain, which arouses great interest as the British population became extinct some 60 years ago. *WS:* 56–68 mm; *Flight:* May–June; *Gen:* 1; *FP:* Hawthorn (*Crataegus*), Cherry, Blackthorn (*Prunus*) and others. *D:* Europe (migrant to Britain, N Scand).

# Bath white

## *Pontia daplidice*

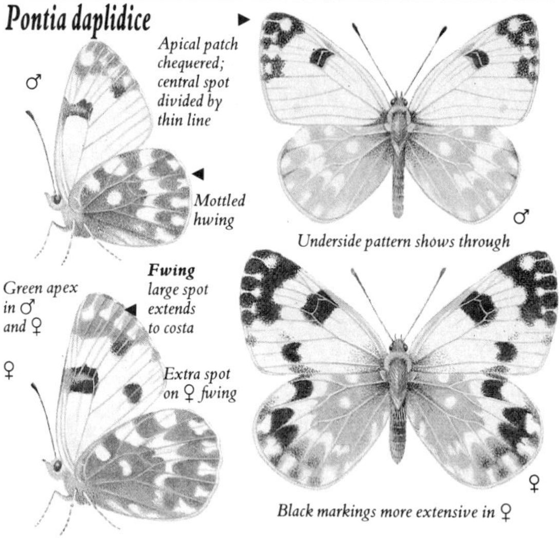

Apical patch chequered; central spot divided by thin line
♂
Mottled hwing
Underside pattern shows through
♂
**Fwing** large spot extends to costa
Green apex in ♂ and ♀
♀
Extra spot on ♀ fwing
♀
Black markings more extensive in ♀


A rare migrant to southern Britain, this species derives its name from an eighteenth-century embroidery made in Bath, in which it is clearly shown. It has a rapid flight and may be seen bobbing around in clover fields. *WS:* 42–48 mm; *Flight:* Feb–Sept; *Gen:* 2–3; *FP:* Cruciferae, esp Rock cress (*Arabis*), Mustard (*Sinapis*); *D:* C and S Europe (migrant to Britain, Holland, Scand).

# Small Bath white

## *P. chloridice*

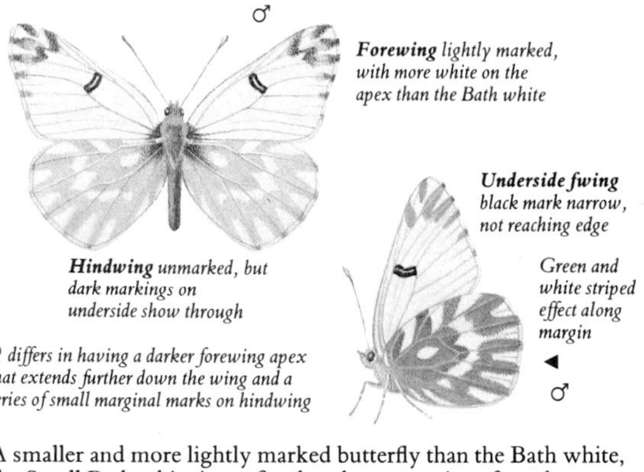

♂
**Forewing** lightly marked, with more white on the apex than the Bath white
**Underside fwing** black mark narrow, not reaching edge
**Hindwing** unmarked, but dark markings on underside show through
Green and white striped effect along margin
♀ differs in having a darker forewing apex that extends further down the wing and a series of small marginal marks on hindwing
♂


A smaller and more lightly marked butterfly than the Bath white, the Small Bath white is confined to the mountains of southeastern Europe, being more widespread in central Asia. The second generation is larger than the first and the upperside markings are better developed. *WS:* 40–44 mm; *Flight:* Apr–July; *Gen:* 2; *FP:* unknown; *D:* Bulgaria, Albania, Turkey, Greece.

# Peak white

## *Pontia callidice*

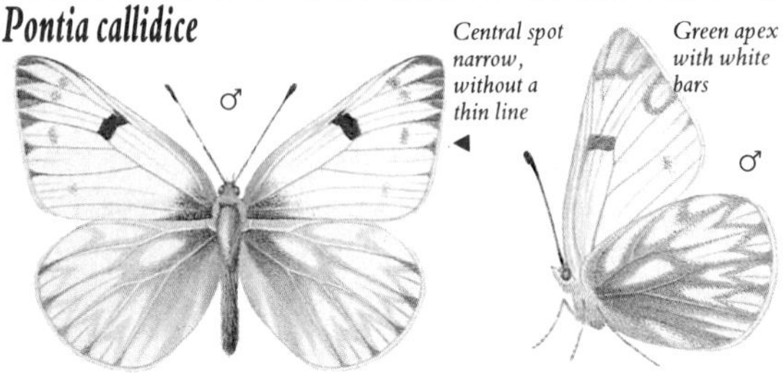
♂
Central spot narrow, without a thin line
Green apex with white bars
♂

*♂ sparsely marked, mostly white. ♀ darker, underside pattern very distinct through hwing*

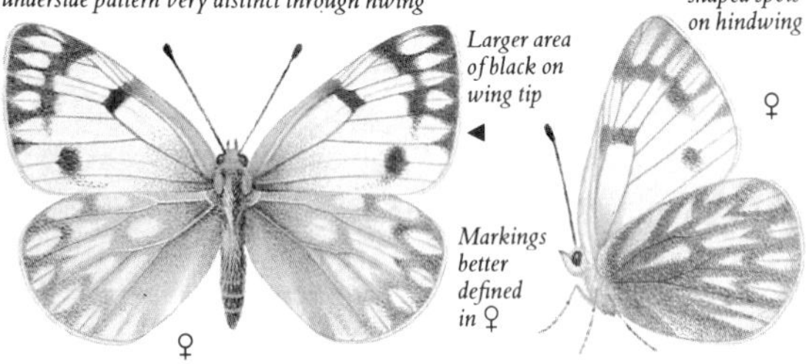
Spearhead-shaped spots on hindwing
Larger area of black on wing tip
♀
Markings better defined in ♀
♀

The Peak white is a butterfly of mountains and Alpine valleys from 1,500 up to 3,000 m. It closely resembles the Bath white and the Small Bath white, differing most noticeably in the shape of the markings on the green underside of the hindwing. In the male these spearhead-shaped marks are white, while in the female they are yellowish. Although there is usually only one generation, a second may occur at lower altitudes in August if conditions are favourable. *WS:* 42–52 mm; *Flight:* June–July; *Gen:* 1–2; *FP:* Dwarf treacle mustard (*Erysimum pumilum*), Mignonette (*Reseda*), other Cruciferae; *D:* Pyrenees and Alps (NE Spain, France, Switzerland, Austria, N Italy).

# Desert orange tip

## *Colotis evagore*

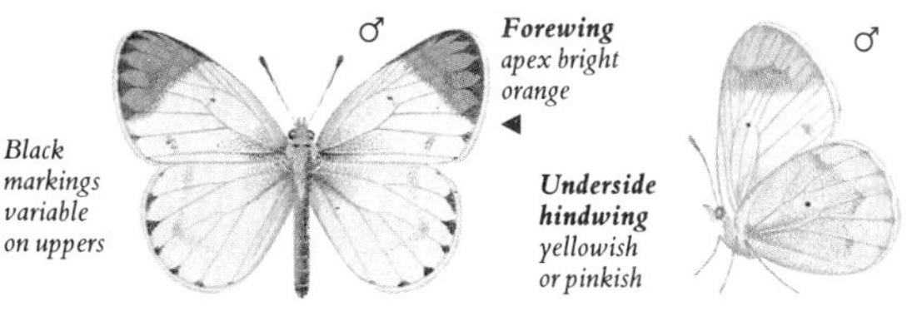
♂
Forewing apex bright orange
♂
Black markings variable on uppers
Underside hindwing yellowish or pinkish

Far more common in Africa than in Europe, the Desert orange tip has extended its range to include a pocket in southern Spain. This is a smaller, more delicate butterfly than the Orange tip (p 36), with less orange on its wings. The female is similar to the male but for a narrower orange patch, while later generations are smaller and paler. *WS:* 30–36 mm; *Flight:* Feb–Aug; *Gen:* several; *FP:* Caper (*Capparis spinosa*); *D:* S Spain.

# Dappled white

## *Euchloe simplonia*

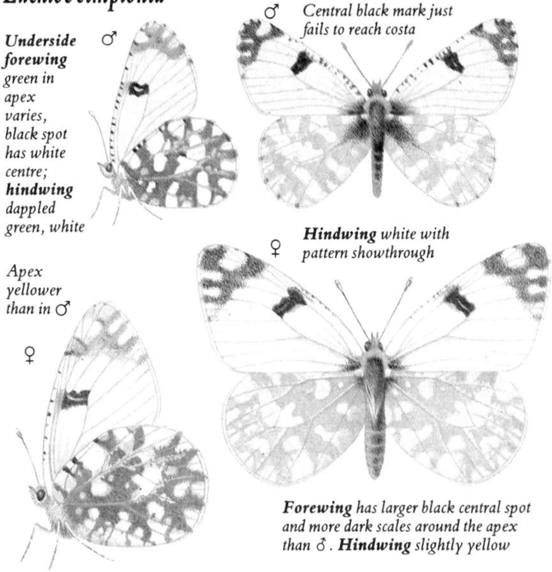
**Underside** ♂
**forewing** green in apex varies, black spot has white centre; **hindwing** dappled green, white
♂ Central black mark just fails to reach costa
♀ **Hindwing** white with pattern showthrough
Apex yellower than in ♂
♀
**Forewing** has larger black central spot and more dark scales around the apex than ♂. **Hindwing** slightly yellow

A widespread butterfly of grassy slopes up to 1,400 m, with many subspecies based on small differences in pattern. *WS:* 40–48 mm; *Flight:* Mar–June; *Gen:* 2; *FP:* Cruciferae, esp Candytuft (*Iberis*); *D:* Spain, Portugal, C and S France, Italy, Switz, SE Europe.
***E. ausonia*** (Mountain dappled white) is distinguished by the black spot on the forewing which actually reaches the costa and spreads a little way along it. Flies over mountains from 1,500 to 2,000 m. *WS:* 40–48 mm; *Flight:* June; *Gen:* 1; *D:* Pyrenees, Alps.

# Portuguese dappled white

## *E. tagis*

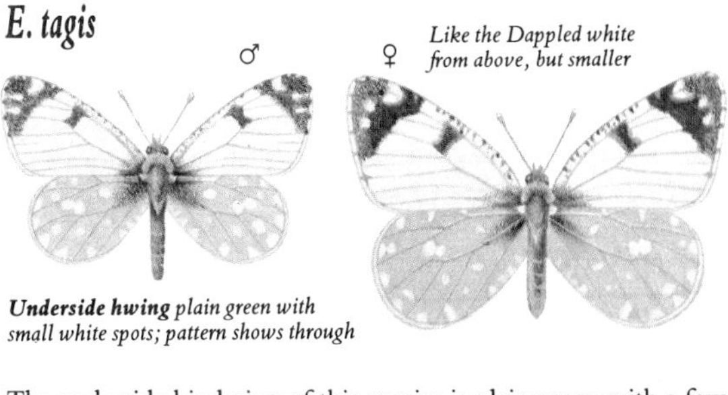
♂
♀ Like the Dappled white from above, but smaller
**Underside hwing** plain green with small white spots; pattern shows through

The underside hindwing of this species is plain green with a few small white spots, separating it from the Dappled white. Found in rough meadows up to 1,000 m. *WS:* 30–44 mm; *Flight:* Feb–May; *Gen:* 1; *FP:* Candytuft (*Iberis*); *D:* Spain, Portugal, S France.
***E. belemia*** (Green-striped white) is similar but with white stripes running across the green underside hindwing. *WS:* 36–44 mm; *Flight:* Feb–May; *Gen:* 2; *FP:* unknown; *D:* S Spain, Portugal.

## Greenish black tip

## *Elphinstonia charlonia*

♂


***Uppers*** *lime yellow in both sexes with a broad black patch at the forewing apex*

*♀ has larger black spot in cell of forewing*

Strictly speaking this is an African butterfly, but the subspecies *E. charlonia penia* is found in a few isolated rocky places in Europe and is larger than its North African counterparts. *WS:* 32–36 mm; *Flight:* Apr–June; *Gen:* 2; *FP: Matthiola tessala*; *D:* SE Yugoslavia, N Greece, Bulgaria.

## Orange tip

## *Anthocharis cardamines*

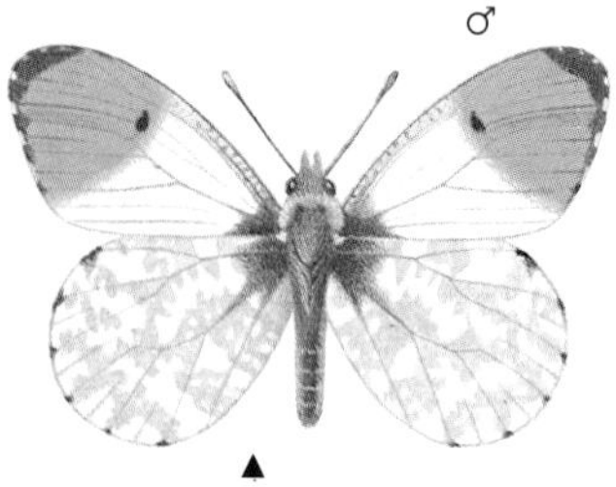

♂
▲


*Extreme tip is black*

*Apex dappled green and white*

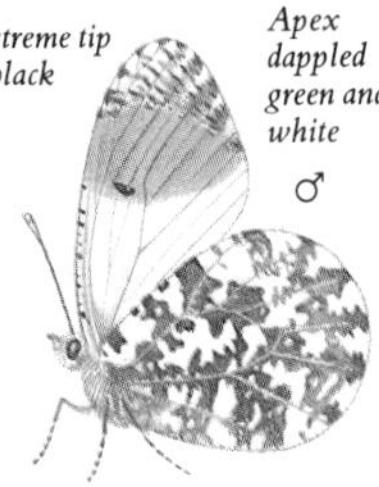

♂


***Forewing*** *large orange patch on outer third just encloses small black spot.* ***Hindwing*** *dappled grey-green effect caused by underside pattern*

***Underside hindwing*** *mottled green and white in ♂ and ♀*

***Forewing*** *lacks orange patch; central spot bigger, often crescent-shaped;* ***underside*** *white, poorly marked, with grey apex*

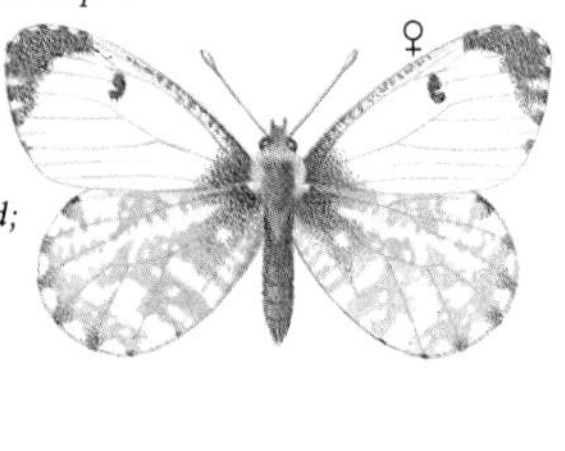

♀


*Grey apex does not have any distinct white spots; this distinguishes it from the Dappled white*

***Hindwing*** *may have yellow tinge*

Common in damp meadows, woodland edges and country lanes, the Orange tip is the only species in Britain with a distinctive dappled green underside. This coloration is a peculiar effect of the mixing of black and yellow scales which serves as a useful camouflage. Occasionally drawn to the ornamental Cruciferae of urban parks, the sight of this butterfly is thought by many to be a true sign of spring. *WS:* 38–48 mm; *Flight:* Apr–July; *Gen:* 1; *FP:* Cruciferae, esp Tower mustard (*Arabis glabra*), Lady's smock (*Cardamine pratensis*); *D:* Europe (but not N Scand, N Scotland). ***A. gruneri*** (Gruner's orange tip) is smaller with a pale yellow ground colour. *WS:* 30–36 mm; *Flight:* Mar–May; *FP: Aethionema saxatilis*; *D:* Greece, Albania, SE Yugoslavia, Turkey.

# Moroccan orange tip

## *A. belia*

♂

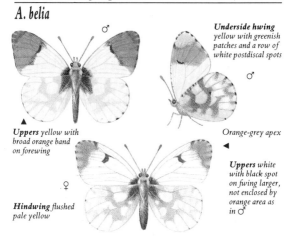

**Uppers** *yellow with broad orange band on forewing*

*Underside hwing yellow with greenish patches and a row of white postdiscal spots*

♂

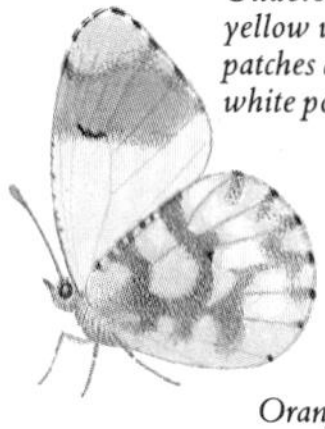

*Orange-grey apex*

♀

***Hindwing** flushed pale yellow*

***Uppers** white with black spot on fwing larger, not enclosed by orange area as in ♂*

There are two subspecies of the Moroccan orange tip, the European one being *A. belia euphenoides* (illustrated). Usually found in mountainous regions up to 2,000 m, it is sometimes mistaken for the Eastern orange tip, even though their ranges do not overlap. The latter has a bolder underside hindwing pattern. *WS:* 36–40 mm; *Flight:* May–July; *Gen:* 1; *FP:* Buckler mustard (*Biscutella laevigata*); *D:* Spain, Portugal, S France, Italy, Switz.

# Eastern orange tip

## *A. damone*

***Uppers** similar to Moroccan orange tip*

***Underside hindwing** strongly mottled green and yellow, in irregular pattern like that of the Orange tip*

♂

♀

***Uppers** white, lacking orange patch near forewing apex*

***Underside** markings as in ♂*

Very little is known about this local orange tip which flies on rocky mountain slopes up to 1,000 m. *WS:* 38–40 mm; *Flight:* Apr–June; *Gen:* 1; *FP:* Woad (*Isatis tinctoria*); *D:* Sicily, S Italy, Greece, SE Yugoslavia.

# Sooty orange tip

## *Zegris eupheme*

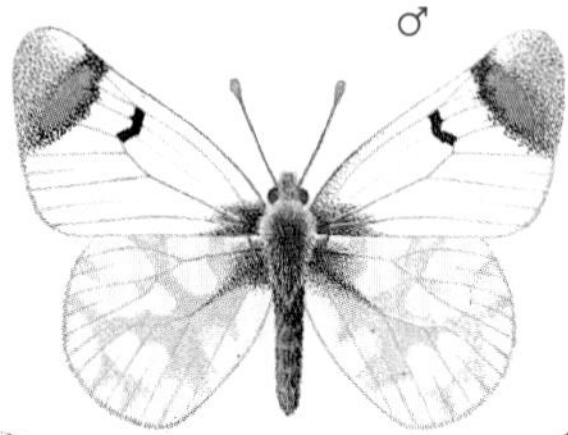

♂

***Forewing*** *apical area grey-green enclosing small orange patch; central black mark curved*

***Underside hindwing*** *yellow, marbled grey-green as in Moroccan orange tip*

***Forewing*** *orange patch smaller than in ♂, often absent;* ***underside*** *apex yellow in both sexes*

♀

♀ *often larger than* ♂

Very local in southern Europe, this species has a fast flight which carries it over rough flowery slopes up to 1,000 m. At lower altitudes in southern Spain it may be on the wing as early as April, becoming later with increasing altitude. *WS:* 46–50 mm; *Flight:* Apr–June; *Gen:* 1; *FP:* Hoary mustard (*Sinapis incana*); *D:* S Spain, S Portugal.

# Mountain clouded yellow

## *Colias phicomone*

♂

***Forewing*** *row of pale submarginal spots stands out against dark border*

***Uppers*** *yellowish green with heavy dusting of grey scales*

***Hindwing*** *darker, bright spot visible from underside*

♀

***Uppers*** *paler whitish green but otherwise similar to ♂; amount of grey variable*

***Underside hindwing*** *bright yellow in both sexes with clear orange central spot*

Found on Alpine meadows from 2,000 m upwards, this species occasionally produces a second brood in September. *WS:* 40–50 mm; *Flight:* June–Aug; *Gen:* 1; *FP:* Leguminosae, esp *Vicia*; *D:* Spain (Cantabrians, Pyrenees), Switz, Austria, S France (Alps).

# Moorland clouded yellow

## C. palaeno

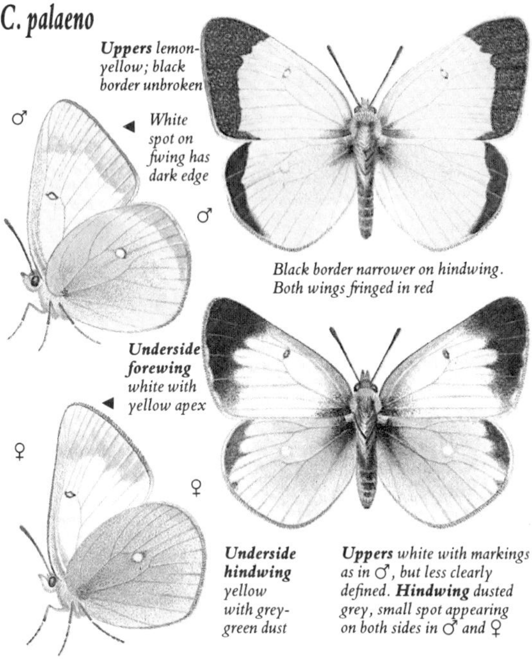

**Uppers** *lemon-yellow; black border unbroken*
♂
*White spot on fwing has dark edge*
♂
*Black border narrower on hindwing. Both wings fringed in red*
***Underside forewing*** *white with yellow apex*
♀
♀
***Underside hindwing*** *yellow with grey-green dust*
***Uppers*** *white with markings as in ♂, but less clearly defined.* ***Hindwing*** *dusted grey, small spot appearing on both sides in ♂ and ♀*


Several subspecies based on small differences in colour and pattern have been described. The Moorland clouded yellow is a strong flier, found in lowland bogs. *WS:* 48–64 mm; *Flight:* June–July; *Gen:* 1; *FP:* Bog whortleberry (*Vaccinium uliginosum*); *D:* Scand, NE France, Germany, Poland, Czech, Alps.

# Pale Arctic clouded yellow

## C. nastes

***Uppers*** *lemon yellow without heavy dusting of dark scales*
♂
*Wing fringes usually red*
***Hindwing*** *tiny round yellow spot near centre*


The Pale Arctic clouded yellow is, as its name suggests, strictly an Arctic species and for this reason is unlikely to be mistaken in the field for the Mountain clouded yellow, which only flies in the Pyrenees and Alps. The female is whiter with more grey scales on the hindwing. Found on mountainous moorland above 400 m. *WS:* 44–48 mm; *Flight:* June–July; *Gen:* 1; *FP:* Alpine milk vetch (*Astragalus alpinus*); *D:* N Scandinavia.

# Lesser clouded yellow

## *Colias chrysotheme*

♂

***Forewing*** *central spot small, often reddish*

*Dark wing borders crossed by yellow veins*

***Underside*** *yellow with row of black postdiscal spots on both wings*

The female is closer in appearance to the female Danube clouded yellow, except that the more pointed forewing has a broad, greenish grey costal margin. Flies over grassland up to 1,000 m. *WS:* 40–48 mm; *Flight:* May–Aug; *Gen:* 2; *FP:* Hairy tare (*Vicia hirsuta*); *D:* Austria, Hungary, Romania, Czech.

# Danube clouded yellow

## *C. myrmidone*

*Wide black borders not crossed by yellow veins*

♂

▲

***Underside*** *series of black postdiscal spots small or absent*

***Uppers*** *deep orange-yellow.* ***Forewing*** *dark spot is generally quite small*

*♀ has yellow spots in dark forewing border* ▶

***Uppers*** *not as dark as ♂.* ***Hindwing*** *row of yellow submarginal spots conspicuous*

*Greenish white ♀s also exist*

♀

The main features to look out for when identifying this species are its deep orange uppers and the apparent lack of venation on the wing borders. It has the typical fast flight of the clouded yellows and is found mainly in the Danube basin. *WS:* 44–50 mm; *Flight:* May–Aug; *Gen:* 2; *FP:* Broom (*Cytisus*); *D:* Romania, Hungary, S Germany, Czech, Austria, Bulgaria.

# Balkan clouded yellow

## C. balcanica

♂

*Deeper in colour and with a duskier hindwing than the Danube clouded yellow; otherwise similar*

*Pale submarginal marks along the inside of the dark hindwing border are slightly more noticeable*

A very local species which is associated with the open woodland of the Balkan mountain range. The female is larger and darker than the female Danube clouded yellow. *WS:* 50–54 mm; *Flight:* July–Aug; *Gen:* 1; *FP:* unknown; *D:* Yugoslavia, Bulgaria (but not Greece).

# Greek clouded yellow

## C. libanotica

♂

***Uppers** dark orange with black border crossed by yellow veins*

*Very pale purple reflection on wing at certain angles*

***Underside** dull yellow-green, with red-edged spot on hindwing*

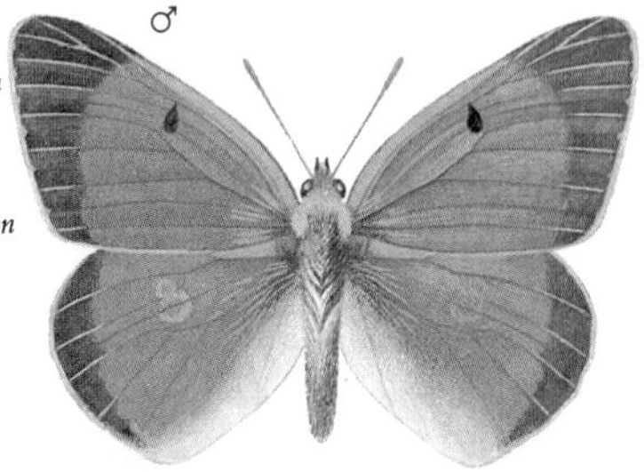

♀

*Black border broken by fairly large spots which form a regular series on hindwing*

***Underside hindwing** pale grey-green with small white central spot*

Like many of the other clouded yellows, the females may vary in colour, with some rare forms almost white. The pale purple sheen on the male upperside is an attractive and characteristic feature of this species. It occurs locally on mountain slopes from 1,600 to 2,600 m. *WS:* 54–56 mm; *Flight:* June–July; *Gen:* 1; *FP:* Milk vetch (*Astragalus*); *D:* Greece.

# Clouded yellow

## *Colias crocea*

♂

***Uppers** bright orange-yellow with broad black margins crossed by yellow veins*

***Underside** yellow with green tinge on forewing margin and all over hindwing*

♀

*Differs from ♂ in having wider black margins enclosing yellow spots of uneven size*

***Hindwing** dusky with prominent orange spots*

♀

**C. crocea** ***f.*** **helice,** *a ♀ form, has pale green-white uppers with grey suffusion over hindwings*

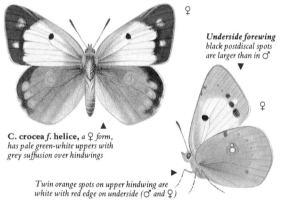

***Underside forewing** black postdiscal spots are larger than in ♂*

♀

*Twin orange spots on upper hindwing are white with red edge on underside (♂ and ♀)*

The Clouded yellow is a powerful, fast-flying butterfly which is strongly migratory and may appear anywhere in Europe except for the more northerly areas of Scandinavia. Unable to survive the northern winter, the British population depends each year on fresh migrations from the Mediterranean, the first butterflies usually arriving in late May. These migrants breed to produce a "native" generation in August and September and are most commonly seen along the south coast. The Clouded yellow prefers open spaces, and is attracted to fields of clover or lucerne. *WS:* 46–54 mm; *Flight:* Apr–Sept; *Gen:* several; *FP:* Birdsfoot trefoil (*Lotus corniculatus*), Lucerne (*Medicago sativa*), Clover (*Trifolium*); *D:* Europe (migrant to Britain, Holland, S Scand).

# Northern clouded yellow

## C. hecla

♂

***Uppers*** *orange-yellow with dark wing borders crossed by yellow veins and dusted with yellow scales on forewing*

***Underside*** *grey-green except for pale orange-yellow discal area in forewing*

♀

***Forewing*** *paler than ♂ with dark veins and yellow-green spots in margin*

***Hindwing*** *dusted with grey scales; submarginal spots in regular series*

Locally common up to 1,000 m, the Northern clouded yellow is probably circumpolar, occurring in Arctic Europe and N America. White females are unknown. *WS:* 40–46 mm; *Flight:* June–July; *Gen:* 1; *FP:* Alpine milk vetch (*Astragalus alpinus*); *D:* N Scand.

# Pale clouded yellow

## C. hyale

♂

▲ ***Underside hindwing*** *golden yellow with white, red-edged spot shaped like figure of 8*

*♀ white with slight green tint; otherwise similar to ♂*

♂ ***Uppers*** *pale yellow with spots in forewing border*

♀

***Hindwing*** *lacks grey suffusion, distinguishing it from ♀ Clouded yellow* ▶

Originates in southern Europe and migrates northwards, feeding on clover. Probably replaced in Italy and Spain by *C. australis* (p 44). A rare migrant to Britain. *WS:* 42–50 mm; *Flight:* May–Sept; *Gen:* 2–3; *FP:* Clover (*Trifolium*); *D:* Europe (not N Scand).

# Berger's clouded yellow

## *Colias australis*

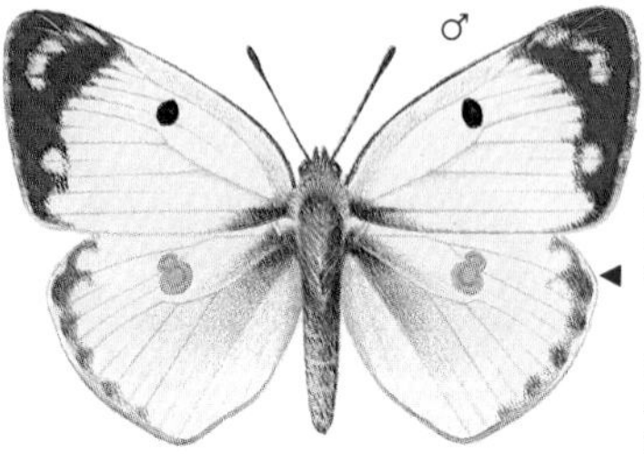

♂

*Distinguished from very similar* C. hyale *by brighter, lemon-yellow ground colour*

***Hindwing*** *has large, bright orange central spot and narrow dark margin*

*♀ greenish white, pattern as in ♂; difficult to separate from ♀* C. hyale

The range of this species is uncertain because of its similarity to *C. hyale* (p 43). The latter prefers lucerne fields while Berger's clouded yellow is commoner on downs. *WS:* 42–54 mm; *Flight:* May–Sept; *Gen:* 2; *FP:* Horseshoe vetch (*Hippocrepis comosa*); *D:* W and C Europe (not Scand; migrant to S Britain, Holland).
***C. erate*** (Eastern pale clouded yellow) is yellow with unbroken dark borders in the male. *WS:* 46–52 mm; *D:* SE Europe.

# Cleopatra

## *Gonepteryx cleopatra*

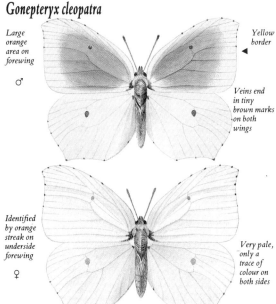

*Large orange area on forewing*

♂

*Yellow border*

*Veins end in tiny brown marks on both wings*

*Identified by orange streak on underside forewing*

♀

*Very pale, only a trace of colour on both sides*

Cleopatra is a rapid flier, similar in shape and colouring to the commoner Brimstone (p 45). Overwinters in the adult form and is locally common on open, lightly wooded slopes. There are several subspecies. *WS:* 50–68 mm; *Flight:* Feb–Aug; *Gen:* 1; *FP:* Buckthorn (*Rhamnus*); *D:* Spain, S France, Italy, Greece, Yugoslavia.

# Brimstone

## G. rhamni

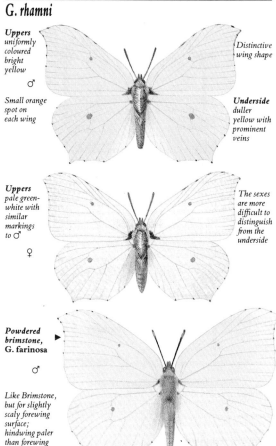

***Uppers*** *uniformly coloured bright yellow*

♂

*Small orange spot on each wing*

*Distinctive wing shape*

***Underside*** *duller yellow with prominent veins*

***Uppers*** *pale green-white with similar markings to ♂*

♀

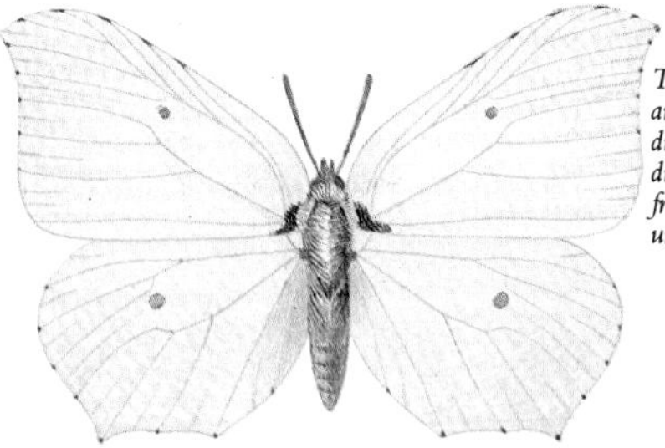

*The sexes are more difficult to distinguish from the underside*

**Powdered brimstone, G. farinosa** ►

♂

*Like Brimstone, but for slightly scaly forewing surface; hindwing paler than forewing*

***G. rhamni.*** In Britain, any bright yellow butterfly seen in early spring is likely to be the male of this species. The female usually emerges a little later and is sometimes mistaken for a white, but on settling the leaf-like shape of the wing instantly identifies her. It is possible that the Brimstone was once known as the "butter-coloured fly" and that the contracted form gave rise to the word "butterfly". The species has a powerful flight and is common in woods, gardens and roadsides up to 2,000 m. It is one of the few butterflies to hibernate in the adult form, hiding in evergreen plants such as Ivy, where its closed wings provide an effective camouflage. *WS:* 52–60 mm; *Flight:* July–Sept (hibernated specimens appear in April to lay eggs); *Gen:* 1; *FP:* Buckthorn (*Rhamnus catharticus*), Alder buckthorn (*R. frangula*); *D:* Europe (but not N Scandinavia, Scotland).

***G. farinosa.*** Rarer; on mountains. *WS:* 56–64 mm; *Flight:* May–June; *Gen:* 1; *FP:* Buckthorn (*Rhamnus*); *D:* SE Europe.

# Wood white

## *Leptidea sinapis*

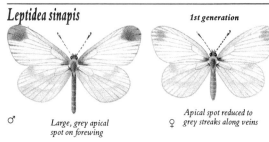

***1st generation***

♂ *Large, grey apical spot on forewing*

♀ *Apical spot reduced to grey streaks along veins*

Smaller, more fragile than the other whites, the Wood white may be found flying close to the ground in forest clearings and woodland edges. The second generation is whiter with smaller but blacker apical spots. *WS:* 36–48 mm; *Flight:* May–Aug; *Gen:* 2 or more; *FP:* Everlasting pea (*Lathyrus*), Birdsfoot trefoil (*Lotus*); *D:* Europe (but not Scotland, Holland, Denmark, N Scand).

# Eastern wood white

## *L. duponcheli*

***1st generation***

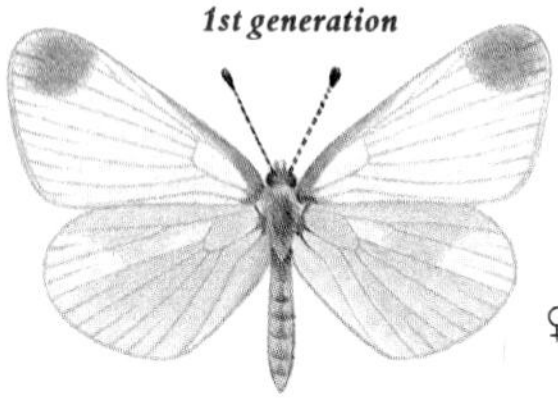

♀

♂

*Wings slightly pointed, tinged yellow*

*Grey spot reduced in 2nd gen*

The antennal clubs of this species are dark underneath, unlike those of the Wood white which have a white mark. Flies over open slopes. *WS:* 34–42 mm; *Flight:* Apr–Aug; *Gen:* 2; *FP:* Sainfoin (*Onobrychis viciifolia*); *D:* S France, SE Europe.

# Fenton's wood white

## *L. morsei*

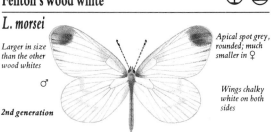

*Larger in size than the other wood whites*

♂

***2nd generation***

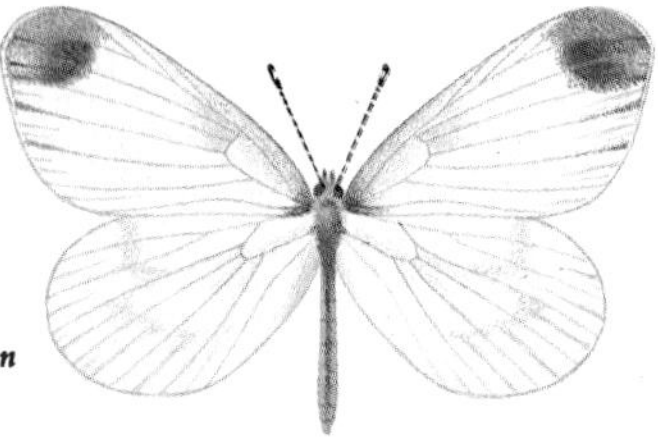

*Apical spot grey, rounded; much smaller in ♀*

*Wings chalky white on both sides*

The antennal clubs are white underneath, as in the Wood white. It is also mainly a woodland species, with a typical weak flight. The first generation is usually greyer than the second. *WS:* 42–46 mm; *Flight:* Apr–July; *Gen:* 2; *FP:* Spring pea (*Lathyrus vernus*); *D:* Austria, Hungary, Romania, NW Yugoslavia.

# Monarch butterflies Danaidae

Most of the species in this family occur in the tropics of Africa and southeast Asia, but there are a few which originate in the New World continents of North and South America. One of these, the Monarch, is famous for its remarkable annual migration from Mexico to Canada. Occasionally some migrants stray off-course and arrive in Europe, but there is some debate over whether these butterflies come from America or from the nearer Canary Islands. The adults tend to be large, brightly coloured butterflies with a powerful but unhurried flight. They are distasteful to predators and are extremely tough, being able to withstand the odd trial peck from a curious bird without shortening their adult life of 8 or 9 months. In both sexes the front legs are small and not used for walking.

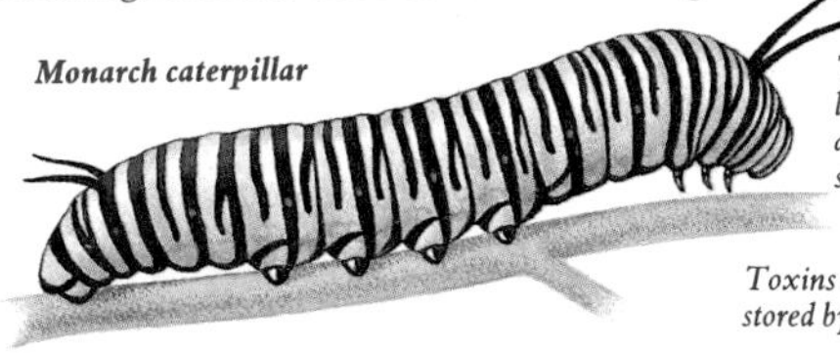
Monarch caterpillar
Two pairs of long black horns at each end of smooth body
Toxins in foodplant are stored by caterpillar

## Monarch

## *Danaus plexippus*

Chestnut-brown wings with black veins; 2 rows of white spots in wide black borders
♂

The infrequent but regular occurrence of this large and beautiful butterfly in Europe often gives rise to much local interest. Unfortunately it is unable to breed in the wild in Europe because its foodplant does not grow here. However, in other parts of the world such as Australia, Java and the Philippines, the Monarch or Milkweed has successfully established itself by adapting to new foodplants. In America the butterflies move in large numbers and some of their winter tree roosts have become tourist attractions. *WS:* 75–100 mm; *Flight:* all year (late summer in Europe); *Gen:* several; *FP:* Milkweed (*Asclepias curassavica*); *D:* migrant to W Europe, incl Britain.

***D. chrysippus*** (Plain tiger) is an African species, similar in colouring but less prominently marked. *WS:* 70–84 mm; *Flight:* summer; *D:* migrant to Mediterranean, esp Greece and S Italy.

# Snout butterflies Libytheidae

This is a family of comparatively few species, with one in Europe, one in North America, and the rest in the Old World tropics of Africa and Asia. The butterflies tend to be small in size, and are characterized by the long palps that project in front of the head like a beak or snout, giving the family its popular name. The wing borders are serrated, with a prominent tooth on the forewing. Many species are migratory and of similar appearance, usually with a dark brown ground colour and orange markings. The forelegs are reduced in the male, as in the Nymphalidae, but in the female they are of normal length.

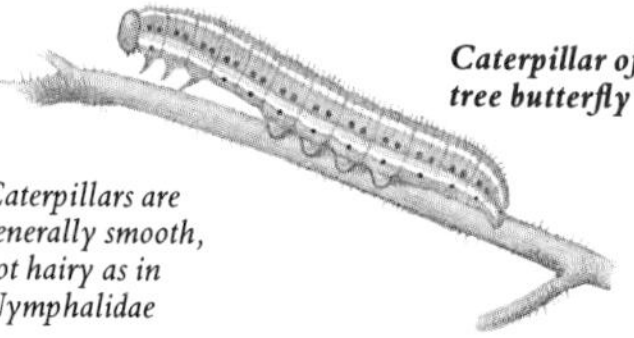

***Caterpillar of Nettle-tree butterfly***

*Caterpillars are generally smooth, not hairy as in Nymphalidae*

## Nettle-tree butterfly

## *Libythea celtis*

♂

♂

*Long snout protrudes from below the head*

***Underside hindwing*** *greyish brown, with thin white central line*

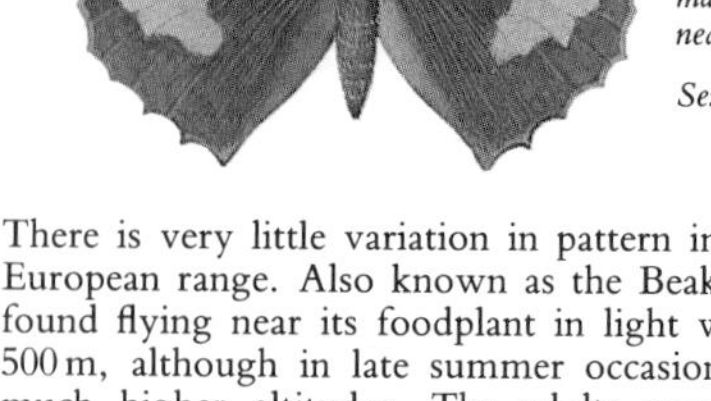
♀

▲ *Distinguished by prominent tooth on forewing border*

***Uppers*** *brown with orange markings and white spot near forewing apex*

*Sexes are similar*

There is very little variation in pattern in this species over its European range. Also known as the Beak butterfly, it may be found flying near its foodplant in light woodland areas up to 500 m, although in late summer occasional vagrants occur at much higher altitudes. The adults spend a long period in hibernation, from September until March when they fly again to lay their eggs for the next generation. The distinctive toothing on the forewing border and the protruding snout easily distinguish it from other European butterflies. *WS:* 34–44 mm; *Flight:* Mar–Apr, June–Sept; *Gen:* 1; *FP:* Nettle tree (*Celtis australis*); *D:* Spain, Portugal, S France, Italy, Sicily, Austria, Romania, Yugoslavia, Bulgaria, Hungary, Greece, Corsica, Sardinia.

# **Brush-footed butterflies** Nymphalidae

This family, by far the largest, has been divided into many subfamilies, with species occurring all over the world. They are medium to large in size, often brightly coloured, and include some of the best-known butterflies, such as the tortoiseshells, admirals and peacocks. The adults in both sexes have reduced forelegs which are tucked up against the thorax, so that only four legs are used for walking. Attached to these forelegs, especially in the male, are dense tufts of scales, which give a "brush-footed" appearance. The caterpillars are usually spiny and often very striking, but vary considerably. Some, such as the Small tortoiseshell (p 57), live in large groups in silken webs.

*Gregarious. Black spiny body speckled with white*

***Peacock caterpillar***

## Two-tailed pasha

## *Charaxes jasius*

***Forewing*** *row of orange postdiscal spots diminishes towards hind margin*

*Wide orange border on both wings*

♂

***Hindwing*** *border edged in black with proximal blue spots*

The underside of this butterfly bears little resemblance to the upperside, being conspicuously marked with black spots and streaks outlined in white and set against a chocolate-brown ground colour. The two short tails on the hindwing are quite conspicuous, but usually it is the rapid and powerful flight that is first noticed. The Two-tailed pasha is the only representative in Europe of a widespread African group, with a range confined mainly to the coastal regions and islands of the Mediterranean. It rarely flies above 800 m and is very local in distribution. The female is larger than the male but otherwise similar in markings. *WS:* 76–83 mm; *Flight:* May–Sept; *Gen:* 2; *FP:* Strawberry tree (*Arbutus unedo*); *D:* Spain, Portugal, S France, Italy (west coast only), Greece, Yugoslavia, Albania, Corsica, Sardinia, Sicily.

# Purple emperor

## *Apatura iris*

♂
Purple iridescence seen only from certain angles; otherwise wings appear brownish
**Forewing** has obscure round black spot near middle of outer margin

♀
♀ not as dark as ♂ and lacking purple sheen
White markings larger than ♂

Considered to be a rare species, this large and beautiful butterfly has a powerful flight and is much sought-after by collectors. Elusive rather than rare would perhaps be a more apt description, as it spends most of its time in the tree tops, the males occasionally coming down to feed at damp patches such as sap, dung and carrion. The females seldom descend except to deposit their eggs on young willow trees. Well-established oakwoods up to 1,000 m form the main breeding grounds, within which an adequate supply of foodplant must be found. In Britain the species has only been recorded in the south and east. There is a recurrent rare form, f. *iole*, which lacks any white marks on its upperside. *WS:* 62–74 mm; *Flight:* July–Aug; *Gen:* 1; *FP:* Sallow (*Salix caprea*), Grey willow (*S. cinerea*); *D:* Europe (but not Italy, Balkans, Norway, Sweden).

# Lesser purple emperor

## A. ilia

♂

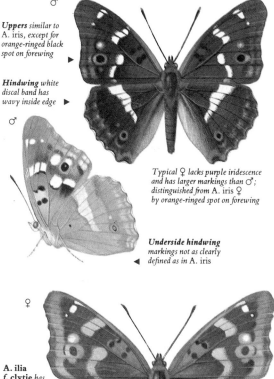

***Uppers** similar to* A. iris, *except for orange-ringed black spot on forewing* ▶

***Hindwing** white discal band has wavy inside edge* ▶

♂

*Typical ♀ lacks purple iridescence and has larger markings than ♂; distinguished from* A. iris ♀ *by orange-ringed spot on forewing*

◀ ***Underside hindwing** markings not as clearly defined as in* A. iris

♀

**A. ilia *f.* clytie** *has pale yellow-brown markings on uppers in ♂ and ♀, except for white apical spots on forewing*

Both sexes occur in two distinct forms in most localities: the "typical" dark brown form which resembles the Purple emperor (p 50) and the yellowish brown form, f. *clytie*. There are also several subspecies which vary slightly in pattern; *A. ilia barcina*, for example, has more extensive white markings. The Lesser purple emperor is a widespread woodland species, with similar habits to the Purple emperor. *WS:* 64–70 mm; *Flight:* May–June, Aug–Sept; *Gen:* 2 (1 in north); *FP:* Poplar (*Populus*), Willow (*Salix*); *D:* Europe (but not Britain, Holland, Scand).
***A. metis*** (Freyer's purple emperor) is similar but smaller, and its upper hindwing lacks a broad dark postdiscal band. Rare. *WS:* 60–64 mm; *Flight, Gen, FP:* as above; *D:* SE Europe.

# Poplar admiral

## *Ladoga populi*

**Forewing** white markings indistinct, often absent except for 3 apical spots
♂
**Hindwing** row of orange-red lunules distinctive

Full complement of white spots in ♀
♀
Markings more prominent than in ♂, especially white discal band on hindwing

Although the female has more white on the upperside than the male, it still has comparatively less than the White admiral (p 53). The row of orange-red, crescent-shaped marks on the hindwing is also diagnostic. During the day this butterfly is active in the tree tops, but the pungent smell of carrion or dung will often attract it down to the ground. Open woodland, especially along the edges of streams where poplars grow, is the preferred habitat, where it is most likely to be seen early in the day. The bright orange underside with white bands and dark spots contrasts markedly with the dark brown upperside. *WS:* 70–80 mm; *Flight:* June–Aug; *Gen:* 1; *FP:* Poplar (*Populus*), esp Aspen (*P. tremula*); *D:* C and E Europe (rare in W France, Denmark, Holland; absent from Spain, Portugal, Britain, peninsular Italy, Greece, N Scand).

# Southern white admiral

## *L. reducta*

**Forewing** *distinct white spot in cell; amount of white may vary*

***Uppers** with bluish tint; row of black submarginal spots edged in blue on both wings*

***Underside hwing** single row of black submarginal spots*

Distinguished from the White admiral by the single row of black spots on the hindwing underside and the central white spot on the forewing. It flies slowly and gracefully in lightly wooded areas, feeding at flowers with its wings outspread. The sexes are similar. *WS:* 46–54 mm; *Flight:* May–Sept; *Gen:* 2; *FP:* Honeysuckle (*Lonicera periclymenum*); *D:* S and C Europe (rare in N and W France; absent from Britain, Holland, N Germany, Scand).

# White admiral

## *L. camilla*

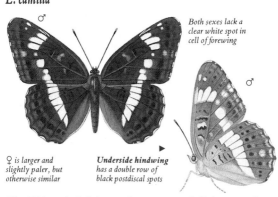

*Both sexes lack a clear white spot in cell of forewing*

*♀ is larger and slightly paler, but otherwise similar*

***Underside hindwing** has a double row of black postdiscal spots*

The White admiral has a slow, measured flight, sometimes gliding, and is locally common in woodland glades, where it feeds freely on blackberry blossom. In Britain its range in the south seems to be increasing, most noticeably in the Forest of Dean. Generally it occurs singly, but sometimes numbers may congregate in shady places, especially when feeding. *WS:* 52–60 mm; *Flight:* June–July; *Gen:* 1; *FP:* Honeysuckle (*Lonicera*); *D:* C Europe, incl S Britain, S Sweden (but not Ireland, Norway, Finland, S Italy).

# Common glider

## *Neptis sappho*

♂
▲ **Hindwing** clearly marked with large white discal band and narrower postdiscal band

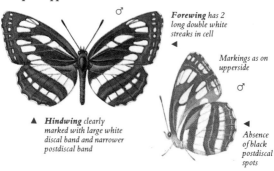

**Forewing** has 2 long double white streaks in cell ◀
Markings as on upperside
♂
◀ Absence of black postdiscal spots

The flight is steady with, as its name implies, a gliding as well as a flapping movement. It flies in woodlands and shrub-covered hillsides at low altitudes, and is commonly associated with Fenton's wood white (p 46), as they both share the same foodplant and distribution. The female is similar to the male and is readily distinguished from the Hungarian glider by the presence of two transverse white bands on the upper hindwing. Also popularly known as the Common sailer. *WS:* 44–48 mm; *Flight:* May–June, July–Sept; *Gen:* 2; *FP:* Spring pea (*Lathyrus vernus*); *D:* lower Austria, Hungary, Yugoslavia, Romania.

# Hungarian glider

## *N. rivularis*

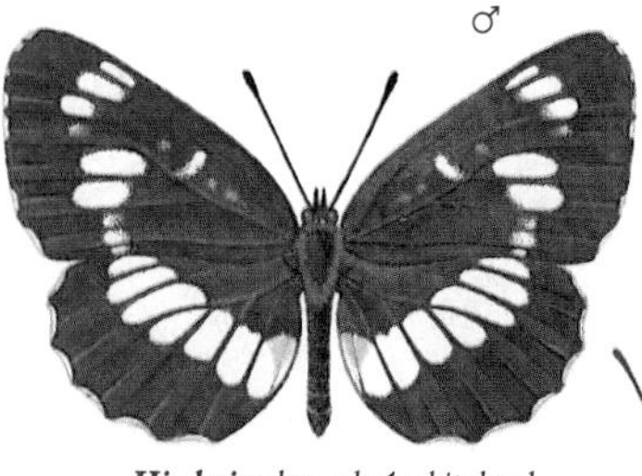
♂
**Hindwing** has only 1 white band, unlike Common glider which has 2

**Forewing** has reduced white marks in cell
Row of white submarginal spots absent ◀
♂

This species is similar in flight and distribution to the Common glider, but whereas the latter is found on shrubby hill slopes, the Hungarian glider is more restricted to woodlands and their edges. The reduced amount of white on the wings, notably the single white discal band on the hindwing, is characteristic. Although there are only two examples of this genus in Europe, many more are to be found in Africa. All are blackish with white markings and have a gliding flight. *WS:* 50–54 mm; *Flight:* June–July; *Gen:* 1; *FP: Spiraea*, possibly Meadowsweet (*Filipendula*); *D:* Austria, Switzerland, Czechoslovakia, Yugoslavia, Hungary, Romania, Bulgaria, N Greece.

# Camberwell beauty

## *Nymphalis antiopa*

Sexes are similar
♂
Wide, creamy yellow border
Row of violet-blue spots just inside margin on both wings

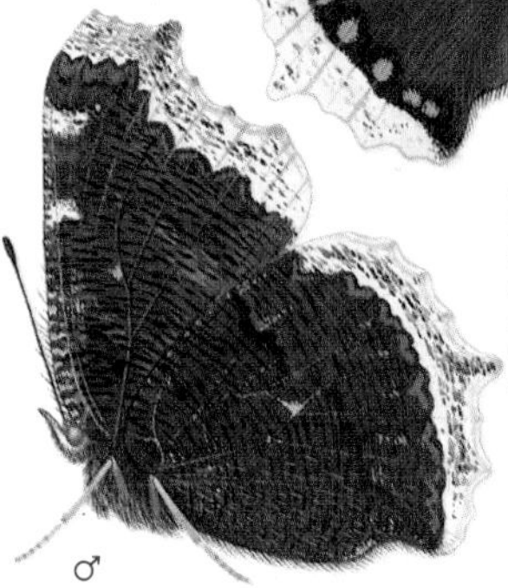
♂

*Once known as "Grand surprise" because of its unexpected and striking appearance, which is quite unlike that of any other European species. Originally discovered in Camberwell, but may appear anywhere*

***Underside*** *dark brown, relieved by almost-white border*

◀

A regular migrant with a powerful flight, it occurs throughout Europe, although its appearance in Britain is rare. The adults feed on tree sap and bask in sun with wings outspread. *WS:* 60–65 mm; *Flight:* June–Sept; *Gen:* 1; *FP:* Willow (*Salix*); *D:* Europe.

# Yellow-legged tortoiseshell

## *N. xanthomelas*

♂
Sharply angled wing
Distinguished by yellowish hair covering middle and hind legs
Black margins slightly wider than in Large tortoiseshell

Differs only slightly in pattern from the Large tortoiseshell (p 56), the most reliable diagnostic feature being its yellowish legs. Flies in damp woods. *WS:* 60–64 mm; *Flight:* July–Sept; *Gen:* 1; *FP:* Willow (*Salix*); *D:* E and SE Europe (migrates west).

# Large tortoiseshell

## *Nymphalis polychloros*

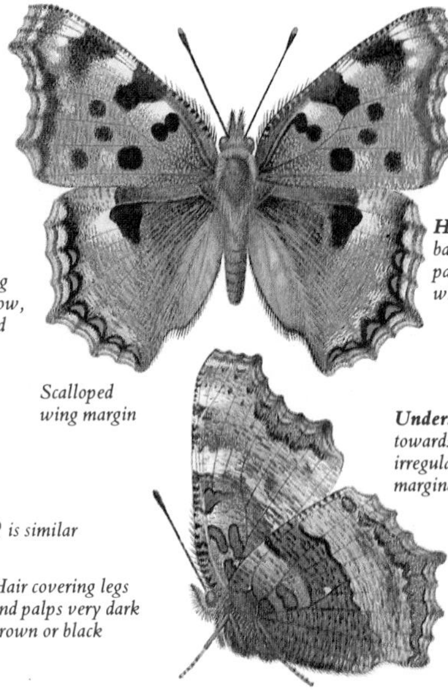
♂
**Forewing** *spots rounded*
*Inner edge of dark wing border narrow, well-defined*
**Hindwing** *basal area pale brown with long hairs*
*Scalloped wing margin*
**Underside** *darker towards base with irregular blue-grey marginal band*
♀ *is similar*
♂
*Hair covering legs and palps very dark brown or black*

Less common over its range than in former years; in Britain it is found in southern England and in parts of the Midlands. *WS:* 50–63 mm; *Flight:* June–Oct; *Gen:* 1; *FP:* Elm (*Ulmus*), Poplar (*Populus*), Willow (*Salix*); *D:* Europe (not Ireland; rare in Scand).

# False comma

## *N. vau-album*

♂
*More black on wings than in Large tortoise-shell*
*White spots near forewing apex and on costa of hindwing*
**Hindwing** *lacks any blue spots*

The white costal mark on the upper hindwing distinguishes this butterfly from the similar tortoiseshells. A rare and local species, it flies mainly over lowland meadows near woods. *WS:* 60–66 mm; *Flight:* July–Sept; *Gen:* 1; *FP:* Elm (*Ulmus*), Beech (*Fagus*); *D:* Romania, Bulgaria, Hungary (migrant to Poland, S Scand).

## Small tortoiseshell

# *Aglais urticae*

***Forewing*** *has distinctive white spot near apex*
*Blue spots border both wings*
♂
♂
***Underside*** *dark brown with yellowish area near margin*
***Hindwing*** *has large black basal area; cp Large tortoiseshell which has single black costal patch*

This colourful butterfly is one of the commonest in Europe, and is generally easy to recognize. Apart from being smaller than the Large tortoiseshell (p 56), it is usually brighter in colour, but this may vary between specimens. The adults are common in gardens and often hibernate in houses. *WS:* 44–50 mm; *Flight:* Mar–Apr, June–Oct; *Gen:* 1–2; *FP:* Nettle (*Urtica*); *D:* Europe.

## Comma

# *Polygonia c-album*

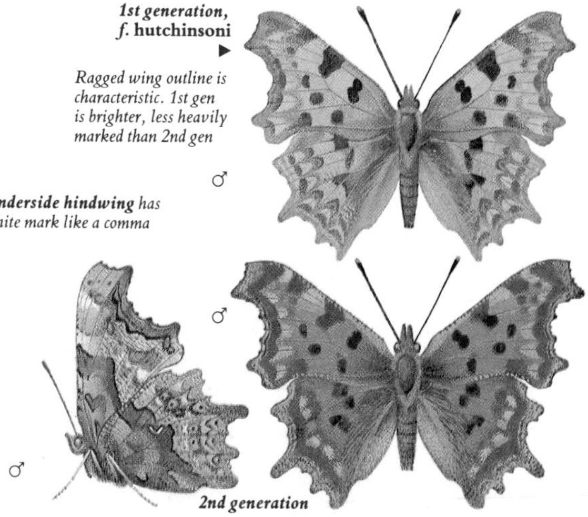
***1st generation, f.*** **hutchinsoni**
*Ragged wing outline is characteristic. 1st gen is brighter, less heavily marked than 2nd gen*
♂
***Underside hindwing*** *has white mark like a comma*
♂
♂
***2nd generation***

The lighter-coloured first generation is produced from the eggs laid by the overwintering butterflies in the spring. A rapid flier, attracted into gardens by buddleia and Michaelmas daisies. The British population seems to be increasing, but the species is rarely abundant. *WS:* 44–48 mm; *Flight:* Mar–July; *Gen:* 2; *FP:* Nettle (*Urtica*), Hop (*Humulus*); *D:* Europe (not Scotland, N Scand).

# Southern comma

## *Polygonia egea*

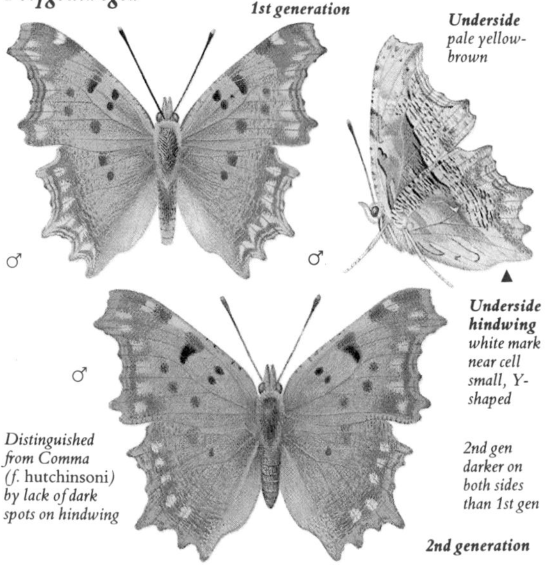

1st generation
Underside pale yellow-brown
♂
♂
Underside hindwing white mark near cell small, Y-shaped
♂
Distinguished from Comma (f. hutchinsoni) by lack of dark spots on hindwing
2nd gen darker on both sides than 1st gen
2nd generation


This species is generally paler and less heavily marked than the Comma (p 57). It has a rapid flight, often settling on the ground, and is locally common in hot, dry valleys and on slopes up to 1,400 m. Female is similar. *WS:* 44–46 mm; *Flight:* Apr–Sept; *Gen:* 2; *FP:* Pellitory of the wall (*Parietaria*); *D:* SE France, Italy, Corsica, Sardinia, Sicily, Greece, Yugoslavia.

# Map butterfly

## *Araschnia levana*

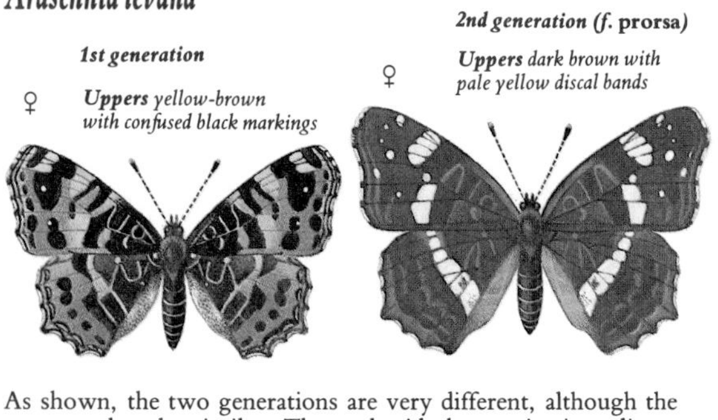

2nd generation (f. prorsa)
1st generation
♀
Uppers dark brown with pale yellow discal bands
♀
Uppers yellow-brown with confused black markings


As shown, the two generations are very different, although the sexes tend to be similar. The underside has an intricate linear pattern, with more purple in the margin of the first generation. Flies in light woods up to 900 m. *WS:* 32–38 mm; *Flight:* May–June, Aug–Sept; *Gen:* 2; *FP:* Nettle (*Urtica*); *D:* C Europe (but not Britain, Scand, S France, Italy, SE Balkans).

# Painted lady

## *Cynthia cardui*

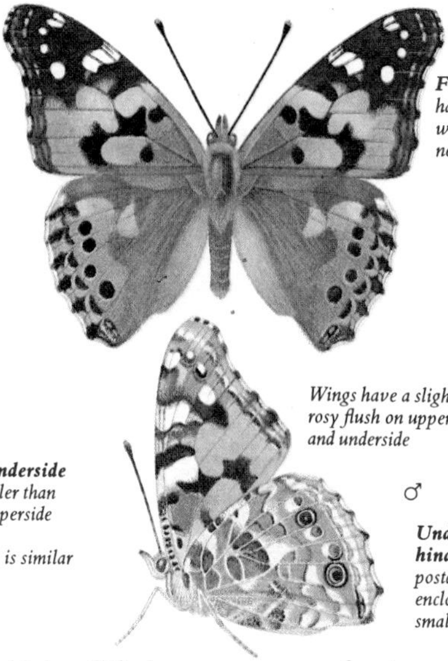
♂
**Uppers** yellowish brown with irregular black-brown markings
**Forewing** has small white spots near apex
Wings have a slight rosy flush on upper- and underside
**Underside** paler than upperside
♀ is similar
♂
**Underside hindwing** postdiscal area encloses 5 small eye-spots

The Painted lady will feed on many sources of nectar and so will frequent a variety of habitats. A rapid flier and strong migrant, it may appear and breed anywhere in Europe, but tends to be scarcer further north. The first migrants may not arrive in Britain until June. *WS:* 54–58 mm; *Flight:* Apr–Oct; *Gen:* 2–3; *FP:* Thistle (*Carduus*); *D:* Europe (as migrant from N Africa).

# American painted lady

## *C. virginiensis*

**Uppers** lack a rosy flush
**Underside hwing** has 2 large eye-spots in postdiscal band
♂
Blue eye-spots on hwing
♂

Common and widespread in America, this butterfly is an occasional migrant to Europe. It is smaller than the Painted lady and is found on flowery slopes. There have been several records of its appearance in Britain, the earliest one being in 1828. *WS:* 40–50 mm; *Flight:* June–Oct; *Gen:* 1; *FP:* Cudweed (*Gnaphalium*), other Compositae; *D:* migrant to SW Europe.

# Red admiral

## *Vanessa atalanta*

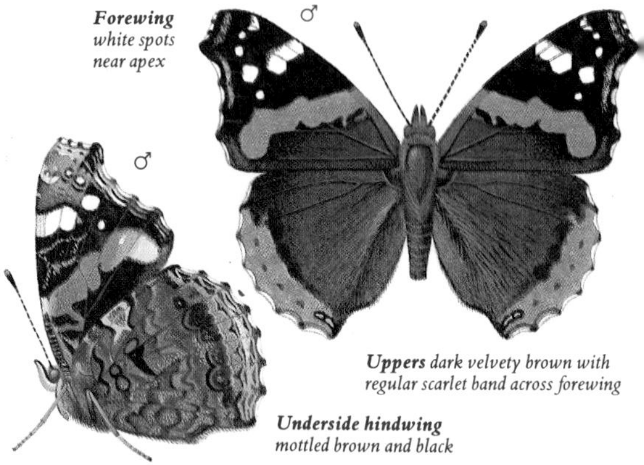

♂
♂
**Forewing** white spots near apex
**Uppers** dark velvety brown with regular scarlet band across forewing
**Underside hindwing** mottled brown and black


At rest, the Red admiral is unmistakable, with its red and black wings outspread. A visitor to gardens and parkland, it is attracted to a variety of flowers and, when in season, over-ripe fruit. It is a strong migrant and may appear anywhere in Europe, moving north each spring from its breeding grounds in the south. Few, if any, survive the northern winter. The butterfly is territorial in habit and may be observed patrolling the same area each day. The sexes are similar. *WS:* 56–63 mm; *Flight:* May–Oct (hibernated specimens appear early spring); *Gen:* 2–3; *FP:* Nettle (*Urtica*); *D:* Europe (rare in N Scand).

# Indian red admiral

## *V. indica vulcania*

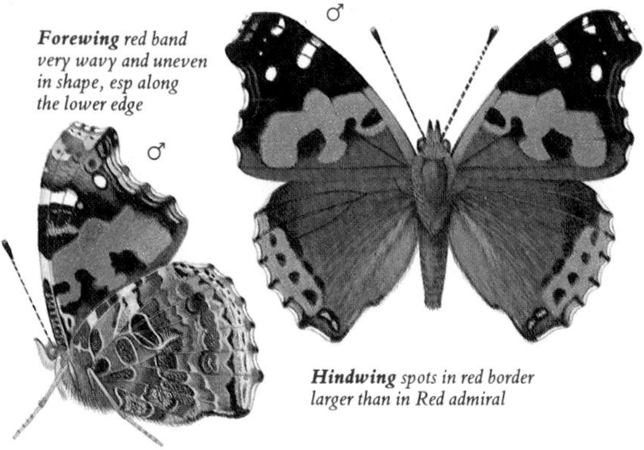

♂
♂
**Forewing** red band very wavy and uneven in shape, esp along the lower edge
**Hindwing** spots in red border larger than in Red admiral


Does not breed in Europe, but has been known to occur in the south as a vagrant (possibly from the Canaries). It has a powerful flight, similar to the Red admiral, and may be separated by the irregular shape of the red band on the forewing. *WS:* 54–60 mm; *Flight:* May–Oct; *Gen:* 2–3; *FP:* unknown; *D:* S Europe.

## Peacock butterfly

## *Inachis io*

*Large "peacock eye" on each wing is characteristic*

♂

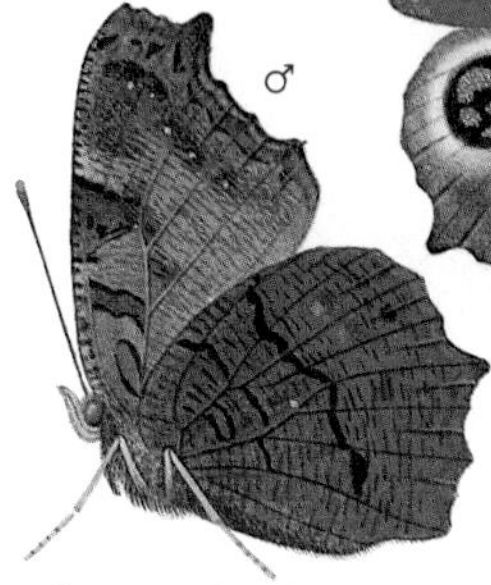

*♀ is similar but slightly larger*

***Underside** very dark, contrasting with bright upperside*

Well camouflaged by its dark underside when at rest but, if disturbed, the eye-spots on the upperside can startle predators. The Peacock must be one of the most conspicuous European butterflies, impossible to confuse with any other. Although not migratory, it is both common and widespread in many habitats. Adult overwinters. *WS:* 54–60 mm; *Flight:* July–Oct, spring; *Gen:* 1; *FP:* Nettle (*Urtica*); *D:* Europe (but not N Scand, N Scot).

## Pallas's fritillary

## *Argyronome laodice*

♂

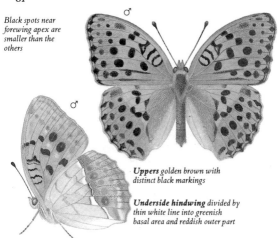

*Black spots near forewing apex are smaller than the others*

♂

***Uppers** golden brown with distinct black markings*

***Underside hindwing** divided by thin white line into greenish basal area and reddish outer part*

The female is paler with a small white spot near the forewing apex. A fast-flying species, found in damp woodland clearings. *WS:* 54–58 mm; *Flight:* July–Aug; *Gen:* 1; *FP:* Bog violet (*Viola palustris*); *D:* SE Finland, Poland, Hungary, Romania, Czech.

## *Pandoriana pandora*

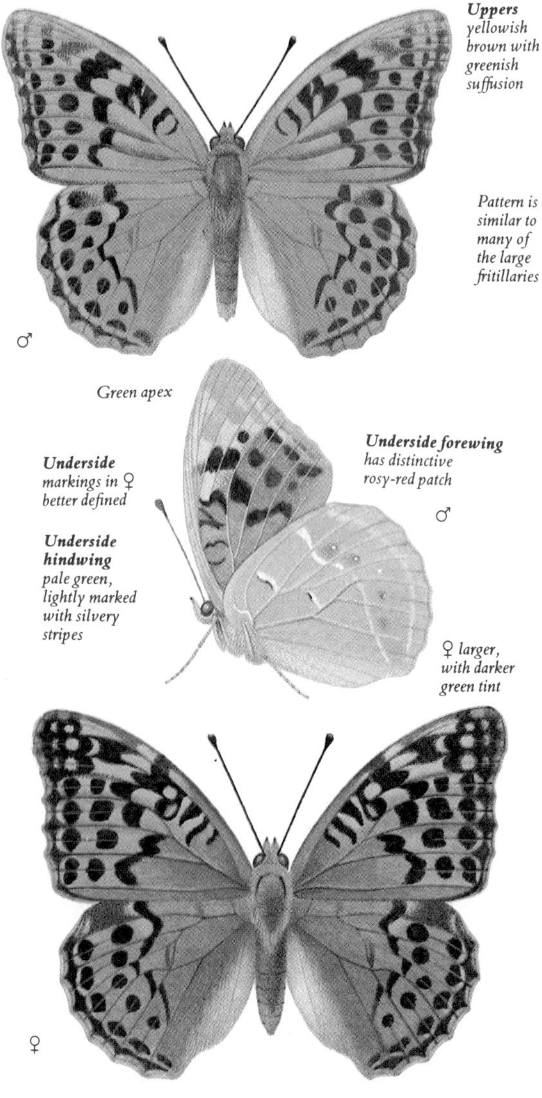
***Uppers***
*yellowish brown with greenish suffusion*
*Pattern is similar to many of the large fritillaries*
♂
*Green apex*
***Underside***
*markings in ♀ better defined*
***Underside hindwing***
*pale green, lightly marked with silvery stripes*
***Underside forewing***
*has distinctive rosy-red patch*
♂
*♀ larger, with darker green tint*
♀

The silvery bands on the underside hindwing of the Cardinal vary in different individuals and may even be absent. It has a rapid flight and is locally common in flowery meadows up to 1,200 m. *WS:* 64–80 mm; *Flight:* June–July; *Gen:* 1; *FP:* Violet (*Viola*); *D:* Spain, Portugal, S France, Italy, Sicily, Corsica, Sardinia, Austria, Hungary, Czechoslovakia, Balkans, Greece.

# Silver-washed fritillary

## *Argynnis paphia*

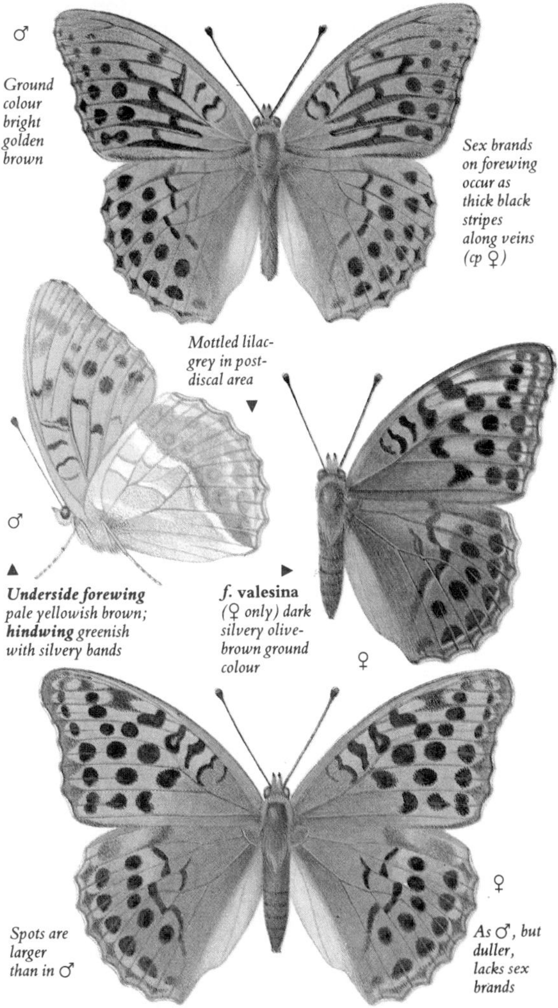
♂
Ground colour bright golden brown
Sex brands on forewing occur as thick black stripes along veins (cp ♀)
Mottled lilac-grey in post-discal area
♂
Underside forewing pale yellowish brown; hindwing greenish with silvery bands
f. valesina (♀ only) dark silvery olive-brown ground colour
♀
♀
Spots are larger than in ♂
As ♂, but duller, lacks sex brands

This fritillary derives its name from the silvery markings on its underside. Two female forms are illustrated; the dark form, f. *valesina*, is less common and only occurs in certain localities. In Britain, the butterfly is usually found in woods, mainly in the south and southwest. The adults are partial to bramble blossom and on sunny days they may be seen descending from the trees to feed. The female lays her eggs not on the foodplant but on near-by tree trunks, where the caterpillar hibernates until spring. *WS:* 54–70 mm; *Flight:* June–Aug; *Gen:* 1; *FP:* Violet (*Viola*); *D:* Europe (but not Scotland, N Scandinavia).

# Dark green fritillary

## *Mesoacidalia aglaja*

*Markings very variable*

♂

***Uppers*** *have typical intricate pattern of fritillaries*

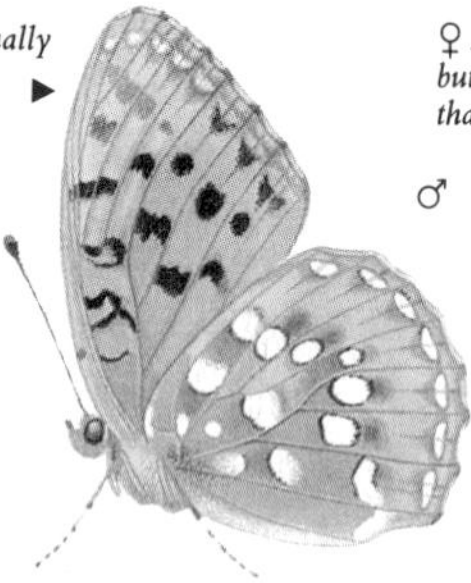

*Apex usually greenish* ▶

*♀ similar but paler than ♂*

♂

***Underside hindwing*** *has green suffusion around silvery spots*

◀ *Postdiscal spots absent (cp High brown fritillary)*

Difficult to distinguish from the High brown fritillary (p 65) without closely examining the underside of the hindwing, which in this species has silvery spots set against a greenish background. The females tend to vary more in colour on the upperside than the males, with some very pale naturally occurring forms. A rapid flier, often found in open countryside, but also in woodlands. *WS:* 48–58 mm; *Flight:* June–July; *Gen:* 1; *FP:* Violet (*Viola*); *D:* Europe (but not Corsica, Sardinia).

# Corsican fritillary

## *Fabriciana elisa*

♂ *Black marks small*

***Underside hwing*** *spots small, silver*

♂

Although not known outside Corsica and Sardinia, it is quite widespread on these islands. The species is characterized by the small size of the spots on the uppers and the numerous small silver spots on the underside hindwing. *WS:* 46–52 mm; *Flight:* June–July; *Gen:* 1; *FP:* Violet (*Viola*); *D:* Corsica, Sardinia.

# High brown fritillary

## *F. adippe*

♂

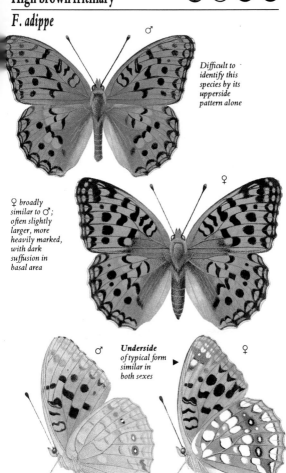

*Difficult to identify this species by its upperside pattern alone*

♀

*♀ broadly similar to ♂; often slightly larger, more heavily marked, with dark suffusion in basal area*

♂

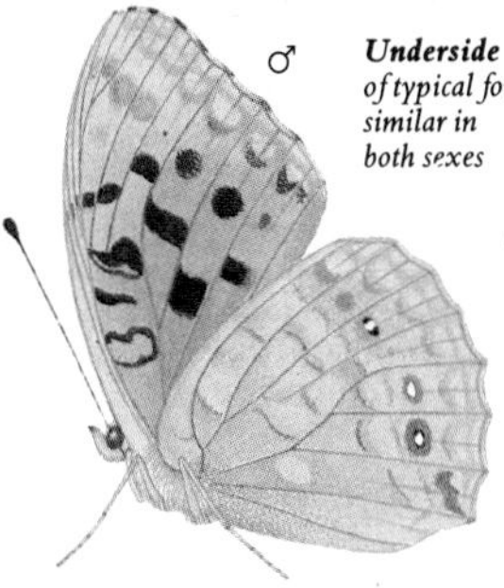

***Underside** of typical form similar in both sexes* ▶

♀

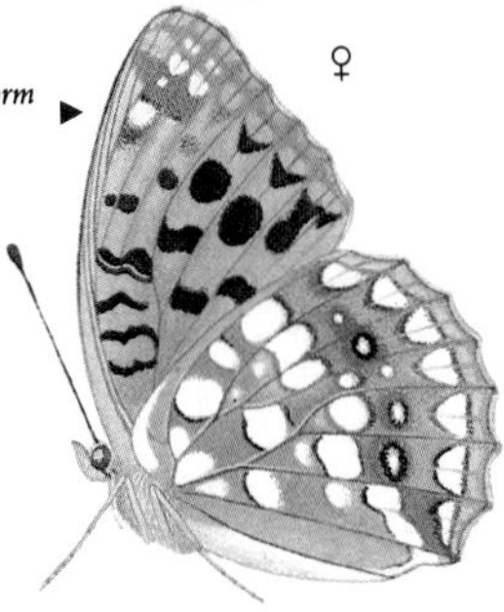

**F. adippe *f.* cleodoxa** *lacks typical silver spotting on underside*

*Distinguished by small, reddish, silver-centred postdiscal spots on hwing*

The most distinctive features of this species are on the underside hindwing, notably the row of reddish, silver-centred postdiscal spots which separate it from the Dark green fritillary (p 64). Several subspecies of the High brown fritillary have been described based on the presence or absence of silvery spots on the underside; for example, f. *cleodoxa*, a rare form in northern Europe, has pale spots without any silver (except in the postdiscal series). Recently the species has become less common in Britain and is found mainly in wooded areas of southern England. *WS:* 50–62 mm; *Flight:* June–July; *Gen:* 1; *FP:* Violet (*Viola*); *D:* Europe (but not Ireland, Scotland, N Scandinavia).

# Niobe fritillary

## *Fabriciana niobe*

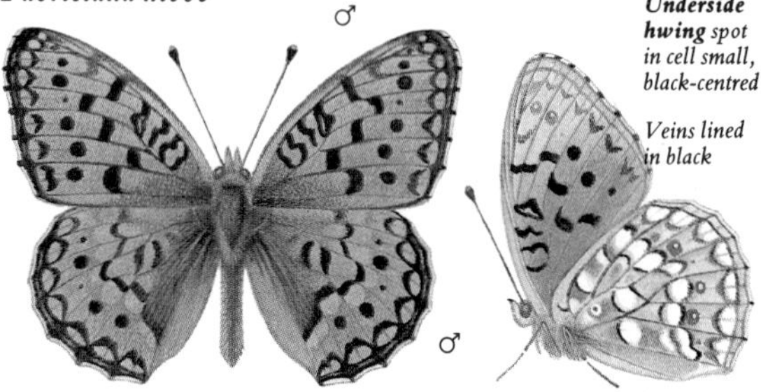
♂
♂
Underside hwing spot in cell small, black-centred
Veins lined in black

Very similar to the High brown fritillary (p 65), except that the underside hindwing is usually more greenish near the base and the silvery spots are smaller. *WS:* 46–60 mm; *Flight:* June–July; *Gen:* 1; *FP:* Violet (*Viola*); *D:* Europe (not Britain, N Scand).

# Queen of Spain fritillary

## *Issoria lathonia*

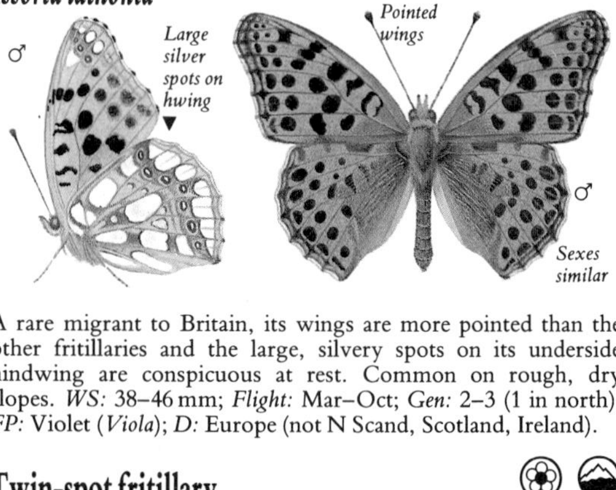
♂
Large silver spots on hwing
Pointed wings
♂
Sexes similar

A rare migrant to Britain, its wings are more pointed than the other fritillaries and the large, silvery spots on its underside hindwing are conspicuous at rest. Common on rough, dry slopes. *WS:* 38–46 mm; *Flight:* Mar–Oct; *Gen:* 2–3 (1 in north); *FP:* Violet (*Viola*); *D:* Europe (not N Scand, Scotland, Ireland).

# Twin-spot fritillary

## *Brenthis hecate*

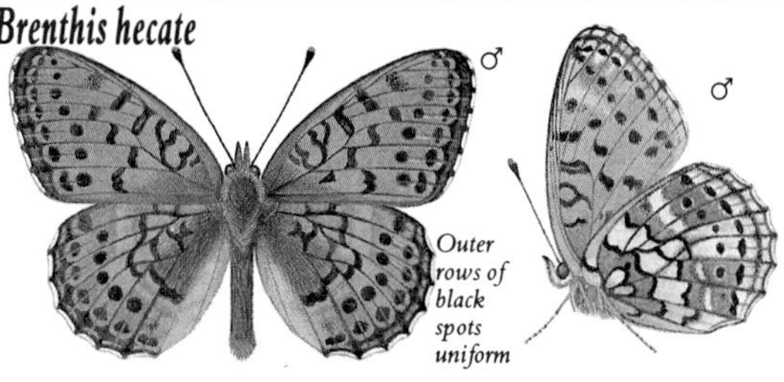
♂
♂
Outer rows of black spots uniform

The two uniform rows of black spots running parallel to the wing edge are distinctive. Occurs in small colonies on dry slopes between 600 and 1,500 m. *WS:* 36–44 mm; *Flight:* May–June; *Gen:* 1; *FP: Dorycnium*; *D:* Spain, S France, Italy, E Europe.

# Marbled fritillary

## *B. daphne*

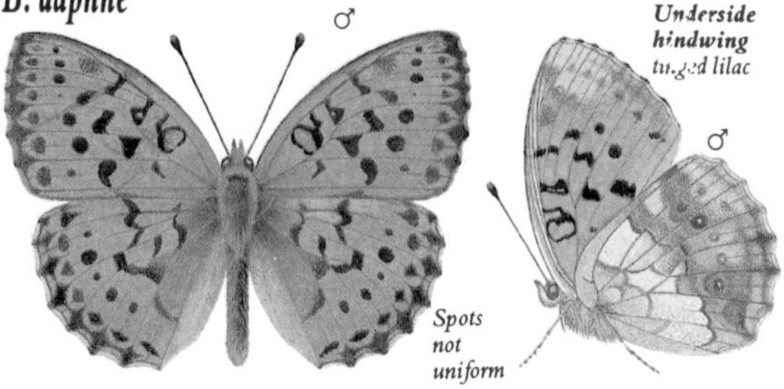
♂
Underside hindwing tinged lilac
♂
Spots not uniform

Distinguished from the Twin-spot fritillary (p 66) by the less distinct markings on the underside hindwing and the uneven row of postdiscal spots in the upper forewing. Flies in valleys up to 1,200 m. Common in eastern part of range. *WS:* 42–52 mm; *Flight:* June–July; *Gen:* 1; *FP:* Bramble (*Rubus*), Violet (*Viola*); *D:* N Spain, S France, Italy, Austria, Czech, Balkans, Greece.

# Lesser marbled fritillary

## *B. ino*

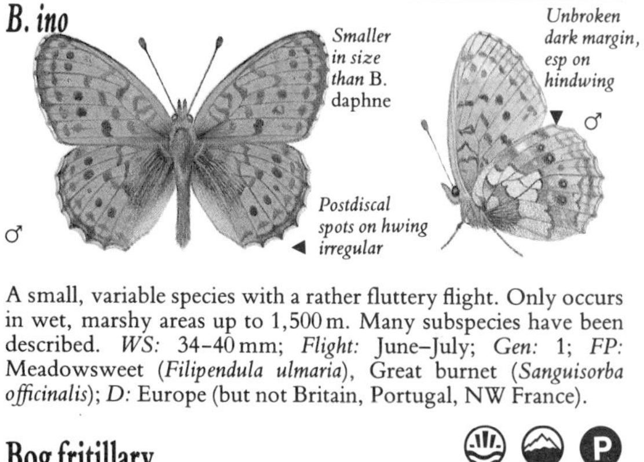
Smaller in size than B. daphne
Unbroken dark margin, esp on hindwing
♂
Postdiscal spots on hwing irregular
♂

A small, variable species with a rather fluttery flight. Only occurs in wet, marshy areas up to 1,500 m. Many subspecies have been described. *WS:* 34–40 mm; *Flight:* June–July; *Gen:* 1; *FP:* Meadowsweet (*Filipendula ulmaria*), Great burnet (*Sanguisorba officinalis*); *D:* Europe (but not Britain, Portugal, NW France).

# Bog fritillary

## *Proclossiana eunomia*

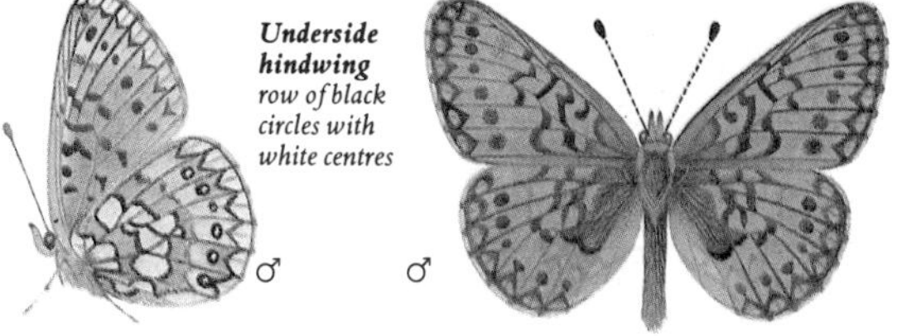
Underside hindwing row of black circles with white centres
♂
♂

The markings on the upperside are neat and regular with a zig-zag border. Life cycle unusually long: takes 2 years to develop from egg to adult. Found in boggy areas up to 1,500 m. *WS:* 40–46 mm; *Flight:* June–July; *Gen:* 1; *FP:* Bistort (*Polygonum bistorta*); *D:* Scand; local in France, Germany, Austria, Czech, Bulgaria.

# Shepherd's fritillary

## *Boloria pales*

♂
Spots round or squarish, not elongate
Hindwing has large, dark basal area
Underside forewing black marks ill defined
♂
♀
Underside hindwing brightly marked
♀
Slightly paler ground colour than ♂

Widespread over the central and southern European mountain ranges, this butterfly rarely flies below altitudes of 1,500 m. Subspecies from different localities vary in colour and pattern on the upperside; in the Pyrenees it is orange-brown with a small, dark basal area on the hindwing, while in the Apennines the subspecies is yellowish with more linear markings. *WS:* 32–40 mm; *Flight:* June–Aug; *Gen:* 1; *FP:* Violet (*Viola*); *D:* Spain, France, Italy, Austria, Switz, Poland, Germany, SE Europe.

# Mountain fritillary

## *B. napaea*

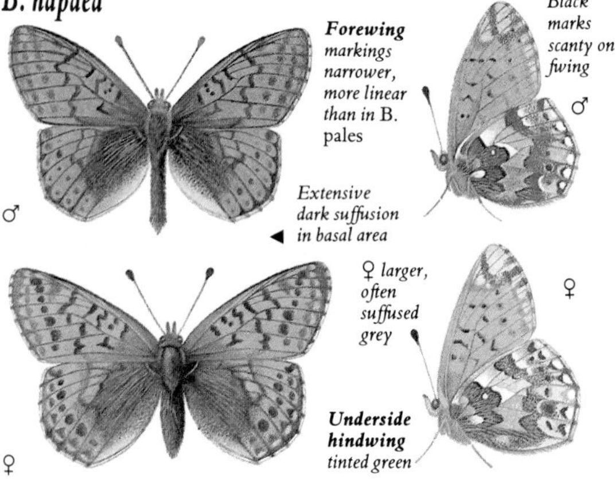
Forewing markings narrower, more linear than in B. pales
Black marks scanty on fwing
♂
♂
Extensive dark suffusion in basal area
♀ larger, often suffused grey
♀
Underside hindwing tinted green
♀

A true mountain species, found in small colonies usually in the wet areas at or above the tree-line from 1,500 to 3,000 m. The red and yellow on the underside hindwing are never as bright as in the Shepherd's fritillary (above). The life cycle from egg to adult usually takes 2 years. *WS:* 34–42 mm; *Flight:* July–Aug; *Gen:* 1; *FP:* Alpine bistort (*Polygonum viviparum*); *D:* France (Alps, Pyrenees), Switz, Austria, Italy (Alps), Scand (not Denmark).

# Cranberry fritillary

## B. aquilonaris

♂

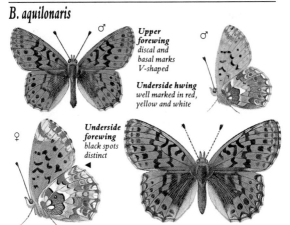

***Upper forewing*** *discal and basal marks V-shaped*

***Underside hwing*** *well marked in red, yellow and white*

♂

♀

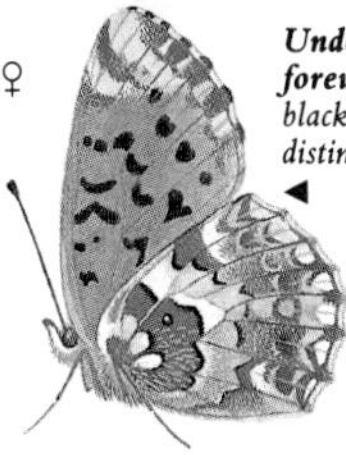

***Underside forewing*** *black spots distinct* ◀

♀ **B. aquilonaris** ***f.*** **alethea,** *a large form*

This species is found in boggy areas rich in sphagnum moss where the foodplant grows, from lowlands up to 1,800 m. The black markings on both sides are generally more prominent than in other *Boloria* species, although identification can still be difficult. Colonies tend to be small and isolated; specimens found in the north are often smaller than those further south. *WS:* 32–42 mm; *Flight:* June–July; *Gen:* 1; *FP:* Cranberry (*Vaccinium oxycoccus*); *D:* Scand, Poland, Czech, Austria, Germany, France, Switz.

# Balkan fritillary

## B. graeca

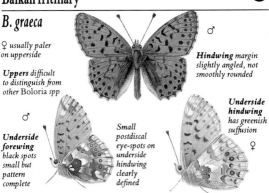

*♀ usually paler on upperside*

***Uppers*** *difficult to distinguish from other* Boloria *spp*

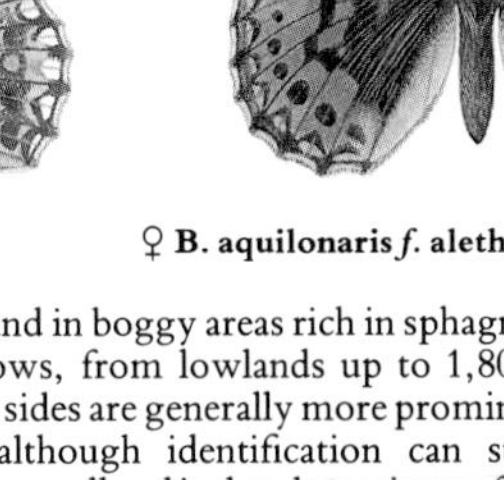

♂

***Hindwing*** *margin slightly angled, not smoothly rounded*

♂

***Underside forewing*** *black spots small but pattern complete*

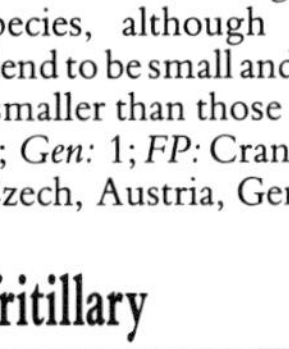

*Small postdiscal eye-spots on underside hindwing clearly defined*

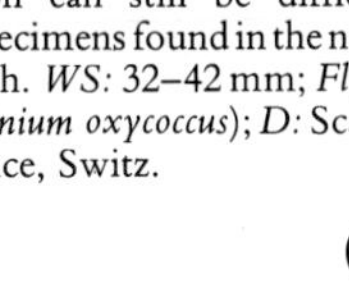

***Underside hindwing*** *has greenish suffusion*

♀

This species is found in the Balkans and southwestern Alps. The subspecies illustrated, *B. graeca graeca*, is restricted to Greece and southern Yugoslavia, and is brighter than the more widespread subspecies, *B. graeca balcanica*. Both fly in high mountainous areas up to the tree-line at 1,500–1,800 m. *WS:* 32–40 mm; *Flight:* July; *Gen:* 1; *FP:* unknown; *D:* SE France, Bulgaria, Romania, Yugoslavia, Greece.

# Pearl-bordered fritillary

## *Clossiana euphrosyne*

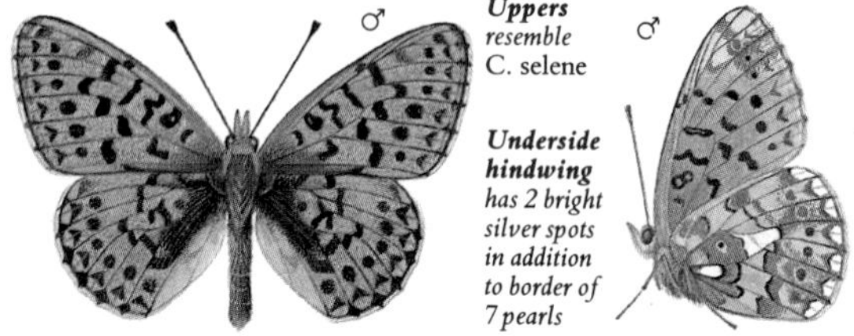
♂
Uppers resemble C. selene
♂
Underside hindwing has 2 bright silver spots in addition to border of 7 pearls

Distinguished from the Small pearl-bordered fritillary (below) by the pattern on the underside hindwing. A common and widespread species in woodlands and meadows up to 1,800 m, although in Britain it is strangely rare in the eastern counties. The sexes are similar. *WS:* 38–46 mm; *Flight:* Apr–Aug; *Gen:* 2 (1 in north); *FP:* Violet (*Viola*); *D:*Europe (but not S Spain).

# Small pearl-bordered fritillary

## *C. selene*

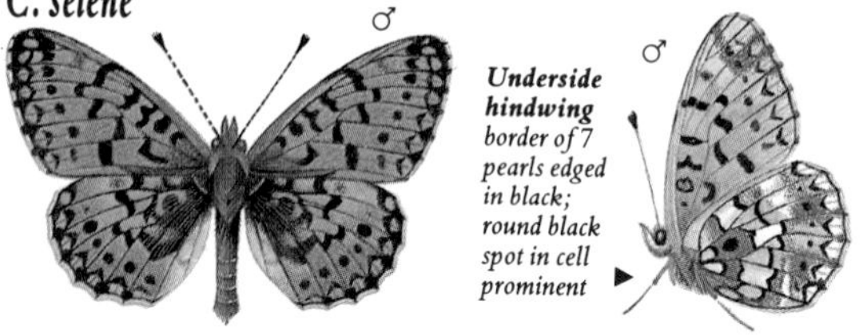
♂
♂
Underside hindwing border of 7 pearls edged in black; round black spot in cell prominent ▶

The Small pearl-bordered fritillary contains more black on its underside hindwing than *C. euphrosyne,* and does not have a prominent central silvery spot on this wing. The two species often fly together, but *C. selene* prefers damper areas. *WS:* 36–42 mm; *Flight:* Apr–Aug; *Gen:* 2 (1 in north); *FP:* Violet (*Viola*); *D:* Europe (not Ireland, S Spain, S Portugal, peninsular Italy, Greece, Mediterranean islands).

# Titania's fritillary

## *C. titania*

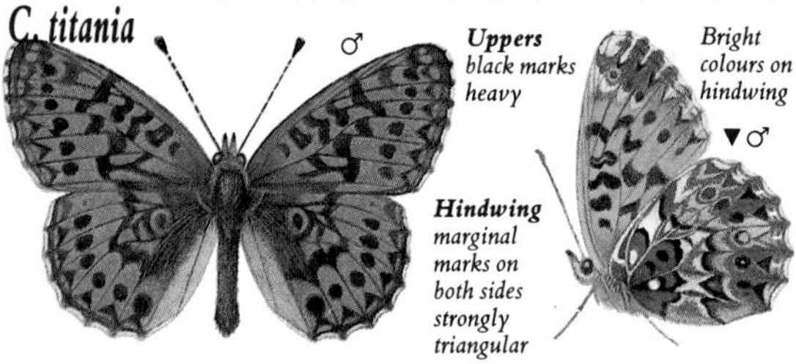
♂
Uppers black marks heavy
Bright colours on hindwing
▼♂
Hindwing marginal marks on both sides strongly triangular

The underside hindwing of *C. titania cypris* (illustrated) is marbled in pink, brown and yellow, although other subspecies may lack such colour contrast. *WS:* 42–48 mm; *Flight:* June–July; *Gen:* 1; *FP:* Violet (*Viola*); *D:* Alps, Balkans, Finland, Baltic states.

# Arctic fritillary

## *C. chariclea*

♂
***Underside hindwing*** *discal band pale with prominent silver spots*

♂
*Sexes similar*

The Arctic fritillary is one of the most northerly species, its capture having been recorded at latitude 81° 42′ N. It has a circumpolar distribution and flies over dry tundra and boggy areas above 300 m. It may be confused with Frejya's fritillary (below) where the two species fly together, but is distinguished by the pale discal band on the underside hindwing. *WS:* 32–36 mm; *Flight:* June–July; *Gen:* 1; *FP:* unknown; *D:* N Scand.

# Frejya's fritillary

## *C. freija*

♂

♂
***Underside hwing*** *has prominent black zig-zag line in lower discal area; white marginal spots large*

Little documentation exists on the life cycle and habits of this species. Its flight is low and slightly hesitant, and it may be found on moorland and tundra in northern Europe. *WS:* 36–44 mm; *Flight:* May–June; *Gen:* 1; *FP:* Cloudberry (*Rubus chamaemorus*), Bog whortleberry (*Vaccinium uliginosum*); *D:* Baltic states, Scandinavia (but not Denmark).

# Violet fritillary

## *C. dia*

♂
***Underside hwing*** *tinged violet; silver spots in discal area and on margin*

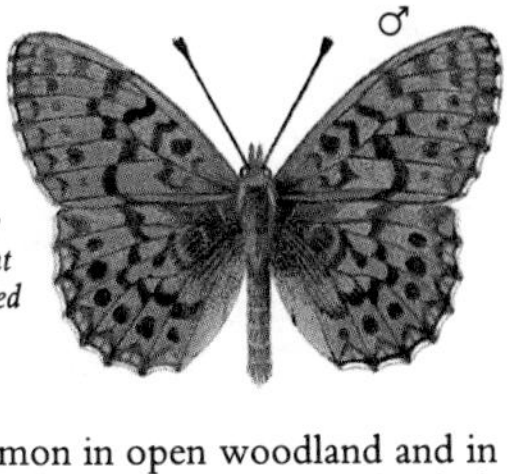
♂
***Hwing*** *sharply angled near front edge, not rounded as in other* Clossiana *spp*

A widespread species, locally common in open woodland and in hilly districts up to 1,200 m. The violet-brown tinge and the dark postdiscal spots on the underside hindwing are diagnostic. The half-grown caterpillar overwinters, feeding up in the spring. *WS:* 32–34 mm; *Flight:* Apr–Oct; *Gen:* 2–3; *FP:* Violet (*Viola*), Blackberry (*Rubus*); *D:* Europe (not Britain, Scand, S Spain, S Italy).

# Polar fritillary

## *Clossiana polaris*

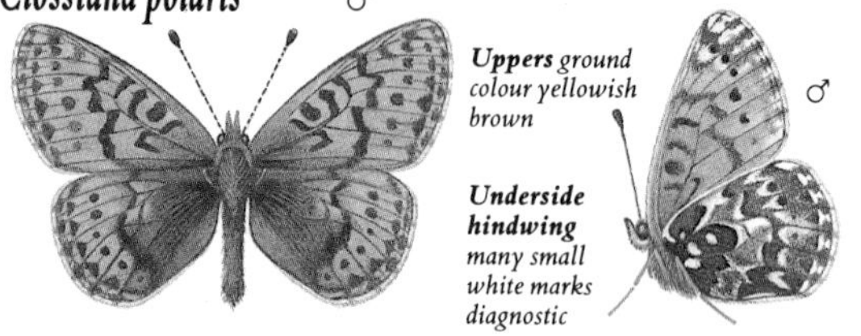
♂
**Uppers** *ground colour yellowish brown*
♂
**Underside hindwing** *many small white marks diagnostic*

A comparatively rare species which occurs in isolated colonies on dry, arctic tundra. The sexes are similar. *WS:* 36–38 mm; *Flight:* June–July; *Gen:* 1; *FP:* possibly Mountain avens (*Dryas octopetala*); *D:* N Scandinavia.

# Thor's fritillary

## *C. thore*

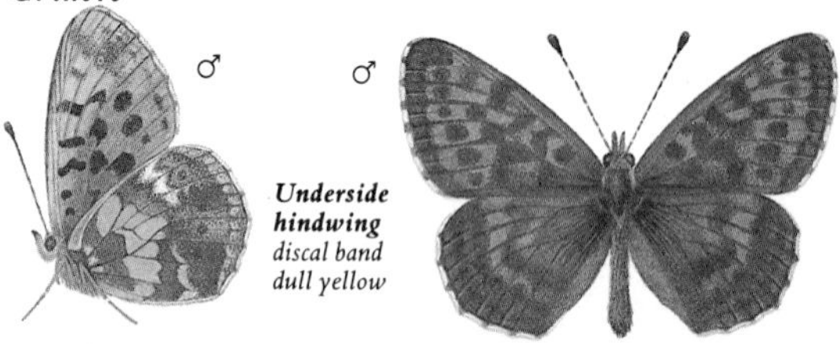
♂
♂
**Underside hindwing** *discal band dull yellow*

The upperside markings on Thor's fritillary are almost obscured by the dark suffusion that covers most of the wing surface. The subspecies *C. thore borealis,* which occurs in Scandinavia, has a much less dense suffusion. The species has a distinctive yellow band on the underside hindwing and occurs on mountains at 900–1,500 m. *WS:* 38–46 mm; *Flight:* June–July; *Gen:* 1; *FP:* Violet (*Viola*); *D:* Alps (Switz, Germany, Austria, Italy), Scand (not Denmark).

# Frigga's fritillary

## *C. frigga*

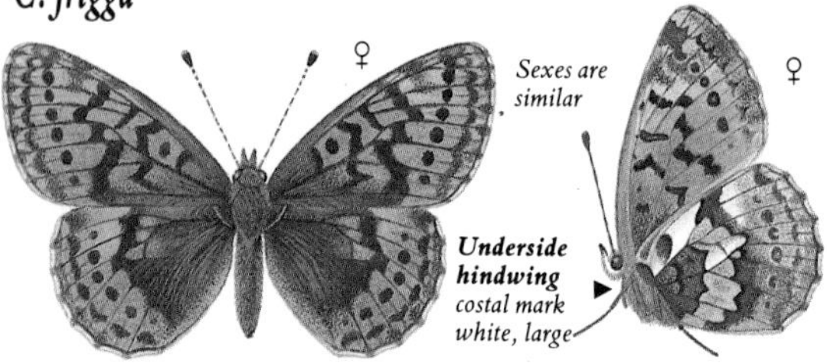
♀
*Sexes are similar*
♀
**Underside hindwing** *costal mark white, large*

This butterfly also occurs in North America where it is known as Saga's fritillary. The upperside markings are generally heavy and regular, while the underside hindwing is attractively coloured red-brown, yellow, white and lilac. Flies over damp moorlands and bogs. *WS:* 40–46 mm; *Flight:* June–July; *Gen:* 1; *FP:* Cloudberry (*Rubus chamaemorus*); *D:* N Scandinavia.

# Dusky-winged fritillary

## C. improba

♂
Uppers grey-brown, markings indistinct

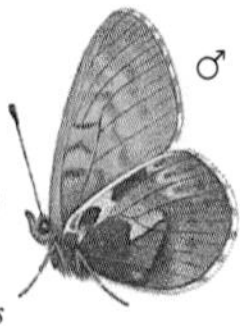
♂
Underside hwing pale red-brown with small white marks

A small fritillary of restricted distribution, confined to drier mountain slopes from 400 to 1,200 m. The lack of clear markings on its upperside distinguishes it from the other fritillaries which have the more regular pattern. There is a narrow, white rim along the front edge of the underside hindwing, which is also a useful identification feature. *WS:* 30–34 mm; *Flight:* July–Aug; *Gen:* 1; *FP:* unknown; *D:* N Scand.

# Aetherie fritillary

## Melitaea aetherie

♂
Marginal marks complete on upperside
Uppers ground colour orange-red

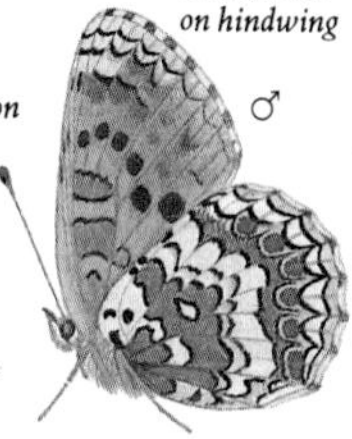
Yellow and red contrast on hindwing
♂

The Aetherie fritillary is a North African species that occurs only very locally in southern Europe. The female is similar but often powdered grey. Prefers light woodlands and meadows at low altitudes. *WS:* 42–46 mm; *Flight:* Apr–July; *Gen:* 1; *FP:* unknown; *D:* S Spain, S Portugal, Sicily (last needs confirmation).

# Freyer's fritillary

## M. arduinna

♀
Uppers reddish brown

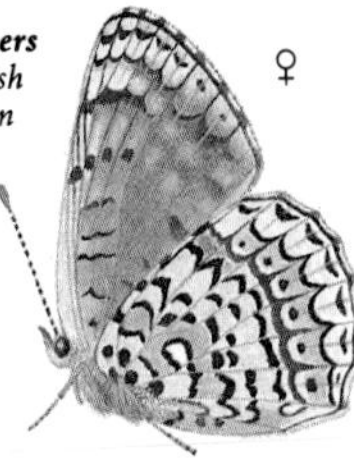
♀
Black spots within orange band on hindwing

A rare and local species in Europe, being more widespread in Asia. It resembles the Glanville fritillary (p 74), but is larger and the underside hindwing pattern differs. In Freyer's fritillary the black lunules, which line the inner border of the orange submarginal band, curve outwards. *WS:* 42–46 mm; *Flight:* May–June; *Gen:* 1; *FP:* Knapweed (*Centaurea*); *D:* SE Europe.

# Knapweed fritillary

## *Melitaea phoebe*

♂

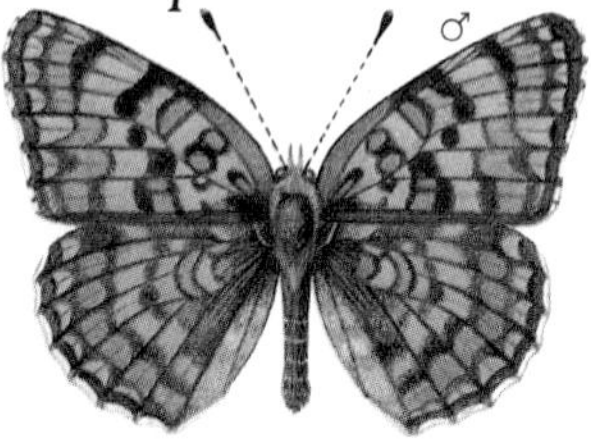

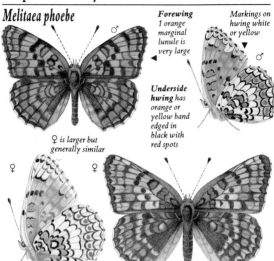

**Forewing** *1 orange marginal lunule is very large*

*Markings on hwing white or yellow*

♂

**Underside hwing** *has orange or yellow band edged in black with red spots*

*♀ is larger but generally similar*

♀

♀

This fritillary is very variable in size and pattern, with several described subspecies. Some specimens are lightly marked on the upperside, and have a reduced amount of black, while others are heavily patterned in black, orange and yellow. The upper hindwing has a distinct row of orange-red marks, normally without dark centres. Flies up to 2,000 m over flowery slopes. *WS:* 34–50 mm; *Flight:* Apr–July; *Gen:* 2–3; *FP:* Knapweed (*Centaurea*); *D:* C and S Europe (not Britain, Scand, Belgium, Holland).

# Glanville fritillary

## *M. cinxia*

♂

**Uppers** *with complete and regular pattern*

♂

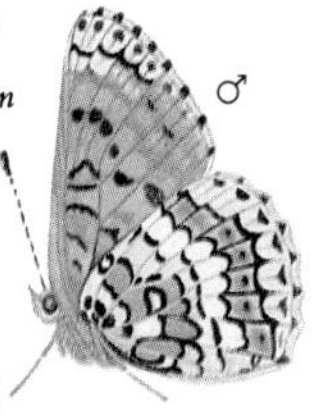

**Hindwing** *has row of black spots in orange submarginal band*

Named after Mrs Eleanor Glanville, a butterfly enthusiast of the eighteenth century (whose Will was contested on the grounds that nobody of sound mind would have such a hobby!), this species, although widespread in central Europe, is restricted to the cliffs of the Isle of Wight in Britain. The black lunules, which form the inner edge of the orange submarginal band on the underside hindwing, curve inwards, distinguishing it from the less common Freyer's fritillary (p 73). *WS:* 28–40 mm; *Flight:* May–Sept; *Gen:* 2 (1 in north); *FP:* Ribwort plantain (*Plantago lanceolata*); *D:* Europe (not S Spain, N Scand, Ireland).

# Spotted fritillary

## *M. didyma*

♂

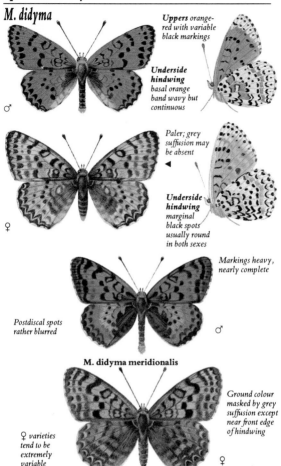

***Uppers** orange-red with variable black markings*

***Underside hindwing** basal orange band wavy but continuous*

♀

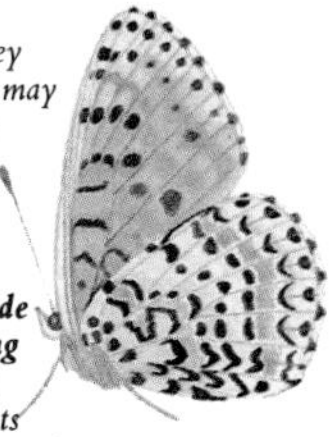

*Paler; grey suffusion may be absent*

◄

***Underside hindwing** marginal black spots usually round in both sexes*

*Markings heavy, nearly complete*

*Postdiscal spots rather blurred*

♂

**M. didyma meridionalis**

*Ground colour masked by grey suffusion except near front edge of hindwing*

*♀ varieties tend to be extremely variable*

♀

**M. didyma meridionalis**

The Spotted fritillary is probably the most variable-patterned butterfly in Europe, with differences occurring not only between subspecies, but also between individuals from neighbouring colonies. Seasonal variation and marked sex differences can create problems of identification even for the experts. The least variable features generally occur on the underside of the hindwing, notably the round black spots in the pale yellow margin and the unbroken orange basal band. *M. didyma meridionalis* is the commonest form in southern Europe and is found in meadows and woodland clearings up to 1,500 m. *WS:* 30–44 mm; *Flight:* May–Sept; *Gen:* 2–3; *FP:* Plantain (*Plantago*), Toadflax (*Linaria*); *D:* Europe (but not Britain, Belgium, Holland, Scandinavia, Corsica, Sardinia).

# Lesser spotted fritillary

## *Melitaea trivia*

♂

♀ *usually larger than* ♂

♂

***Underside hindwing*** *marginal black spots triangular*

Similar to the Spotted fritillary (p 75), except that the marginal spots on the underside hindwing of this species tend to be triangular rather than round. It is variable in colour and pattern, with several named subspecies. Specimens of the first generation are generally larger than those of the second. *WS:* 28–38 mm; *Flight:* May–June, July–Aug; *Gen:* 2; *FP:* Great mullein (*Verbascum thapsus*); *D:* Spain, Portugal, Italy, Austria, Czechoslovakia, Hungary, Romania, Yugoslavia, Bulgaria, Greece.

# False heath fritillary

## *M. diamina*

♂

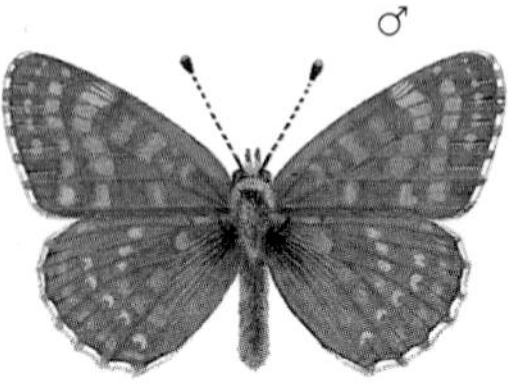

♂ *darker than* ♀

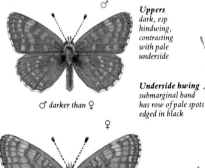

***Uppers*** *dark, esp hindwing, contrasting with pale underside*

♂

***Underside hwing*** *submarginal band has row of pale spots edged in black*

♀

***Hindwing*** *markings pale yellow in* ♀

♀

***Underside hindwing*** *marginal line yellow (*♂ *and* ♀*)*

The pattern and intensity of colour vary considerably between specimens, so that it is very easy to mistake this species in the field for the Heath fritillary (p 77) or Nickerl's fritillary (p 79). It occurs up to 2,000 m and is locally common over Alpine meadows with abundant flowers. A second generation is produced in the south which usually has a smaller wingspan. Overwinters in the caterpillar stage. *WS:* 32–42 mm; *Flight:* May–Aug; *Gen:* Cow-wheat (*Melampyrum*), Plantain (*Plantago*); *FP:* Europe (but not Britain, N Scandinavia, Portugal, S Spain, Holland, W France, peninsular Italy, Greece, Mediterranean islands).

# Heath fritillary

## *Mellicta athalia*

♂

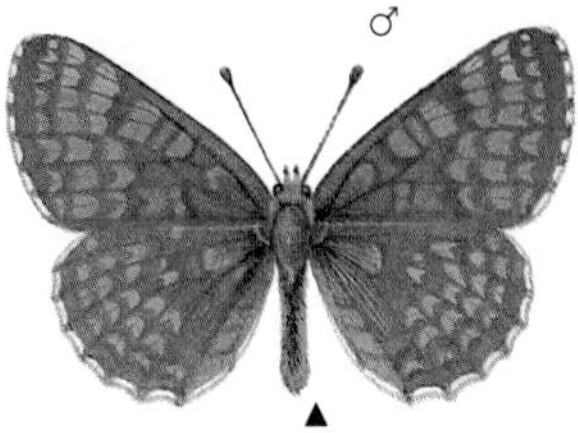

*Black inner edge to yellow lunules*

**M. athalia athalia,** *a northern subspecies*

**M. athalia celadussa,** *a subspecies of SW Europe and Italy*

♀

*Not as dark as those found in north*

*A specimen from Bihar, Hungary*

♂

*Small, with bright orange ground colour*

*A variety found in Portugal*

♀

*Larger and brighter in colour than other forms*

One of the most widespread and variable of the fritillaries. It is usually heavily marked with black in the male but the female is often lighter. Positive identification of the Heath fritillary in the field is difficult, especially in continental Europe where there are many similar species which also show variation in colour, size and pattern. The most constant feature seems to be the yellowish lunules on the underside of the forewing which are edged in black. The species generally occurs in the drier areas of meadowland, but may also be found in woodland clearings up to 2,000 m. In Britain it is restricted to a few counties in southern England. Hibernates in the caterpillar stage. *WS:* 34–46 mm; *Flight:* May–Sept; *Gen:* 1–2; *FP:* Cow-wheat (*Melampyrum*), Plantain (*Plantago*); *D:* Europe (but not Ireland, Scotland, Corsica, Sardinia).

# Provençal fritillary

## *Mellicta deione*

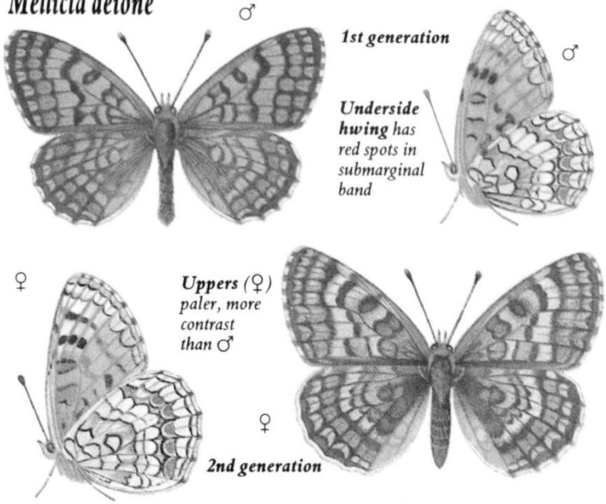
♂
1st generation
♂
Underside hwing has red spots in submarginal band
♀
Uppers (♀) paler, more contrast than ♂
♀
2nd generation

Easily confused with the Heath fritillary (p 77); usually the Provençal fritillary is a paler orange-brown with thinner black markings. One feature that is not always constant (shown in the male specimen above) is a dumb-bell-shaped black mark near the hind margin of the upper forewing. Flies over mountain slopes. *WS:* 32–46 mm; *Flight:* May–Sept; *Gen:* 2; *FP:* Toadflax (*Linaria*) and others; *D:* Spain, Portugal, S France, Alps.

# Meadow fritillary

## *M. parthenoides*

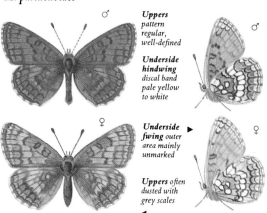

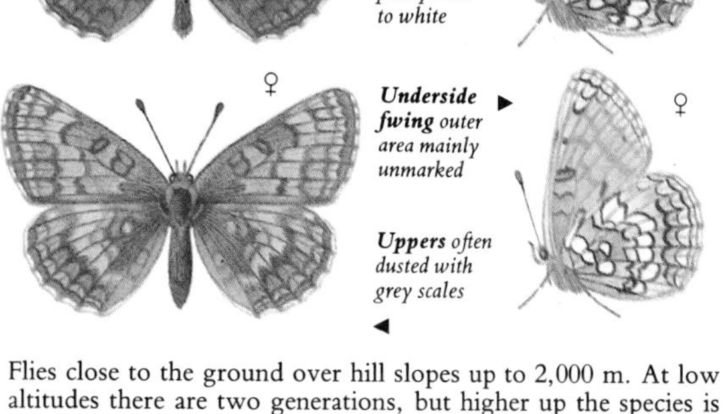
♂
Uppers pattern regular, well-defined
♂
Underside hindwing discal band pale yellow to white
♀
Underside fwing outer area mainly unmarked
♀
Uppers often dusted with grey scales

Flies close to the ground over hill slopes up to 2,000 m. At low altitudes there are two generations, but higher up the species is single-brooded, with dark forms sometimes occurring. *WS:* 30–36 mm; *Flight:* May–Sept; *Gen:* 1–2; *FP:* Toadflax (*Linaria*); *D:* Spain, Portugal, France, S Germany, Switz, N Italy (Alps).

# Grisons fritillary

## *M. varia*

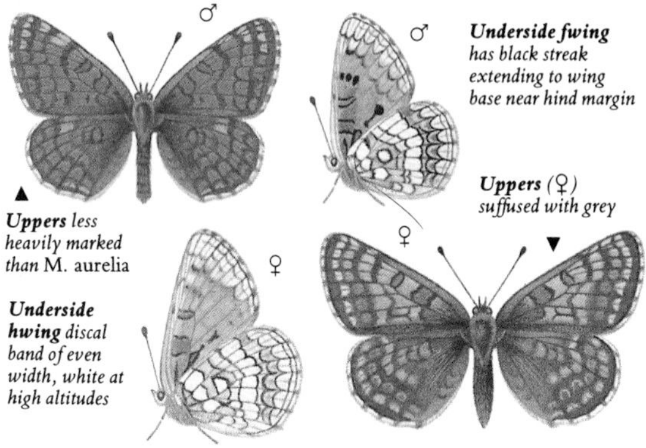
♂
♂
**Underside fwing** *has black streak extending to wing base near hind margin*
**Uppers** *less heavily marked than* M. aurelia
**Uppers** *(♀) suffused with grey*
♀
♀
**Underside hwing** *discal band of even width, white at high altitudes*

Grisons fritillary is found mainly in low vegetation on mountain slopes from 1,000 to 2,000 m. A very difficult species to identify in the field; Nickerl's fritillary (below), which is similar and flies in the same area, tends to have broader wings and more complete markings. *WS:* 30–38 mm; *Flight:* June–Aug; *Gen:* 1; *FP:* Gentian (*Gentiana*); *D:* SE France, Switz, Austria, Italy (Alps, Apennines).

# Nickerl's fritillary

## *M. aurelia*

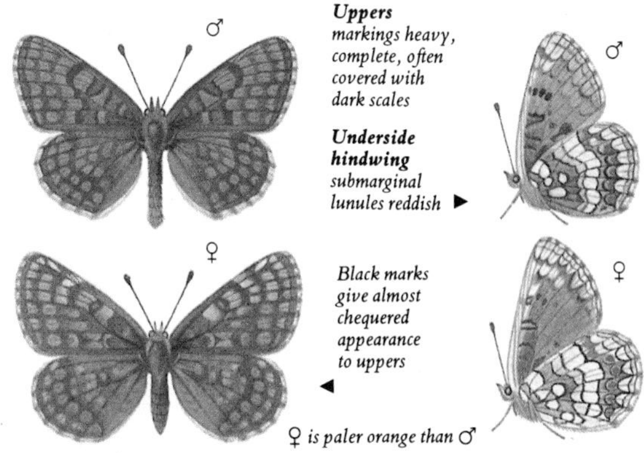
♂
**Uppers** *markings heavy, complete, often covered with dark scales*
♂
**Underside hindwing** *submarginal lunules reddish*
♀
*Black marks give almost chequered appearance to uppers*
♀
*♀ is paler orange than ♂*

Widely distributed in eastern and central Europe, this rather small, dark species can be just as troublesome as the other fritillaries to name correctly. It usually flies in the wetter areas of moorlands up to 1,500 m and over bogs and damp meadows. The species overwinters as a caterpillar, feeding up in the spring before pupating. Occasionally two generations are produced in the south. *WS:* 28–32 mm; *Flight:* June–July; *Gen:* 1–2; *FP:* Plantain (*Plantago*), Speedwell (*Veronica*), Cow-wheat (*Melampyrum*); *D:* N and E France, Germany, Belgium, Switzerland, Czechoslovakia, Austria, N Italy, Hungary, the Balkans.

# Assmann's fritillary

## *Mellicta britomartis*

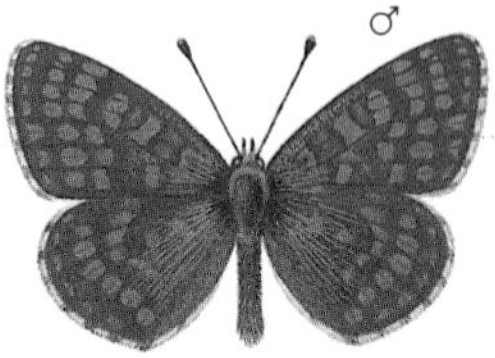

♂

***Uppers** like* M. aurelia, *but slightly darker*

***Underside hwing** orange submarginal lunules have dark inner edge*

♂

Mainly found in eastern Europe, although it does occur locally in north Italy. May be seen on the wing with Nickerl's fritillary (p 79), which is usually smaller, but the two species are not easy to distinguish. The second generation (south only) is smaller than the first. *WS:* 30–36 mm; *Flight:* May–Aug; *Gen:* 2; *FP:* Plantain (*Plantago*) and others; *D:* S Sweden, Poland, Germany, Romania, Hungary, Bulgaria, Czechoslovakia, Italy.

# Little fritillary

## *M. asteria*

***Uppers** very dark in basal area*

***Underside hwing** has single black marginal line*

♂

A very small, dark fritillary, restricted to the eastern Alps. Flies over grassy slopes at altitudes above 2,000 m. The female is usually paler than the male. *WS:* 28–30 mm; *Flight:* May–Aug; *Gen:* 1; *FP:* unknown; *D:* Alps (Switz, N Italy, Austria).

# Scarce fritillary

## *Hypodryas maturna*

***Underside fwing** yellowish lunules along margin are uneven in size*

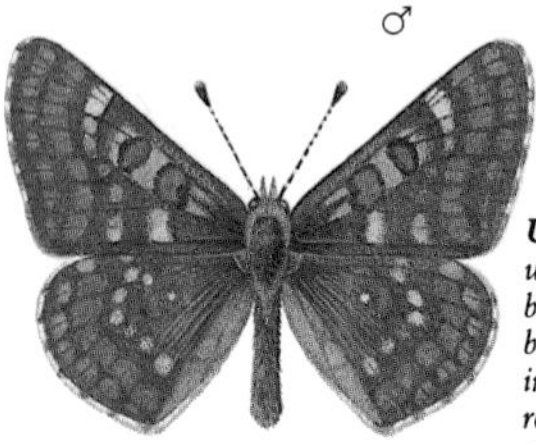

♂

***Uppers** reddish with wide red bands on hwing, bordered internally by row of cream spots*

♂

A species of scattered distribution, with isolated populations occurring in wooded valleys, often near streams. It is a rapid flier and lays its eggs on trees, where the caterpillars then overwinter in colonies beneath a silken web. In spring they disperse and feed on low plants before pupating. *WS:* 42–50 mm; *Flight:* May–July; *Gen:* 1; *FP:* Ash (*Fraxinus*), Poplar (*Populus*), Plantain (*Plantago*); *D:* N France, S Scand, Germany, Poland, Austria, Hungary, Romania, Yugoslavia, Bulgaria, NW Greece.

# Asian fritillary

## *H. intermedia*

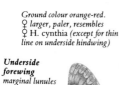

*Ground colour orange-red. ♀ larger, paler, resembles ♀* H. cynthia *(except for thin line on underside hindwing)*

♂

***Underside forewing*** *marginal lunules more regular than in* H. maturna

♂

***Upper hindwing*** *has broad dark margin*

***Underside hindwing*** *central yellow band encloses thin black line*

Risk of confusing this species with the Scarce fritillary (p 80) is unlikely as geographically their ranges do not overlap, and the Asian fritillary flies at higher altitudes, usually above 1,000 m. Confusion is more likely between the females of this species and Cynthia's fritillary (below); the latter lacks a thin black line in the yellow band on the underside hindwing. *WS:* 38–42 mm; *Flight:* June–July; *Gen:* 1; *FP:* unknown; *D:* Alps.

# Cynthia's fritillary

## *H. cynthia*

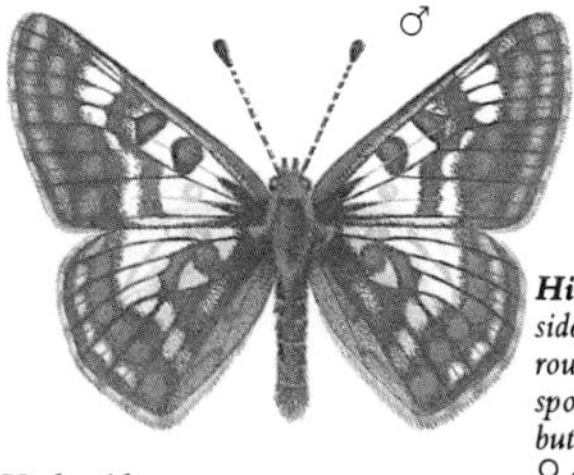

♂

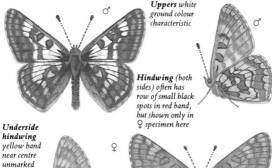

***Uppers*** *white ground colour characteristic*

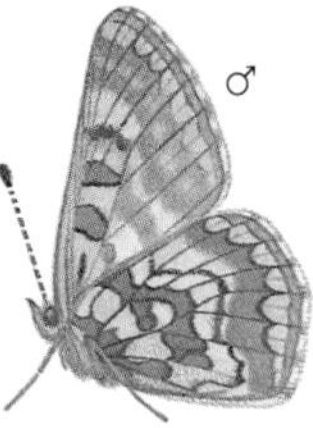

♂

***Hindwing*** *(both sides) often has row of small black spots in red band, but shown only in ♀ specimen here*

***Underside hindwing*** *yellow band near centre unmarked*

♀

♀

Chiefly an Alpine species, although it also occurs in the mountains of Bulgaria. Specimens may be found on sparsely covered slopes as high as 3,000 m, but these tend to be smaller and darker than those which fly lower down. The caterpillars are gregarious and overwinter in a web. *WS:* 32–42 mm; *Flight:* May–Aug; *Gen:* 1; *FP:* Lady's mantle (*Alchemilla*), Plantain (*Plantago*); *D:* Germany, Austria, S France, N Italy, Bulgaria.

# Lapland fritillary

## *Hypodryas iduna*

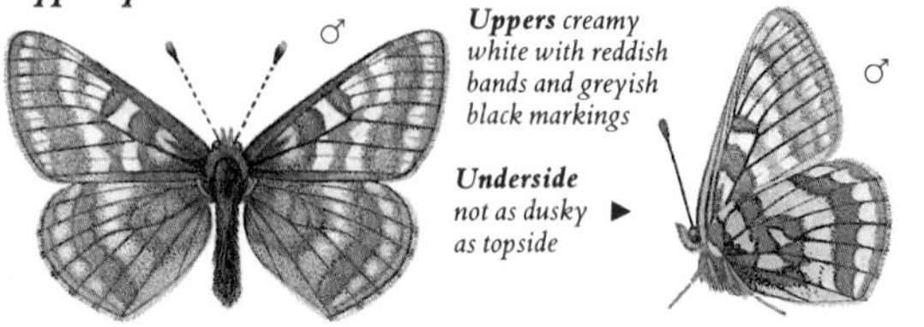
♂
**Uppers** creamy white with reddish bands and greyish black markings
**Underside** not as dusky as topside ▶
♂

Small colonies of the Lapland fritillary are quite common in the far north of Europe, usually in areas with few trees. Always a local species, it is generally found in moorland bogs and on mountainsides up to 800 m. The sexes are similar. *WS:* 36–38 mm; *Flight:* June–July; *Gen:* 1; *FP:* unknown; *D:* N Norway, N Sweden, N Finland.

# Spanish fritillary

## *Eurodryas desfontainii*

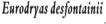

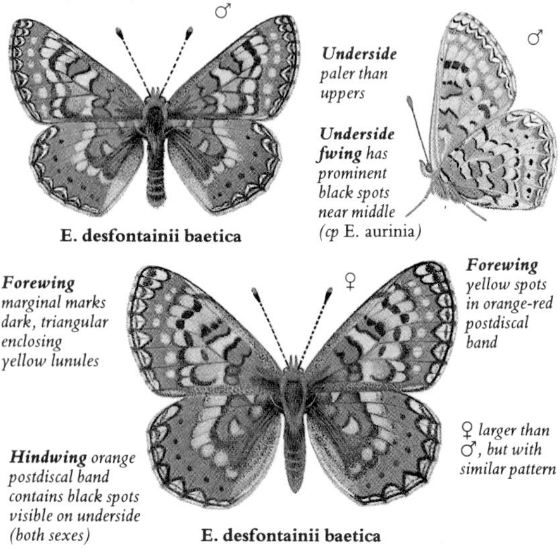
♂
**Underside** paler than uppers
**Underside fwing** has prominent black spots near middle (*cp* E. aurinia)
♂
**Forewing** marginal marks dark, triangular enclosing yellow lunules
♀
**Forewing** yellow spots in orange-red postdiscal band
♀ larger than ♂, but with similar pattern
**Hindwing** orange postdiscal band contains black spots visible on underside (both sexes)

**E. desfontainii baetica**

**E. desfontainii baetica**

This species and the Marsh fritillary (p 83) differ from the preceding fritillaries in always having fairly conspicuous black spots contained within the orange-red postdiscal band on the hindwing. The two species may be separated by the black markings on the underside forewing, which are more prominent in the Spanish fritillary. The European subspecies, illustrated above, is paler red than the nominate subspecies, *E. desfontainii desfontainii,* which occurs in North Africa. In Europe the colonies are widely separated and often show variation in colour and pattern. The adults fly in hilly areas between 600 and 1,200 m. *WS:* 40–48 mm; *Flight:* May–June; *Gen:* 1; *FP:* unknown; *D:* S and E Spain (up to Pyrenees).

# Marsh fritillary

## *E. aurinia*

♂

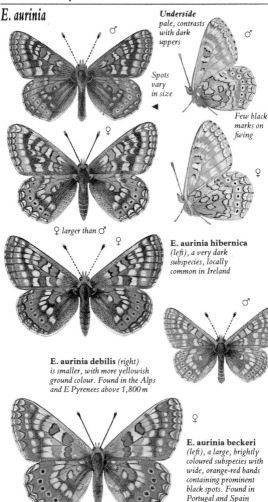

**Underside** *pale, contrasts with dark uppers*

♂

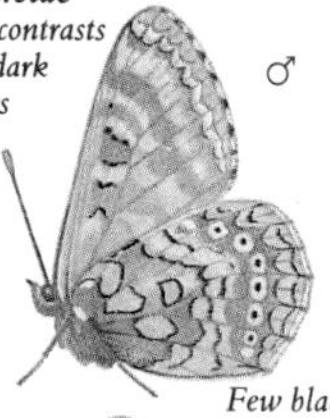

*Spots vary in size* ◄

*Few black marks on fwing*

♀

♀

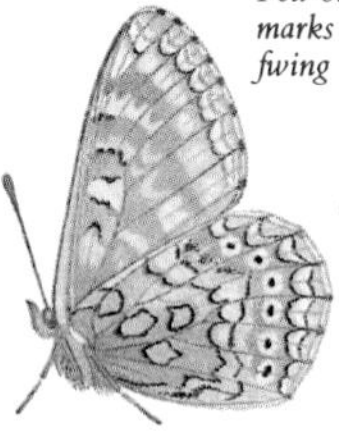

♀ *larger than* ♂

♀

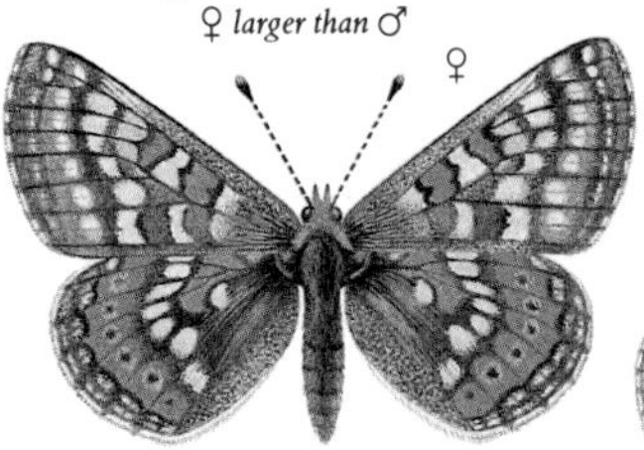

**E. aurinia hibernica** *(left), a very dark subspecies, locally common in Ireland*

♂

**E. aurinia debilis** *(right) is smaller, with more yellowish ground colour. Found in the Alps and E Pyrenees above 1,800 m*

♀

**E. aurinia beckeri** *(left), a large, brightly coloured subspecies with wide, orange-red bands containing prominent black spots. Found in Portugal and Spain*

A local and variable species with many described subspecies, a few examples of which are shown. Differences may even occur between individuals of neighbouring colonies, but generally the species is easy to recognize. As well as having a liking for wet, boggy areas, the Marsh fritillary also flies over dry mountain slopes up to 1,500 m. In Britain it is commoner in the west, with a few isolated populations occurring as far north as west Scotland. The caterpillars live gregariously under a silken web, and hibernate in this form. *WS:* 30–46 mm; *Flight:* May–June; *Gen:* 1; *FP:* Plantain (*Plantago*), Devilsbit scabious (*Succisa pratensis*); *D:* Europe (but not Norway or Mediterranean islands; rare in peninsular Italy).

# Brown butterflies Satyridae

Although most species in this family are some shade of brown, there are exceptions, notably the Marbled white (p 85) which at first looks more like a Pierid. Generally they are medium-sized, darkly coloured butterflies with intricately patterned wings, incorporating black and white ringed eye-spots. One feature of the forewing peculiar to the Browns is the veins which are swollen at the base. The caterpillars taper at both ends, and often have fork-shaped tails.

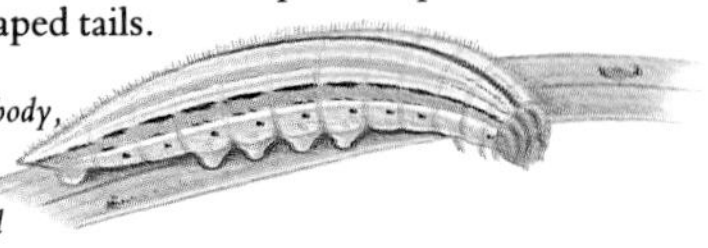
*Sandy-coloured body, covered in down, with several dark longitudinal stripes*
*Active by day and night*

***Grayling caterpillar***

## Esper's marbled white

## *Melanargia russiae*

***Forewing*** *black mark across cell usually a narrow zig-zag*
♂
***Hindwing*** *large white spot in dark basal area; 2 or 3 eye-spots visible*
***Uppers*** *delicate black markings on white background*

♂
*♀ has darker, more extensive black markings and is usually more yellowish*
*Ground colour varies from white to yellow*
***Underside hindwing*** *pale grey markings strongly outlined in black; eye-spots very distinct*

Esper's marbled white is less common and much more delicately marked than the Marbled white (p 85). Several subspecies have been described based on differences in size and pattern; the subspecies *M. russiae japygia,* which is found very locally in the Apennines of southern Italy and in Sicily, is slightly smaller and more heavily marked with black than the specimen shown above (from western Europe). The species occurs in widely scattered colonies on dry, stony mountainous slopes between 1,000 and 2,000 m. *WS:* 50–60 mm; *Flight:* July; *Gen:* 1; *FP:* Annual meadow grass (*Poa annua*); *D:* Spain, Portugal, S and C France, Italy (Apennines), Sicily, Albania, Balkans.

# Marbled white

## *M. galathea*

*Forewing central cell lacks any narrow black cross-bars*

***Uppers** have distinctive black and white chequered pattern; extent of black may vary in both sexes*

***Underside hindwing** submarginal band enclosing eye-spots broken in middle; eye-spots not always visible on uppers*

*♀ usually larger than ♂*

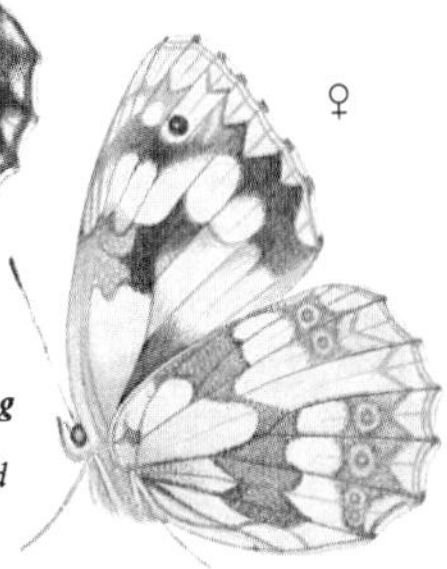

***Underside hindwing** tinted ochre-yellow in ♀; dark discal band very narrow near top of cell (♂ and ♀)*

♂

*Ground colour more yellowish and black markings more extensive*

*Found in S Italy and Balkans*

*f.* **procida**

A variable species, widespread in grassy areas up to 1,800 m. The female lays her eggs in flight; they fall on grasses at random. In Britain it is confined chiefly to southern and central areas, especially chalk downs. Slow in flight, often settling with wings outspread. *WS:* 46–56 mm; *Flight:* June–Aug; *Gen:* 1; *FP:* grasses; *D:* Europe (not Scand, Ireland).

# Balkan marbled white

## *Melanargia larissa*

♂

***Forewing*** *cell crossed by narrow black line*

*Variable amount of black on wings; at times may obscure cell-bar in forewing*

♂

***Uppers*** *basal area of both wings extensively suffused with black*

***Underside hindwing*** *eye-spots distinct; basal area pale grey*

Generally confined to the dry slopes of southeastern Europe, although several subspecies are known to occur in Asia. The females are usually larger with more yellowish undersides. The subspecies *M. larissa herta* is recognized by the greater amount of white on its wings, although there is still a dark suffusion over the basal area. *WS:* 50–60 mm; *Flight:* June–July; *Gen:* 1; *FP:* grasses; *D:* Bulgaria, Greece, Yugoslavia, Albania.

# Western marbled white

## *M. occitanica*

♂

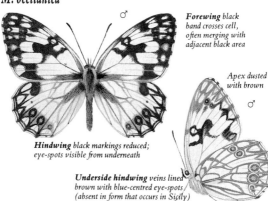

***Forewing*** *black band crosses cell, often merging with adjacent black area*

*Apex dusted with brown*

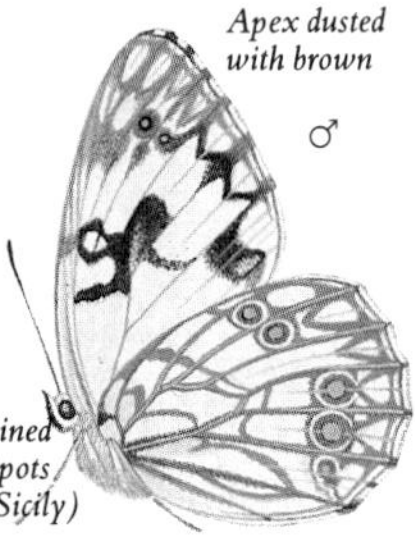
♂

***Hindwing*** *black markings reduced; eye-spots visible from underneath*

***Underside hindwing*** *veins lined brown with blue-centred eye-spots (absent in form that occurs in Sicily)*

Distinguished from other marbled whites by the brown veins on the underside hindwing; also, the patterning tends to be lighter in intensity, with the exception of *M. arge* (p 87). Isolated colonies occur on dry hill slopes up to 1,800 m throughout southern Europe. The flight time is dependent on altitude, being later in the year at higher levels. The females are often bigger with more brown suffusion on the underside. *WS:* 46–56 mm; *Flight:* May–July; *Gen:* 1; *FP:* grasses; *D:* Spain, Portugal, S France, NW Italy (coast), Corsica, Sicily.

# Italian marbled white

## *M. arge*

***Uppers*** *with thin black markings; mark in cell of forewing small, incomplete*

♂ ♂

◀ ***Underside*** *veins thinly lined in black and marginal marks short, right-angled; eye-spots on hindwing brown-centred, visible on upperside*

The Italian marbled white is the most delicately marked of its kind, similar in pattern to *M. occitanica* (p 86) but with much less black on its wings. Isolated populations may be found throughout the mountainous areas of peninsular Italy and Sicily, from quite low altitudes to over 2,000 m. Should not be mistaken in the field for *M. ines* (below) as geographically their ranges are completely separate. The sexes are similar. *WS:* 50–56 mm; *Flight:* May–June; *Gen:* 1; *FP:* unknown, probably grasses; *D:* Italy, Sicily.

# Spanish marbled white

## *M. ines*

*Striations along costa of underside fwing and hwing*

***Forewing*** *black bar across cell well-defined*

♂ ♂

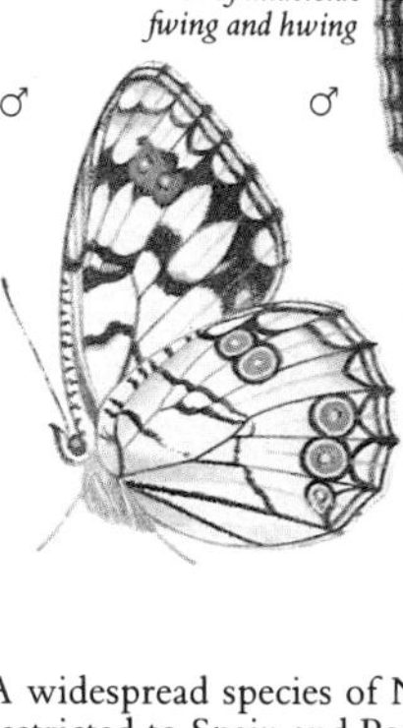

***Underside hindwing*** *eye-spots prominent, black-ringed with blue pupils; marginal marks more rounded than in* M. arge *and* M. occitanica

A widespread species of North Africa but in Europe its range is restricted to Spain and Portugal, where it may be quite common in southern and central regions. It flies over grassy mountain slopes up to 2,000 m, the specimens from higher altitudes being on the wing much later in the year. Two blue-pupilled eye-spots are normally conspicuous on both sides of the forewing, in addition to those that are plainly visible on the hindwing. The female is larger and yellower than the male. *WS:* 46–50 mm; *Flight:* Apr–June; *Gen:* 1; *FP:* unknown; *D:* Spain, Portugal.

# Woodland grayling

## *Hipparchia fagi*

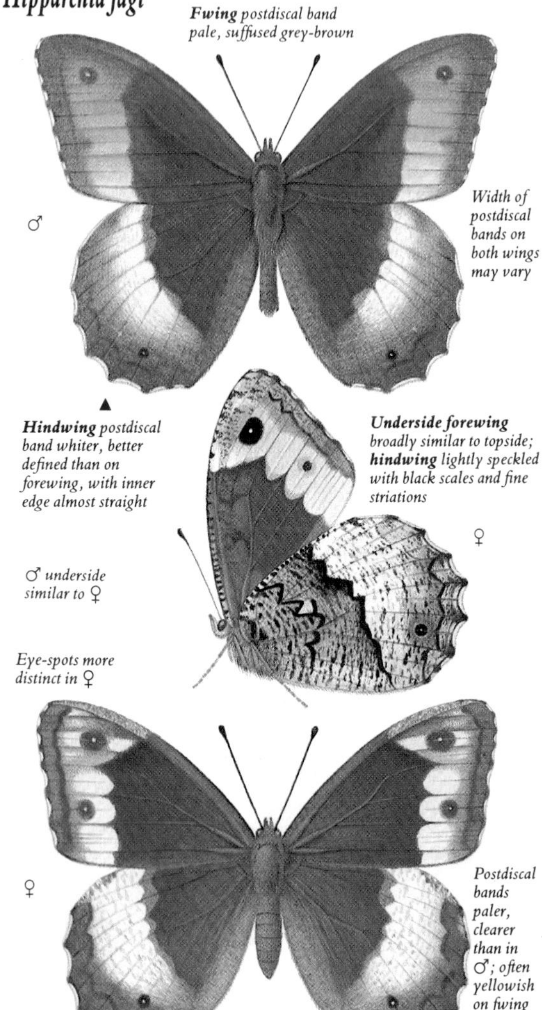

**Fwing** postdiscal band pale, suffused grey-brown
♂
Width of postdiscal bands on both wings may vary
▲
**Hindwing** postdiscal band whiter, better defined than on forewing, with inner edge almost straight
**Underside forewing** broadly similar to topside; **hindwing** lightly speckled with black scales and fine striations
♀
♂ underside similar to ♀
Eye-spots more distinct in ♀
♀
Postdiscal bands paler, clearer than in ♂; often yellowish on fwing


Very difficult to distinguish from the Rock grayling (p 89), especially where the two species fly together, as their distinctive features may vary slightly. Often size is the most reliable guide, the Woodland grayling invariably being the larger. Also, habitat preferences are different, the present species flying in open woods at low altitudes rarely above 1,200 m, frequently settling on trunks with its wings closed. *WS:* 66–76 mm; *Flight:* July–Aug; *Gen:* 1; *FP:* grasses, esp *Holcus*; *D:* S and C Europe (not Britain, Scand, NW France, C and S Spain, Portugal, N Germany).

# Rock grayling

## H. alcyone

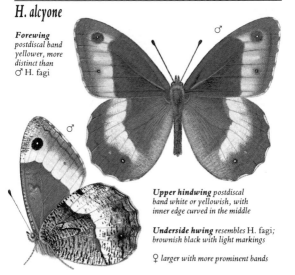

***Forewing*** *postdiscal band yellower, more distinct than* ♂ H. fagi

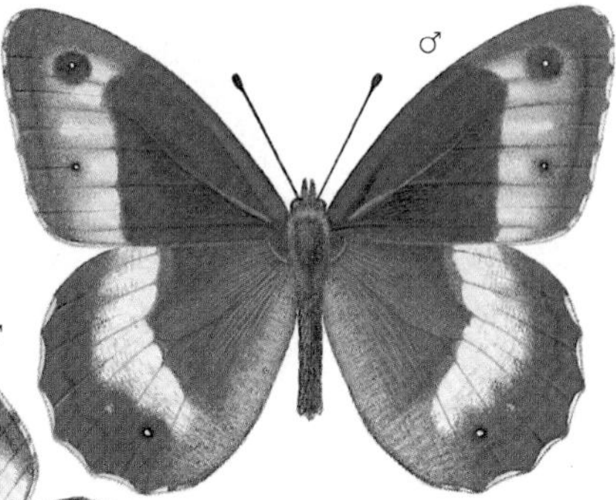

***Upper hindwing*** *postdiscal band white or yellowish, with inner edge curved in the middle*

***Underside hwing*** *resembles* H. fagi*; brownish black with light markings*

♀ *larger with more prominent bands*

Smaller in size and more widespread than the Woodland grayling (p 88), this species flies in mountainous areas up to 1,800 m in the south, but further north it is found at lower levels. *WS:* 56–66 mm; *Flight:* June–July; *Gen:* 1; *FP:* grasses, esp *Brachypodium*; *D:* Spain, Portugal, France, Germany, Austria, Czechoslovakia, Poland, SE Norway (rare in C Italy).
***H. syriaca*** (Eastern rock grayling), formerly a subspecies of *H. alcyone*, cannot be separated from this or *H. fagi* by external features alone. *WS:* 62–66 mm; *D:* Yugoslavia, Greece.

# Corsican grayling

## H. neomiris

***Underside hwing*** *narrow white band merges with dark margin*

***Uppers*** *dark brown with wide orange-yellow bands*

♀ *lighter brown, with less clouding on forewing apex*

This species has only been recorded from a few Mediterranean islands, where it flies mainly in dry mountainous areas between 900 and 2,000 m. In Elba it occurs at lower altitudes. *WS:* 46–50 mm; *Flight:* June–July; *Gen:* 1; *FP:* unknown, probably grasses; *D:* Corsica, Sardinia, Elba.

# Grayling

## *Hipparchia semele*

♂

*2 eye-spots visible on both sides of forewing*

♂

***Fwing*** *yellow postdiscal band poorly defined, suffused with brown in ♂, but more distinct and less dusky in ♀*

*♀ larger than ♂, with bigger eye-spots*

♀

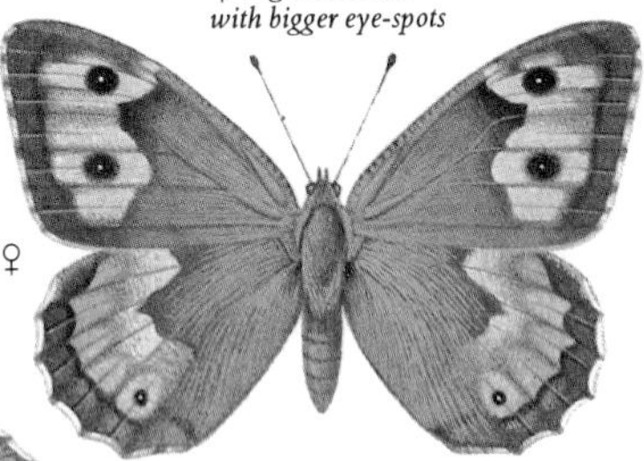

♀

***Underside hwing*** *marbled light and dark grey, darkest in basal area*

***Hindwing*** *has orange-yellow band crossed by dark veins and enclosing 1 small eye-spot*

A complex species with many subspecies: there are several in Britain alone. For example, *H. semele thyone* from North Wales emerges earlier than the typical and is small and subdued in colour, while subsp *atlantica* from the Inner Hebrides is brightly marked. Tends to prefer sandy coastal areas and is difficult to spot when its wings are closed. *WS:* 42–50 mm; *Flight:* May–Aug; *Gen:* 1; *FP:* grasses, esp *Festuca*; *D:* Europe (not N Scand).

# Cretan grayling

## *H. cretica*

♂

*Rather dusky, like* H. semele. *♀ brighter*

♂

Confined to Crete (where the Grayling does not occur). *WS:* 52–60 mm; *Flight:* May–June; *Gen:* 1; *FP:* unknown; *D:* Crete.

# Southern grayling

## *H. aristaeus*

*Variable in colour*

♂ ♂

**Uppers** *very similar to* H. semele*; broad orange band on hindwing more extensive, but only distinguished with certainty by smaller ♂ genitalia*

▲

***Underside hindwing*** *mottled pattern divided by central white band*

♀

*♀ larger, more brightly marked, with yellow areas around eye-spots forming broken postdiscal band*

This species usually has a large amount of orange on its wings; found on rough ground. *WS:* 50–54 mm; *Flight:* June–Aug; *Gen:* 1; *FP:* grasses; *D:* Corsica, Sardinia, Sicily, S Italy, Greece.
***H. delattini*** (Delattin's grayling) is similar, separable by dissection. *WS:* 54–56 mm; *Flight:* June; *D:* Greece, Yugoslavia.

# Tree grayling

## *Neohipparchia statilinus*

♂

***Fwing*** *with 2 white spots; eye-spots blind*

♂

***Uppers*** *dark grey-brown with indistinct markings*

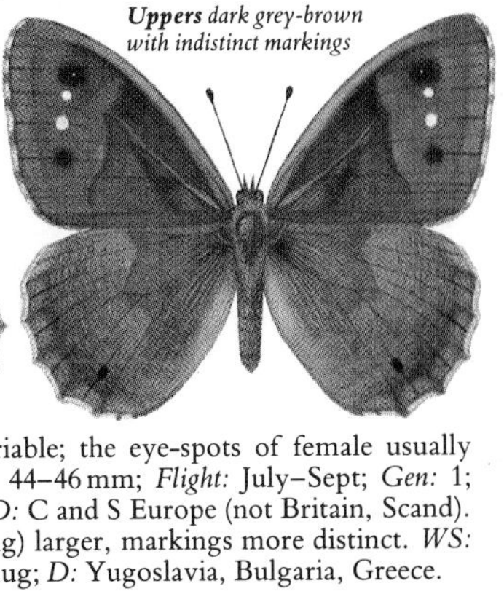

In sparse woodland. Variable; the eye-spots of female usually have white centres. *WS:* 44–46 mm; *Flight:* July–Sept; *Gen:* 1; *FP:* grasses, esp *Bromus*; *D:* C and S Europe (not Britain, Scand).
***N. fatua*** (Freyer's grayling) larger, markings more distinct. *WS:* 60–68 mm; *Flight:* July–Aug; *D:* Yugoslavia, Bulgaria, Greece.

# Striped grayling

## *Pseudotergumia fidia*

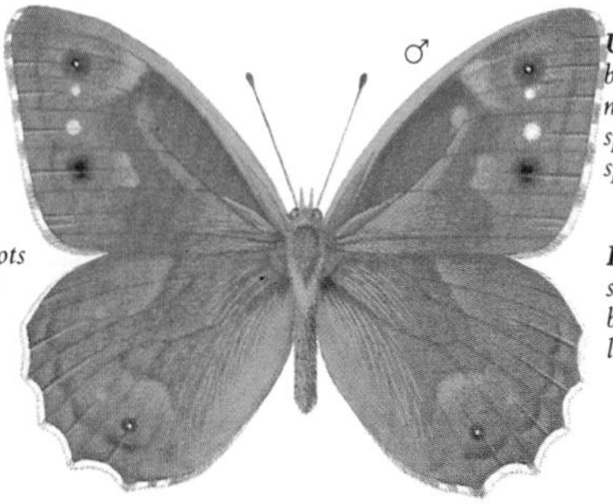
♂
*Uppers* dark grey-brown with obscure markings; 2 white spots between eye-spots larger in ♀
Eye-spots obscure
*Hindwing* margin scalloped; thin black submarginal line just visible

*Underside hindwing* whitish grey and brown with conspicuous dark zig-zag lines
♀ larger, markings better defined on topside, often with few small white spots on hindwing
Pattern on underside is diagnostic
♂

The upperside resembles the Tree grayling (p 91) in colour and markings, the species being distinguished by the zig-zag pattern on the underside hindwing. Occurs in small local colonies on sparsely covered rocky slopes up to 2,000 m. *WS:* 56–62 mm; *Flight:* July–Aug; *Gen:* 1; *FP:* grasses, esp *Oryzopsis*; *D:* Spain, Portugal, S France, N Italy.

# Nevada grayling

## *Pseudochazara hippolyte*

♂
♀ usually larger, with slightly darker basal area
Pale yellow band with well-defined edges stretches across both wings
*Underside* like H. semele, but paler, more yellowish

Flies over mountain slopes between 2,000 and 3,000 m. Very local in western Europe, known only from the Sierra Nevada. *WS:* 50–52 mm; *Flight:* June–July; *FP:* unknown; *D:* Spain. ***P. graeca*** (Grecian grayling) has a darker yellow postdiscal band, and lacks any white marks between its 2 black eye-spots (separating it from *P. amymone* and *P. cingovskii*, p 94). Occurs on mountains. *WS:* 50–52 mm; *Flight:* July–Aug; *D:* Greece.

# The hermit

## *Chazara briseis*

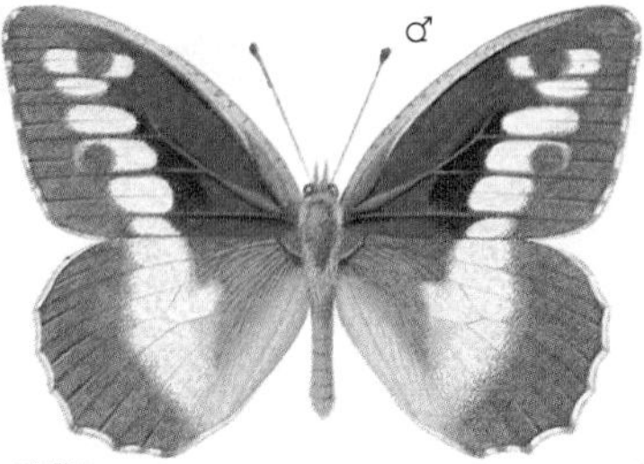

♂


***Forewing*** *front margin pale yellow or whitish*

***Uppers*** *dark brown with creamy white postdiscal band on both wings, divided by dark veins on forewing (not hindwing)*

♀


*Eye-spots in ♀ often have white centres*

*♀ larger, postdiscal band on forewing more uneven than in ♂*

***Underside hindwing*** *has mottled grey-brown pattern, markings obscure*

The size of this butterfly is very variable, with a wingspan difference of as much as 26 mm between a small male specimen and a large female. Locally common on dry stony slopes from lowlands to 2,500 m. *WS:* 42–68 mm; *Flight:* May–Aug; *Gen:* 1; *FP:* grasses, esp Blue moor grass (*Sesleria caerulea*); *D:* C and S Europe (not Britain, N France, Scand, Corsica, Sardinia).

# Southern hermit

## *C. prieuri*

*Eye-spots often blind* ♂

***Underside hwing*** *strongly patterned, with dark V-shaped submarginal marks*

♂


*Separated from* C. briseis *by buff streak in forewing cell (♂ only) and more broken appearance of white postdiscal band*

The female is usually larger with less distinct markings on the underside hindwing. This species has a more restricted range than the Hermit and flies over mountainous terrain above 900 m. *WS:* 54–66 mm; *Flight:* June–July; *Gen:* 1; *FP:*unknown; *D:* C Spain.

# White-banded grayling

## *Pseudochazara anthelea*

***Fwing** has conspicuous black sex brand in cell (♂ only); eye-spots large, may lack white centres*

♂

*White band prominent on forewing, but short with tawny suffusion on hindwing*

*♀ similar but larger*

Flies over rough ground from lowlands up to 1,600 m. *WS:* 46–50 mm; *Flight:* June–July; *Gen:* 1; *FP:* unknown; *D:* Greece, SE Yugoslavia, Albania, Bulgaria, Crete.

# Brown's grayling

## *P. amymone*

♂

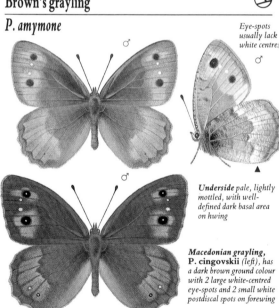

*Eye-spots usually lack white centres*

♂

▲

***Underside** pale, lightly mottled, with well-defined dark basal area on hwing*

♂

***Macedonian grayling,* P. cingovskii** *(left), has a dark brown ground colour with 2 large white-centred eye-spots and 2 small white postdiscal spots on forewing*

Brown's grayling has two small white spots, which are barely discernible, enclosed within the pale orange-yellow band on the forewing. This pale band is very wide where it extends across the hindwing and usually lacks dark cross-veins. An extremely local species, found on rough ground at low altitudes. *WS:* 52–54 mm; *Flight:* July–Aug; *Gen:* 1; *FP:* unknown; *D:* NW Greece.
***P. cingovskii*** flies in more mountainous areas above 1,000 m. The wing bands are more orange in colour with dark venation and two small white-centred eye-spots on the hindwing. *WS:* 50–54 mm; *Flight:* July; *FP:* unknown; *D:* Yugoslavia, NW Greece.

## Grey Asian grayling

### *P. geyeri*

♀

Markings less clear in ♂
Arrow-marks near margin of hwing
♀

A yellowish grey species that occurs locally on dry rocky slopes up to 2,000 m (more widespread in Asia). *WS:* 48–50 mm; *Flight:* July–Aug; *Gen:* 1; *FP:* unknown; *D:* SE Yugoslavia, Albania.

## Norse grayling

### *Oeneis norna*

♂

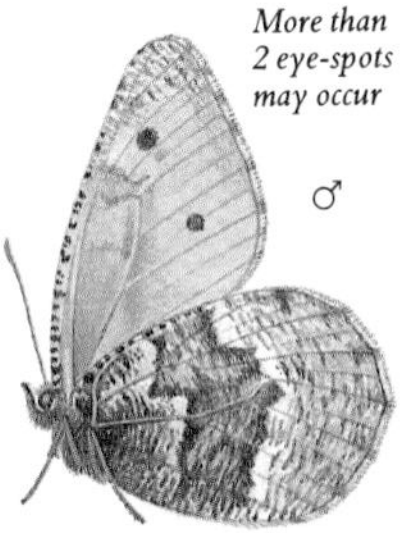
More than 2 eye-spots may occur
♂

This grayling has a dark central band edged with white on its underside hindwing. Flies over bogs from 900 m down to the northern coast. The female is paler with white-centred eye-spots. *WS:* 52–56 mm; *Flight:* July; *Gen:* 1; *FP:* grasses; *D:* N Scand.

## Arctic grayling

### *O. bore*

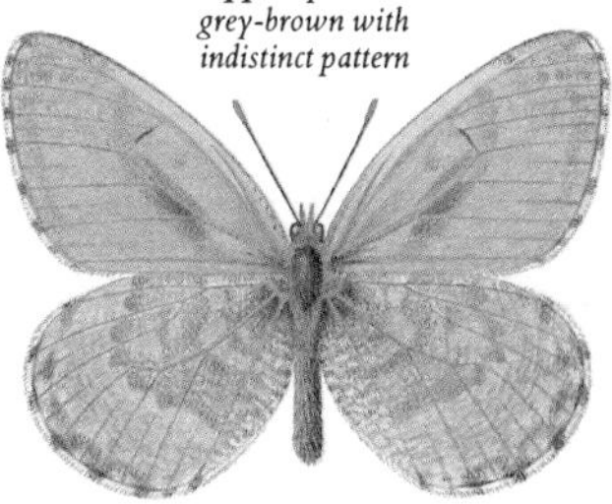
**Uppers** pale grey-brown with indistinct pattern
♂

Eye-spots absent
♂

Often rather worn in appearance, this species is active only in sunshine, and may be found in sandy coastal and mountainous areas. The female is similar but with a yellow flush on the upper forewing. Lives for 2 years as a caterpillar. *WS:* 44–50 mm; *Flight:* July; *Gen:* 1; *FP:* grasses, esp *Festuca ovina*; *D:* N Scand.

# Alpine grayling

## *Oeneis glacialis*

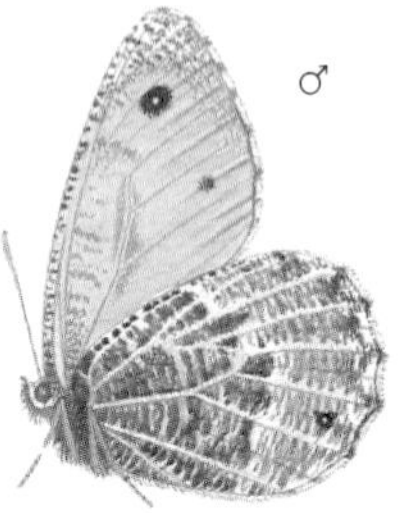

***Underside hwing** mottled dark brown with white-lined veins characteristic*

***Uppers** pale grey-brown with sandy yellow bands, similar to* O. norna*; eye-spots present on both wings, often blind*

Flies at high altitudes (above 2,000 m) over grassy Alpine slopes. Abundant only every other year in some localities, presumably because the caterpillar takes 2 years to grow to full size. *WS:* 50–56 mm; *Flight:* June–Aug; *Gen:* 1; *FP:* grasses, esp Sheep's fescue (*Festuca ovina*); *D:* Alps (Italy, Switz, Austria, Bavaria).

# Baltic grayling

## *O. jutta*

*Prominent dark sex brand on ♂ forewing*

***Hwing** speckled pale grey and dark brown*

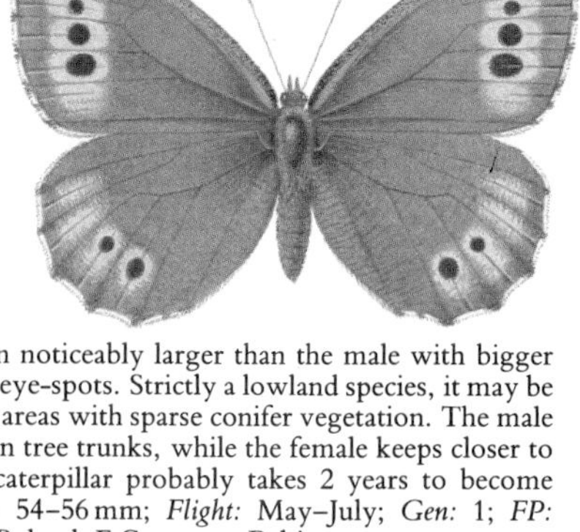

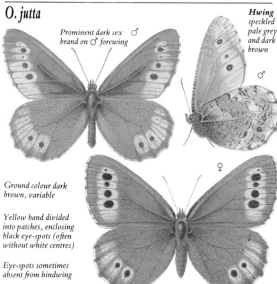

*Ground colour dark brown, variable*

*Yellow band divided into patches, enclosing black eye-spots (often without white centres)*

*Eye-spots sometimes absent from hindwing*

The female is often noticeably larger than the male with bigger and more constant eye-spots. Strictly a lowland species, it may be common in boggy areas with sparse conifer vegetation. The male frequently settles on tree trunks, while the female keeps closer to the ground. The caterpillar probably takes 2 years to become fully grown. *WS:* 54–56 mm; *Flight:* May–July; *Gen:* 1; *FP:* grasses; *D:* Scand, Poland, E Germany, Baltic states.

# Black satyr

## *Satyrus actaea*

***Fwing*** *has single white-centred eye-spot (2 in ♀)*

♂ *Ground colour dark brown to black*

***Underside hwing*** *mottled brown, with 2 narrow grey bands*

♂

A variable species with many local races; in some specimens the eye-spot is very large and a few males may even have an additional spot on the forewing. The females are larger and paler, with two eye-spots ringed in yellow, and an underside forewing which is predominantly brown. Found on dry mountain slopes above 1,000 m. *WS:* 48–56 mm; *Flight:* July–Aug; *Gen:* 1; *FP:* grasses, esp *Bromus*; *D:* Spain, Portugal, S France, N Italy.

# Great sooty satyr

## *S. ferula*

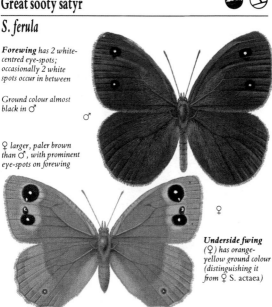

***Forewing*** *has 2 white-centred eye-spots; occasionally 2 white spots occur in between*

*Ground colour almost black in ♂*

♂

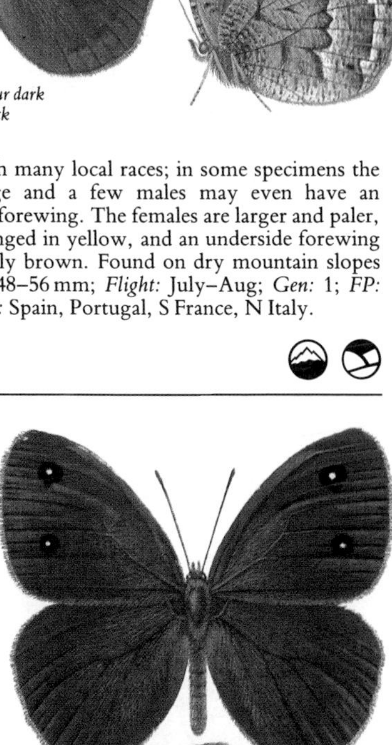

*♀ larger, paler brown than ♂, with prominent eye-spots on forewing*

♀

***Underside fwing*** *(♀) has orange-yellow ground colour (distinguishing it from ♀* S. actaea*)*

Locally common on hillsides up to 1,600 m, especially in stony, sparsely vegetated areas. *WS:* 50–60 mm; *Flight:* July–Aug; *Gen:* 1; *FP:* grasses, esp *Deschampsia caespitosa*; *D:* S France, N Spain, Italy, Switz, Austria, Yugoslavia, Bulgaria, Greece.

# Dryad

## *Minois dryas*

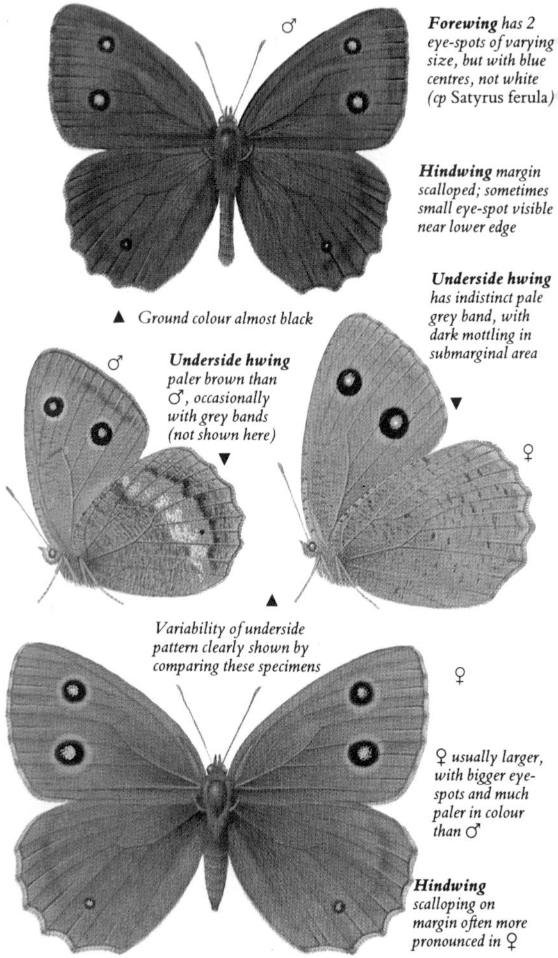
♂
**Forewing** has 2 eye-spots of varying size, but with blue centres, not white (cp Satyrus ferula)
**Hindwing** margin scalloped; sometimes small eye-spot visible near lower edge
▲ Ground colour almost black
♂
**Underside hwing** paler brown than ♂, occasionally with grey bands (not shown here)
**Underside hwing** has indistinct pale grey band, with dark mottling in submarginal area
♀
Variability of underside pattern clearly shown by comparing these specimens
♀
♀ usually larger, with bigger eye-spots and much paler in colour than ♂
**Hindwing** scalloping on margin often more pronounced in ♀

The Dryad has a wider distribution in central Europe than the previous two satyr butterflies, with local colonies scattered throughout most of its range, but sometimes absent from large areas. It has a slow, rather fluttery flight, usually just above the ground, and visits dry shrubland, woodland clearings and grassy slopes up to 1,500 m in the Alps. Both sexes vary in pattern and intensity of colour but are distinguishable from the Great sooty satyr (p 97) by the blue-pupilled eye-spots on the forewing and the scalloped edge of the hindwing. The species overwinters as a caterpillar and pupates in the spring. *WS:* 54–70 mm; *Flight:* June–Sept; *Gen:* 1 (2 in south?); *FP:* grasses; *D:* N Spain, Germany, France, Switz, N Italy, Austria, Yugoslavia, Bulgaria, Romania.

## Great banded grayling

### *Brintesia circe*

**Forewing** has blind eye-spot near apex
♂
Ground colour dark brown to black
Broad white band crossed by veins on both wings
♀ similar but larger

An active flier found in lightly wooded areas up to 1,500 m; if disturbed it usually flies well out of reach before settling again, often on tree trunks. The underside pattern is similar but mottled. *WS:* 66–80 mm; *Flight:* June–Aug; *Gen:* 1; *FP:* grasses, incl *Bromus*; *D:* C and S Europe (not Britain, Scand, Holland).

## Arran brown

### *Erebia ligea*

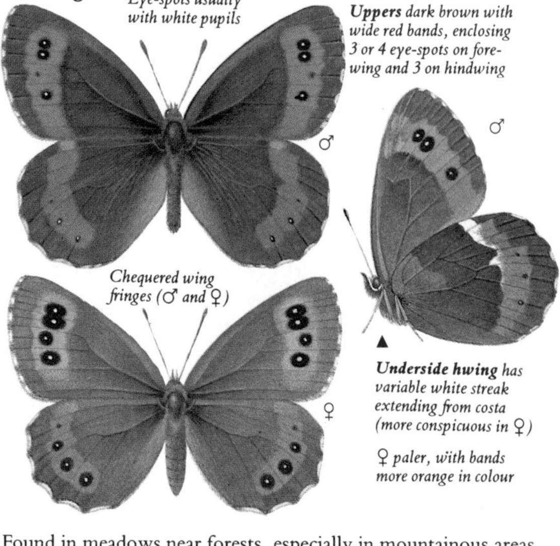
Eye-spots usually with white pupils
**Uppers** dark brown with wide red bands, enclosing 3 or 4 eye-spots on forewing and 3 on hindwing
♂
♂
Chequered wing fringes (♂ and ♀)
♀
**Underside hwing** has variable white streak extending from costa (more conspicuous in ♀)
♀ paler, with bands more orange in colour

Found in meadows near forests, especially in mountainous areas, but further north it prefers lowlands. Reports from Arran in Scotland need confirmation. Spends 2 years as a caterpillar. *WS:* 48–54 mm; *Flight:* June–Aug; *Gen:* 1; *FP:* grasses, esp *Milium*; *D:* Scand, C France, Germany, Italy, Alps, Carpathians, Balkans.

# False grayling

## *Arethusana arethusa*

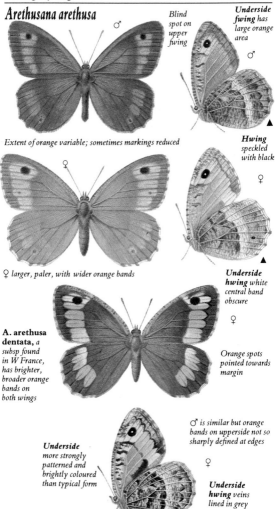

*Blind spot on upper fwing*

***Underside fwing** has large orange area*

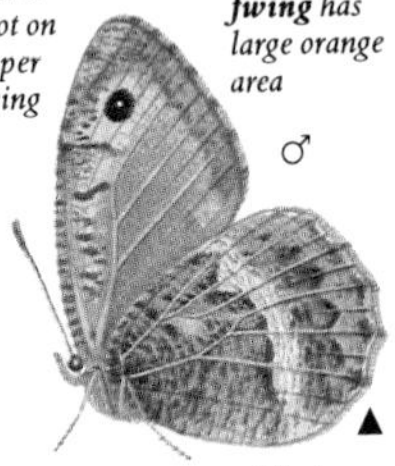

*Extent of orange variable; sometimes markings reduced*

***Hwing** speckled with black*

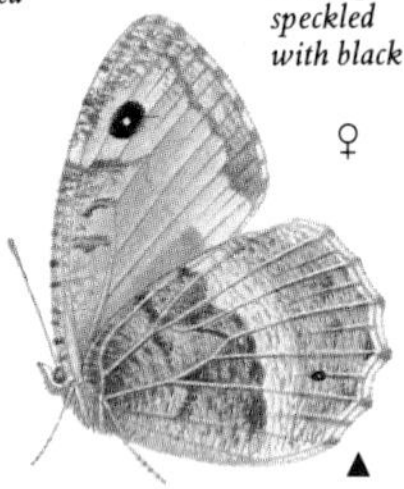

*♀ larger, paler, with wider orange bands*

***Underside hwing** white central band obscure*

**A. arethusa dentata,** *a subsp found in W France, has brighter, broader orange bands on both wings*

*Orange spots pointed towards margin*

*♂ is similar but orange bands on upperside not so sharply defined at edges*

***Underside** more strongly patterned and brightly coloured than typical form*

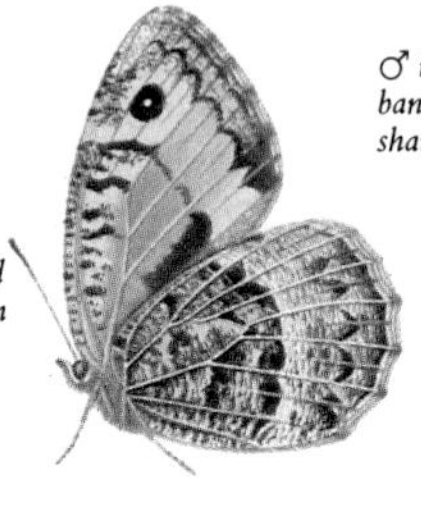

***Underside hwing** veins lined in grey*

The amount of orange on the upperside is extremely variable; some subspecies, such as the one above, have wide bands of brilliant orange-yellow, while others, such as *A. arethusa boabdil* from Andalusia in Spain, have very indistinct markings. The latter has white veins and a conspicuous white central band on its underside hindwing. Widespread but always local, this species flies over heathlands up to 1,500 m, especially in limestone areas. Pupa lies on soil surface. *WS:* 44–48 mm; *Flight:* July–Aug; *Gen:* 1; *FP:* grasses, esp *Festuca*; *D:* Spain, Portugal, France, Switz, N Italy, C Germany, Balkans, Greece, E Europe.

# Large ringlet

## *Erebia euryale*

♂

*Black eye-spots sometimes have white centres*

*Extent of orange and number of eye-spots vary on both sides*

♂

♀

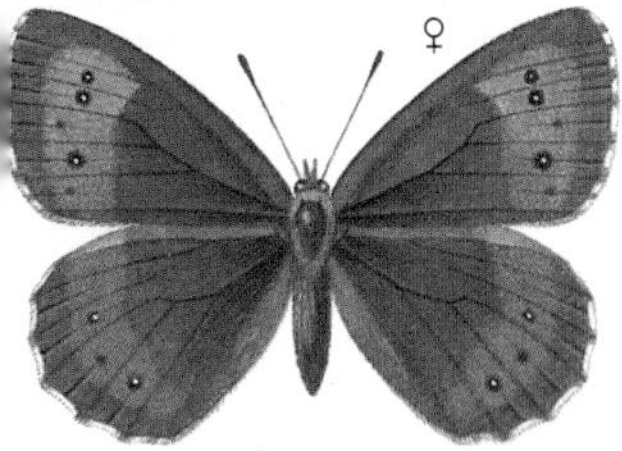

*♀ often has pale band across underside hwing*

*♀ paler than ♂; eye-spots white-centred, enclosed within orange-yellow band*

*Both sexes have chequered fringes*

A variable species, similar to the Arran brown (p 99); where the two species fly together, the Large ringlet is distinguished by its smaller size. There are several subspecies: in some the orange bands are reduced to rings around the eye-spots. Widespread in coniferous forest zone of mountains from 1,000 m up to timber line. *WS:* 42–46 mm; *Flight:* July–Aug; *Gen:* 1; *FP:* grasses; *D:* Cantabrians, Pyrenees, Alps, Balkans, Carpathians, Sudeten mts, Apennines.

# Yellow-spotted ringlet

## *E. manto*

♂

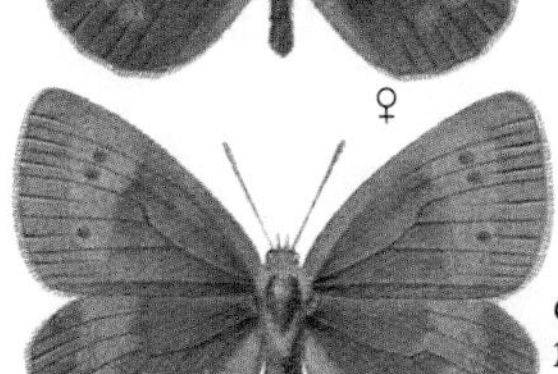

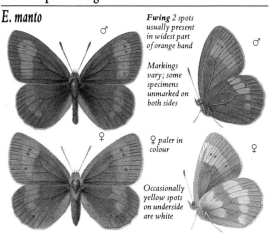

***Fwing*** *2 spots usually present in widest part of orange band*

♂

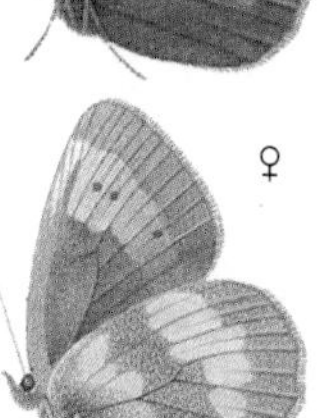

*Markings vary; some specimens unmarked on both sides*

♀

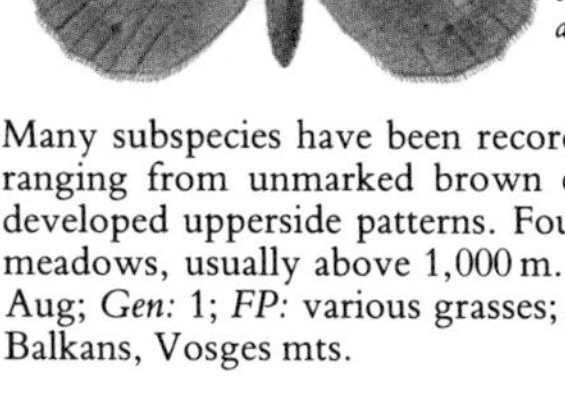

*♀ paler in colour*

♀

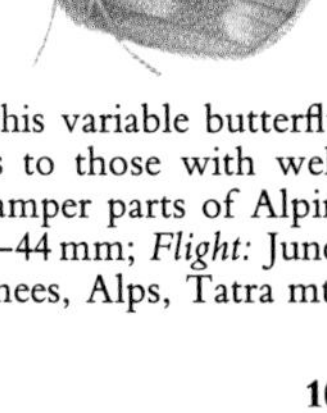

*Occasionally yellow spots on underside are white*

Many subspecies have been recorded for this variable butterfly, ranging from unmarked brown examples to those with well-developed upperside patterns. Found in damper parts of Alpine meadows, usually above 1,000 m. *WS:* 34–44 mm; *Flight:* June–Aug; *Gen:* 1; *FP:* various grasses; *D:* Pyrenees, Alps, Tatra mts, Balkans, Vosges mts.

# Eriphyle ringlet

## *Erebia eriphyle*

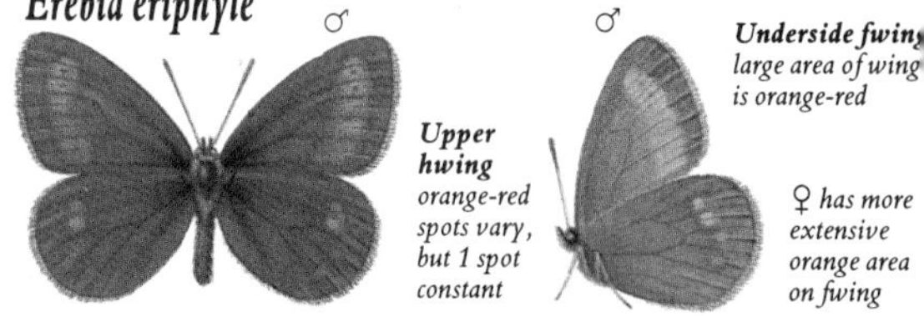
♂
♂
**Underside fwing** large area of wing is orange-red
**Upper hwing** orange-red spots vary, but 1 spot constant
♀ has more extensive orange area on fwing

Some variation occurs in this local Alpine species; specimens from the Bavarian Alps have brighter, better defined markings, often enclosing black points. *WS:* 32–36 mm; *Flight:* July; *Gen:* 1; *FP:* unknown; *D:* Alps (Switz, S Germany, Austria).

# White speck ringlet

## *E. claudina*

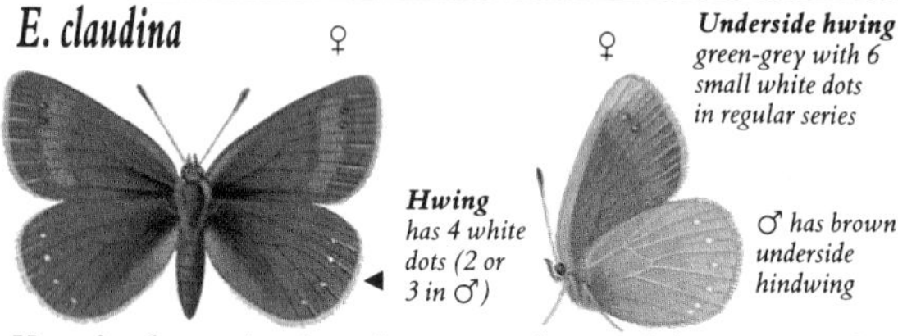
♀
♀
**Underside hwing** green-grey with 6 small white dots in regular series
**Hwing** has 4 white dots (2 or 3 in ♂)
♂ has brown underside hindwing

Very local; restricted to the grassy slopes of the eastern Alps above 1,500 m. Distinguished from other ringlets by the white "specks" on its hindwing. *WS:* 34–36 mm; *Flight:* July; *Gen:* 1; *FP:* grasses, esp *Deschampsia caespitosa*; *D:* Austria.

# Mountain ringlet

## *E. epiphron*

♂
♀
**Uppers** dark brown in ♂, lighter in ♀, with variable amounts of orange or red
♂
Both wings may be unmarked
♀
Spots visible on both sides
♂

The specimens above are of *E. epiphron aetheria*, except for the lower central one, which is the British subspecies *mnemon*. The latter is very local and occurs only in central Scotland and the Lake District, usually above 500 m. The former is one of many subspecies found throughout the European mountain ranges; generally they are dull brown with or without eye-spots. *WS:* 34–42 mm; *Flight:* June–Aug; *FP:* grasses; *D:* Europe (not Scand).

# Yellow-banded ringlet

## E. flavofasciata

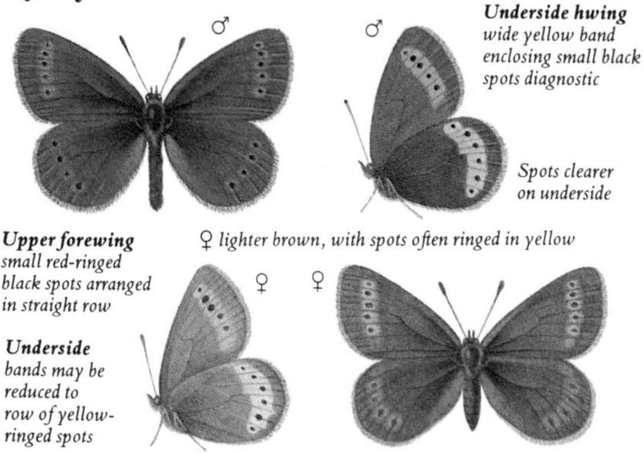
♂
♂
**Underside hwing** wide yellow band enclosing small black spots diagnostic
Spots clearer on underside
**Upper forewing** small red-ringed black spots arranged in straight row
♀ lighter brown, with spots often ringed in yellow
♀
♀
**Underside** bands may be reduced to row of yellow-ringed spots

An extremely local mountain species found only in a few isolated colonies in the Alps above 2,000 m. *WS:* 34–36 mm; *Flight:* July; *Gen:* 1; *FP:* grasses; *D:* Switzerland, ? N Italy.

***E. serotina*** (Descimon's ringlet) is a very rare butterfly recorded only from Cauterets in the Pyrenees. No females have ever been collected and the last specimens were seen about 20 years ago. It has a narrow red band on the topside with eye-spots which usually lack white centres, and is thought by some to be a hybrid of *E. epiphron* (p 102) and *E. pronoe* (p 112). *WS:* 42–44 mm; *Flight:* Sept; *Gen:* 1; *FP:* unknown; *D:* SW France.

# Blind (or Spotless) ringlet

## E. pharte

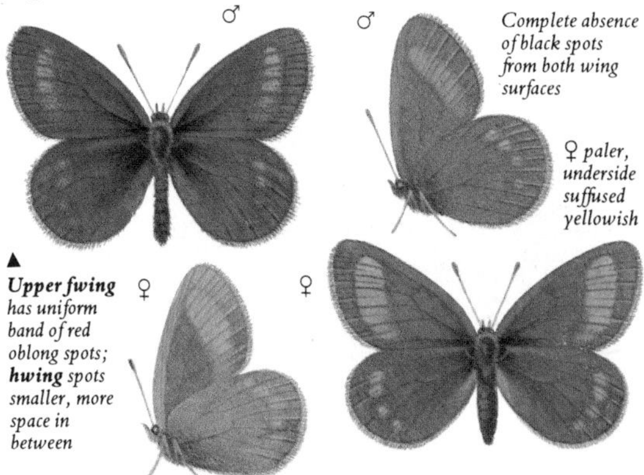
♂
♂
Complete absence of black spots from both wing surfaces
♀ paler, underside suffused yellowish
▲ **Upper fwing** has uniform band of red oblong spots; **hwing** spots smaller, more space in between
♀
♀

Known only from the Alps and Tatra mountains, this species does exhibit a certain amount of variation in its pattern, with some specimens almost unmarked and others with yellow rather than red spots. Found in mountain grassland above 1,600 m. *WS:* 32–40 mm; *Flight:* July–Aug; *Gen:* 1; *FP:* unknown; *D:* Switz, SW France, S Germany, Austria, N Italy, Czech, Poland.

# Rätzer's ringlet

## *Erebia christi*

♂
Red band of uniform width
♂
♀ has wider orange-yellow band on fwing
♀


Similar to *E. epiphron* (p 102) but the underside hindwing has a pale outer area free of spots. Small colonies occur locally on mountains above 1,400 m. *WS:* 36–40 mm; *Flight:* June–July; *Gen:* 1; *FP:* Sheep's fescue (*Festuca ovina*); *D:* S Switzerland.

# Lesser mountain ringlet

## *E. melampus*

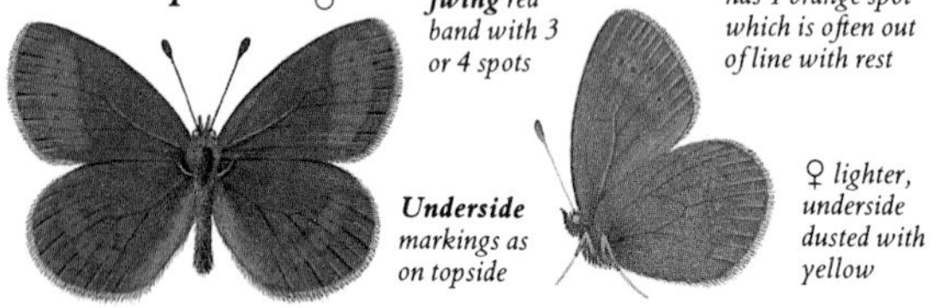

♂
**Upper fwing** red band with 3 or 4 spots
♂
**Underside hwing** has 1 orange spot which is often out of line with rest
**Underside** markings as on topside
♀ lighter, underside dusted with yellow


Specimens from high altitudes are often smaller and darker than those found lower down. A local species of Alpine valleys from 1,000 to 2,000 m. *WS:* 30–36 mm; *Flight:* June–Aug; *Gen:* 1; *FP:* grasses, esp *Poa*; *D:* SW France, Switz, N Italy, Austria.

# Scotch argus

## *E. aethiops*

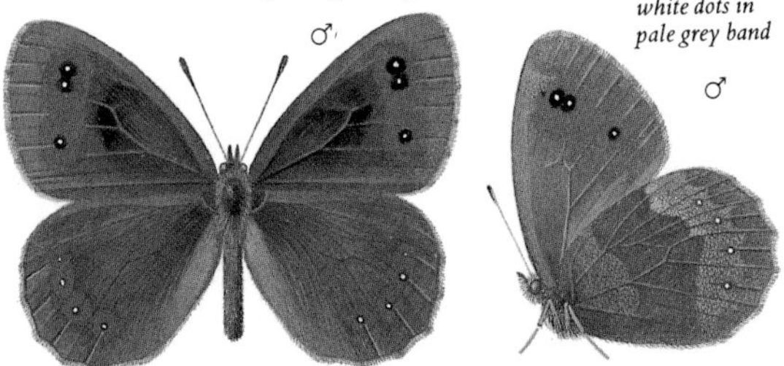

3 white-centred eye-spots on forewing
♂
**Underside hwing** has 4 white dots in pale grey band
♂


A velvety brown butterfly of variable size, generally found in open coniferous woodland up to 1,800 m. It is active in sunshine but disappears into the undergrowth as soon as the weather becomes overcast (unless very warm). The female is a lighter brown and has yellowish bands enclosing bigger eye-spots. May be locally common across Scotland, but in England it is confined mainly to the Lake District. *WS:* 42–52 mm; *Flight:* Aug–Sept; *Gen:* 1; *FP:* grasses, esp *Molinia*; *D:* N Britain, E and C France, Belgium, Germany, Poland, Alps, Carpathians, Balkans.

# de Prunner's ringlet

## E. triaria

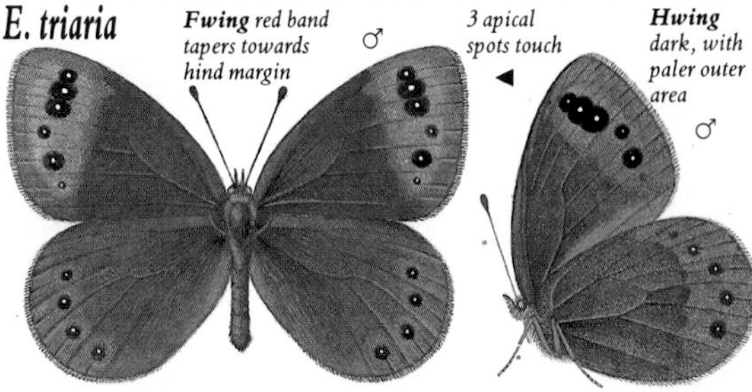
***Fwing*** *red band tapers towards hind margin*
♂
*3 apical spots touch*
***Hwing*** *dark, with paler outer area*
♂

Lives in isolated colonies on grassy slopes up to 2,500 m. *WS:* 44–50 mm; *Flight:* May–July; *Gen:* 1; *FP:* unknown; *D:* Spain, Portugal, S and SE France, Switz, Austria, N Italy, Yugoslavia.

# Lapland ringlet

## E. embla

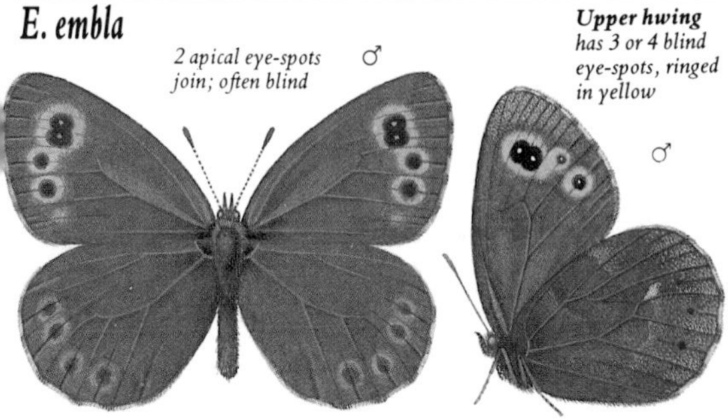
*2 apical eye-spots join; often blind*
♂
***Upper hwing*** *has 3 or 4 blind eye-spots, ringed in yellow*
♂

Locally common in lowland bogs near conifer woods. The female is usually paler, with more yellow around the eye-spots. *WS:* 50–52 mm; *Flight:* June–July; *Gen:* 1; *FP:* unknown; *D:* Scand.

# Arctic ringlet

## E. disa

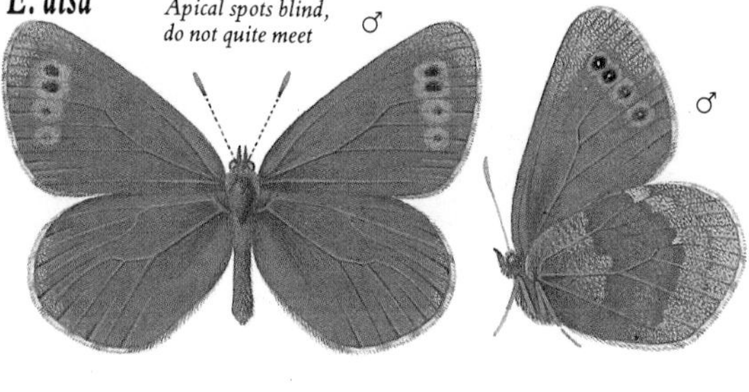
*Apical spots blind, do not quite meet*
♂
♂

Distinguished from *E. embla* by absence of eye-spots on upper hindwing. Flies over wet moorland from sea level to 300 m, occurring most frequently along north coast of Scandinavia. *WS:* 46–50 mm; *Flight:* June–July; *Gen:* 1; *FP:* unknown; *D:* N Scand.

# Woodland ringlet

## *Erebia medusa*

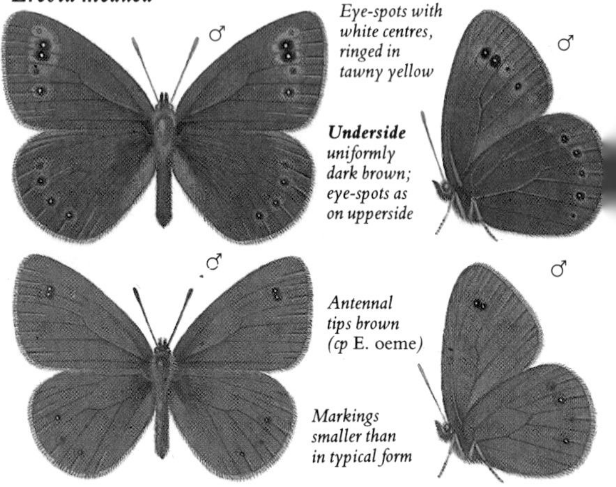
♂
*Eye-spots with white centres, ringed in tawny yellow*
♂
**Underside** *uniformly dark brown; eye-spots as on upperside*
♂
*Antennal tips brown (cp* E. oeme*)*
♂
*Markings smaller than in typical form*

**E. medusa hippomedusa**

There are generally four white-centred eye-spots, one between each vein, on the hindwing of this variable species. Several subspecies have been described based on size and number of these markings; in the subspecies illustrated they are very small, but in subsp *psodea* they are larger and brighter than the typical form. The females are paler than the males with larger spots surrounded by yellow. The butterfly lives in lowland bogs near woods in the north, but further south it is more of a mountain species. *WS:* 38–50 mm; *Flight:* May–July; *Gen:* 1; *FP:* grasses, esp *Digitaria, Milium*; *D:* C and E France, S Belgium, Germany, Poland, Austria, N Italy, Switz, Czech, Hungary, Yugoslavia, Romania, Bulgaria, Greece.

# Arctic woodland ringlet

## *E. polaris*

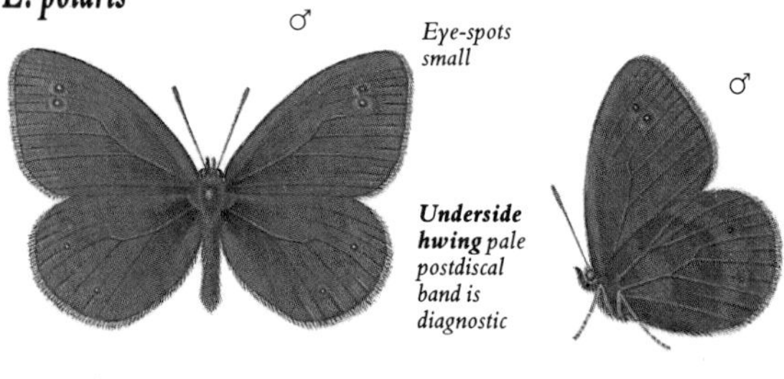
♂
*Eye-spots small*
♂
***Underside hwing*** *pale postdiscal band is diagnostic*

Formerly considered a subspecies of the Woodland ringlet (above) but now regarded as a distinct species. It is very similar to *E. medusa hippomedusa* but has a more northerly distribution and the underside hindwing is not uniformly coloured. Found in dry, lightly wooded areas at low altitudes, rarely above 300 m. The female is paler with more distinct banding on the underside hindwing. *WS:* 40–44 mm; *Flight:* June–July; *Gen:* 1; *FP:* unknown, probably grasses; *D:* N Scandinavia.

## Almond-eyed ringlet

### *E. alberganus*

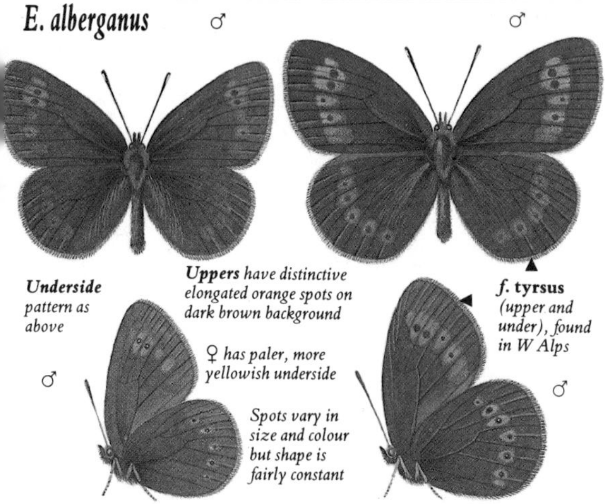
♂
♂
*Underside* pattern as above
**Uppers** have distinctive elongated orange spots on dark brown background
**f. tyrsus** (upper and under), found in W Alps
♀ has paler, more yellowish underside
♂
♂
Spots vary in size and colour but shape is fairly constant

The almond-shaped spots on the upperside make this species identifiable in the field, despite variations in colour and size. The form on the right is an example of a large specimen with bright markings; other forms may be smaller with vestigial orange spots. Found on mountain slopes from 1,000 to 2,000 m. *WS:* 40–46 mm; *Flight:* June–July; *Gen:* 1; *FP:* grasses, esp *Poa*; *D:* N Spain, SE France, Switz, N and C Italy, Austria, Bulgaria.

## Silky ringlet

### *E. gorge*

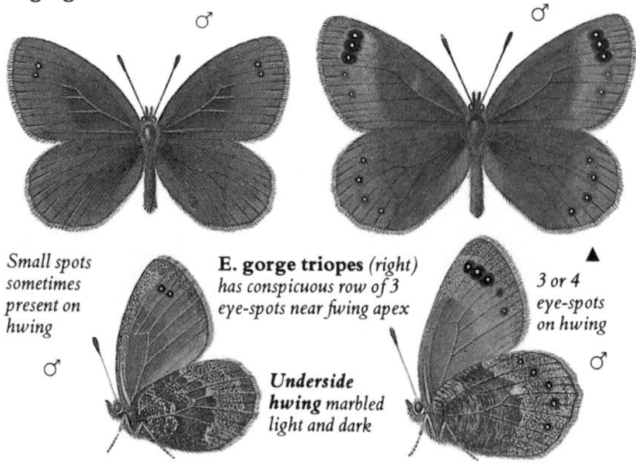
♂
♂
Small spots sometimes present on hwing
**E. gorge triopes** (right) has conspicuous row of 3 eye-spots near fwing apex
3 or 4 eye-spots on hwing
♂
♂
**Underside hwing** marbled light and dark

The red band on the forewing has a silky or gleaming texture. Many subspecies with different combinations of eye-spots have been recorded; occasionally the spots are absent from both wings. Found on rocky slopes with little vegetation from 1,500 to 3,000 m. *WS:* 34–40 mm; *Flight:* June–July; *Gen:* 1; *FP:* grasses; *D:* Cantabrians, Pyrenees, Alps, Apennines, Balkans, Tatra mts.

# Sooty ringlet

## *Erebia pluto*

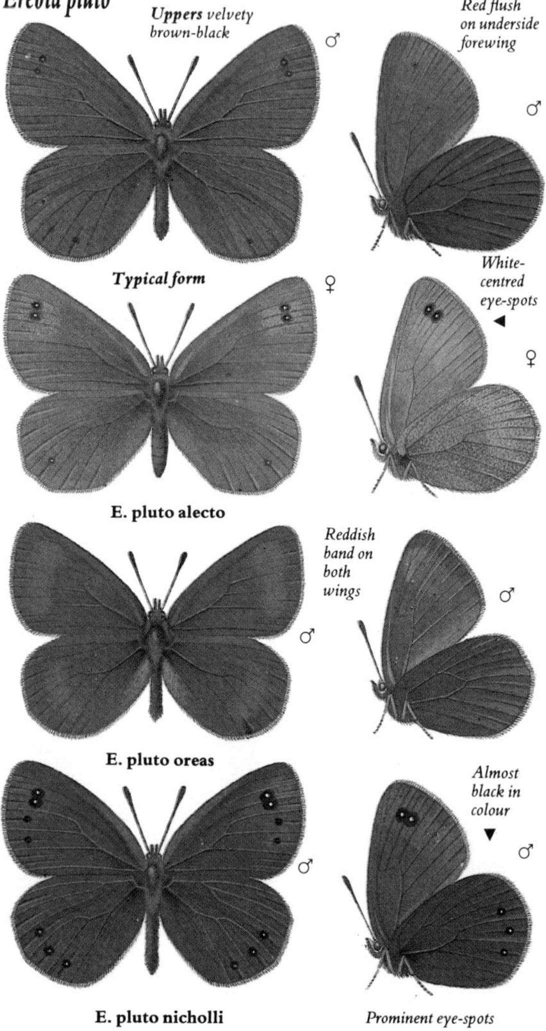
*Uppers* velvety brown-black
♂
*Red flush on underside forewing*
♂
**Typical form**
♀
*White-centred eye-spots*
♀
**E. pluto alecto**
*Reddish band on both wings*
♂
♂
**E. pluto oreas**
*Almost black in colour*
♂
♂
**E. pluto nicholli**
*Prominent eye-spots*

A dark-coloured butterfly with many named subspecies, some of which are illustrated above. The typical form is very distinctive in the field, the male having darker wings than the female, and it may be found on rocky mountainous terrain up to 2,800 m. The various subspecies tend to be associated with different mountain ranges within the Alps, transitional forms occurring in intermediate areas. Generally they are distinguished by colour intensity and number of eye-spots. *WS:* 40–50 mm; *Flight:* June–Aug; *Gen:* 1; *FP:* grasses, esp *Poa*; *D:* Alps, Apennines (Switzerland, Austria, Italy, SE France).

# Mnestra's ringlet

## *E. mnestra*

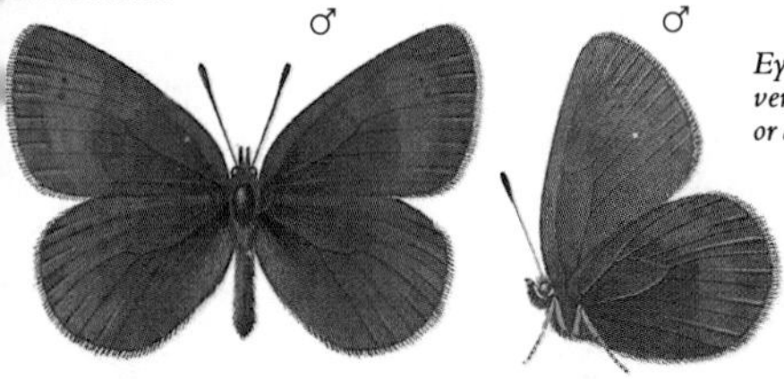
♂
♂
Eye-spots very small or absent
Underside hwing brown, unmarked

The female may be recognized by the presence of two small white-centred eye-spots on the forewing. This very local Alpine species occurs in small colonies on grassy mountain slopes between 1,500 and 2,000 m. *WS:* 34–38 mm; *Flight:* July; *Gen:* 1; *FP:* grasses; *D:* SE France, Austria, Switzerland, S Poland.

# False mnestra ringlet

## *E. aethiopella*

♂
♂
Twin white-centred eye-spots usually present
Underside hwing has pale grey-brown band

The reddish band on the upper hindwing is more distinct than in *E. mnestra* (above) and the underside is well marked in both sexes. This species is even more restricted and local in the Alps than the former, and flies over grassy slopes above 1,800 m. *WS:* 36–40 mm; *Flight:* July–Aug; *Gen:* 1; *FP:* unknown, probably grasses; *D:* SE France, Switzerland, Bulgaria, S Yugoslavia.

# Gavarnie ringlet

## *E. gorgone*

♂
♂
Underside fwing has large dark red area
Ground colour very dark brown
Eye-spots on underside hwing very small

Small colonies of this butterfly occur at altitudes between 1,800 and 2,500 m on the grassy slopes of the Pyrenees. The female is paler than the male with larger eye-spots and buff-coloured veins on the underside hindwing. *WS:* 40–42 mm; *Flight:* July–Aug; *Gen:* 1; *FP:* grasses, esp *Poa*; *D:* N Spain, SW France.

# Spring ringlet

## *Erebia epistygne*

♂

Yellow patch in cell of upper fwing diagnostic
3 eye-spot merge nea fwing ape
♂

The Spring ringlet is on the wing as early as March in hilly, lightly wooded areas up to 2,000 m. The amount of yellow on the upper forewing is distinctive in both sexes. *WS:* 44–50 mm; *Flight:* Mar–June; *Gen:* 2; *FP:* grasses; *D:* S France, Spain.

# Swiss brassy ringlet

## *E. tyndarus*

♂

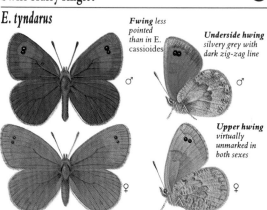

**Fwing** less pointed than in E. cassioides
**Underside hwing** silvery grey with dark zig-zag line
♂

♀

**Upper hwing** virtually unmarked in both sexes
♀

A local species found on grass-covered Alpine slopes above 1,800 m. The brassy ringlets are all very similar but rarely occur together in the same locality. *WS:* 34–36 mm; *Flight:* July–Aug; *Gen:* 1; *FP:* Mat grass (*Nardus stricta*); *D:* Alps.

# De Lesse's brassy ringlet

## *E. nivalis*

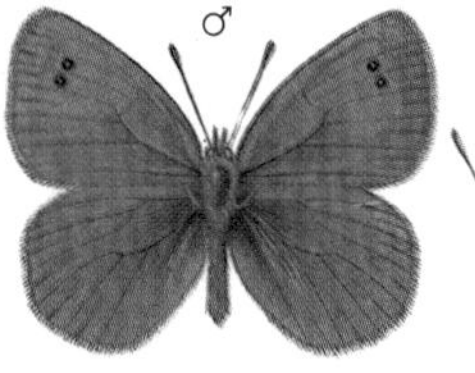
Orange area on forewing extends further in towards wing base than in E. tyndarus
♂

**Underside hwing** has bluish sheen
♂

The lack of eye-spots on the hindwing separates this species from *E. cassioides* (p 111). *WS:* 30–34 mm; *Flight:* July–Aug; *Gen:* 1; *FP:* Mat grass (*Nardus stricta*); *D:* Alps (Austria, Switzerland).

# Common brassy ringlet

## *E. cassioides*

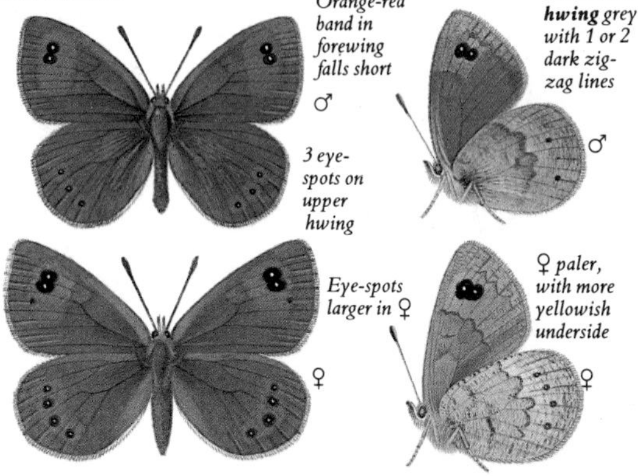
Orange-red band in forewing falls short
♂
3 eye-spots on upper hwing
**Underside hwing** grey with 1 or 2 dark zig-zag lines
♂
Eye-spots larger in ♀
♀
♀ paler, with more yellowish underside
♀

The most widespread of the brassy ringlets, this species may be found on grass slopes at around 1,600 m. Each colony may exhibit small differences, and many forms and subspecies have been named as a result. *WS:* 32–38 mm; *Flight:* June–Aug; *Gen:* 1 (2?); *FP:* Mat grass (*Nardus stricta*); *D:* N Spain, France, Switzerland, Austria, Italy, Yugoslavia, Albania, Romania, Bulgaria.

# Spanish brassy ringlet

## *E. hispania*

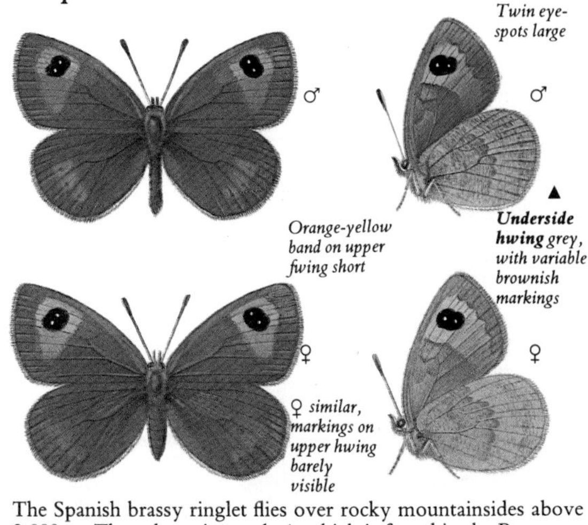
Twin eye-spots large
♂
♂
▲
**Underside hwing** grey, with variable brownish markings
Orange-yellow band on upper fwing short
♀
♀
♀ similar, markings on upper hwing barely visible

The Spanish brassy ringlet flies over rocky mountainsides above 2,000 m. The subspecies *rondoui*, which is found in the Pyrenees, is smaller and more brightly marked. *WS:* 34–42 mm; *Flight:* June–July; *Gen:*1; *FP:* unknown; *D:* S and N Spain, SW France. ***E. calcaria*** (Lorkovic's brassy ringlet) is very dark with small eye-spots. *WS:* 36–40 mm; *Flight:* July; *Gen:* 1; *FP:* grasses, esp *Festuca*; *D:* E Alps (Yugoslavia, NE Italy).

# Ottoman brassy ringlet

## *Erebia ottomana*

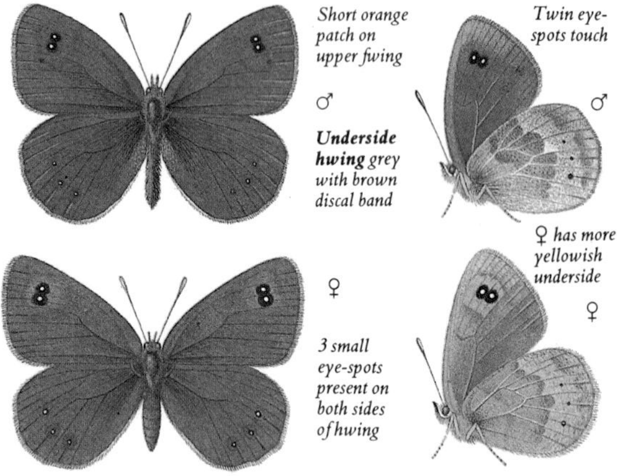
*Short orange patch on upper fwing*
♂
**Underside hwing** *grey with brown discal band*
*Twin eye-spots touch*
♂
♀
*3 small eye-spots present on both sides of hwing*
♀ *has more yellowish underside*
♀

The specimens above are subsp *tardenota* from the Massif Central, France; the more widespread subsp *balcanica* is distinguished by the absence of black spots on the underside hindwing. On grassy slopes above 1,200 m. *WS:* 34–44 mm; *Flight:* July; *Gen:* 1; *FP:* unknown; *D:* C France, NE Italy, Yugoslavia, Bulgaria, Greece.

# Water ringlet

## *E. pronoe*

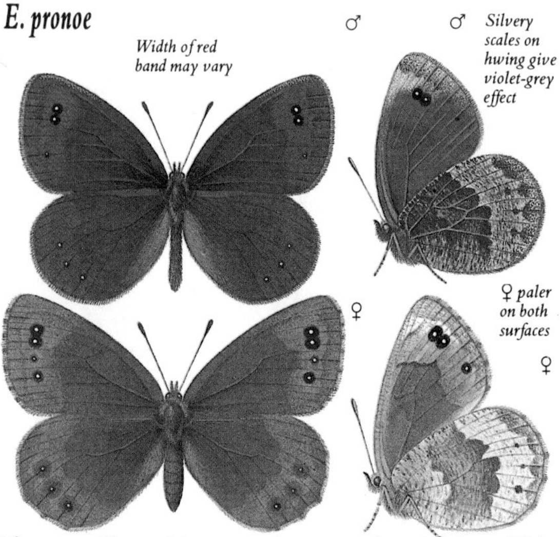
♂
♂ *Silvery scales on hwing give violet-grey effect*
*Width of red band may vary*
♀
♀ *paler on both surfaces*
♀

The upperside markings vary; in some subspecies the reddish band is very faint and the eye-spots are barely visible. The butterfly flies over damp slopes, often near woods, from 1,000 to 1,800 m. *WS:* 42–50 mm; *Flight:* July–Sept; *Gen:* 1; *FP:* Meadow grass (*Poa*); *D:* Pyrenees, Alps, Balkans, Carpathians, Tatra mts.

# Black ringlet

## E. melas

Ground colour almost black
♂
Eye-spots present on both wings
♂


The female has larger eye-spots that are usually surrounded by orange. This species tends to live in limestone areas but little is known of its biology. *WS:* 42–48 mm; *Flight:* July–Aug; *Gen:* 1; *FP:* unknown; *D:* Romania, Yugoslavia, Greece.

# Lefèbvre's ringlet

## E. lefebvrei

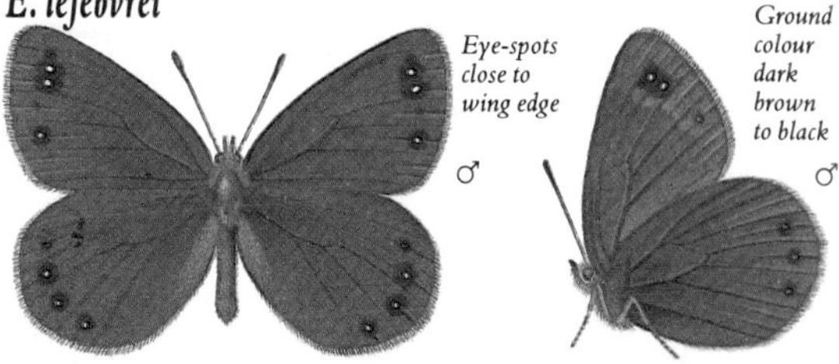

Eye-spots close to wing edge
♂
Ground colour dark brown to black
♂


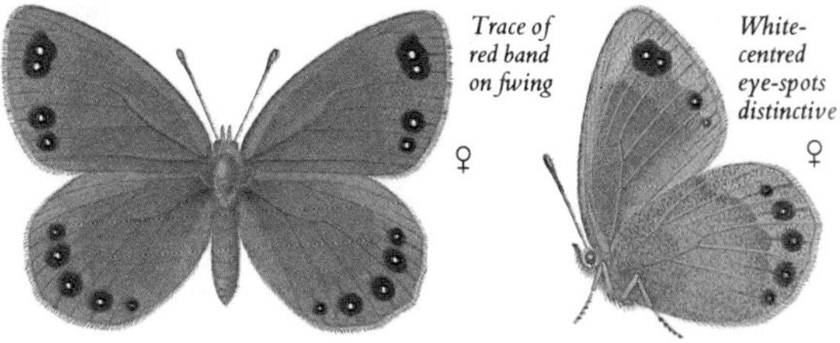

Trace of red band on fwing
♀
White-centred eye-spots distinctive
♀

♂
Eye-spots tend to be small


**E. lefebvrei astur** *f.* **pyrenaea,** *a form that occurs in the Pyrenees*

A mountain species, locally common above 1,800 m in the Pyrenees and Cantabrian mountains. It is less brightly coloured than *E. meolans* (p 117), which flies in the same area, and is unlikely to be confused with *E. melas* (above) as the latter is restricted to southeast Europe. *WS:* 40–48 mm; *Flight:* June–July; *Gen:* 1; *FP:* unknown, probably grasses; *D:* N Spain, SW France.

# Larche ringlet

## *Erebia scipio*

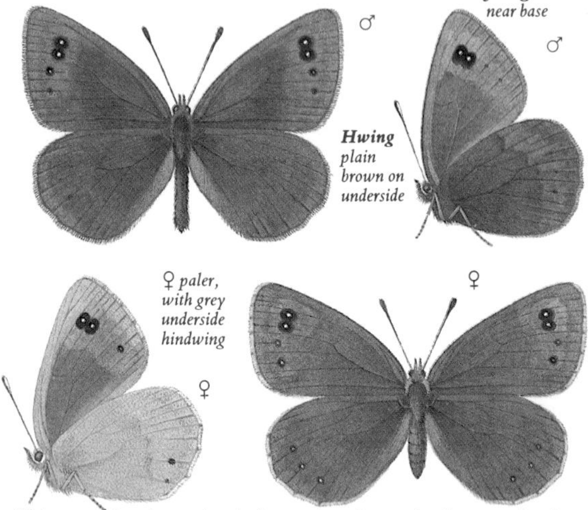
♂
**Underside fwing** red near base
♂
**Hwing** plain brown on underside
♀ paler, with grey underside hindwing
♀
♀

This very local species is becoming increasingly rare, having disappeared from some previous localities. It is found in high rocky areas above 1,500 m. *WS:* 46–50 mm; *Flight:* June–Aug; *Gen:* 1; *FP:* unknown; *D:* S France, NW Italy (Alpes Maritimes).

# Marbled ringlet

## *E. montana*

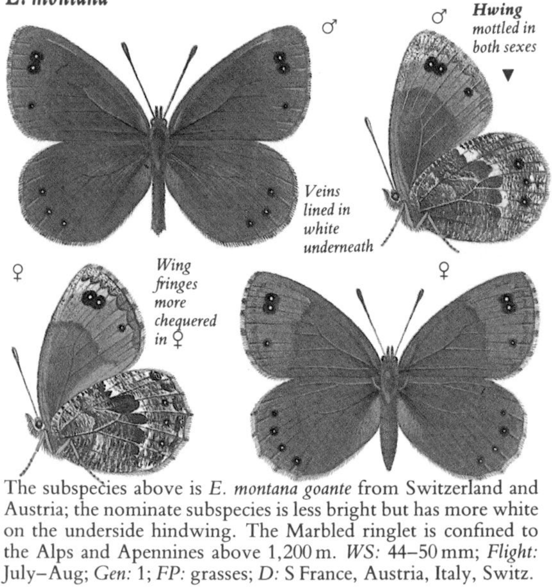
♂
♂
**Hwing** mottled in both sexes
▼
Veins lined in white underneath
♀
Wing fringes more chequered in ♀
♀

The subspecies above is *E. montana goante* from Switzerland and Austria; the nominate subspecies is less bright but has more white on the underside hindwing. The Marbled ringlet is confined to the Alps and Apennines above 1,200 m. *WS:* 44–50 mm; *Flight:* July–Aug; *Gen:* 1; *FP:* grasses; *D:* S France, Austria, Italy, Switz.

# Styrian ringlet

## E. styria

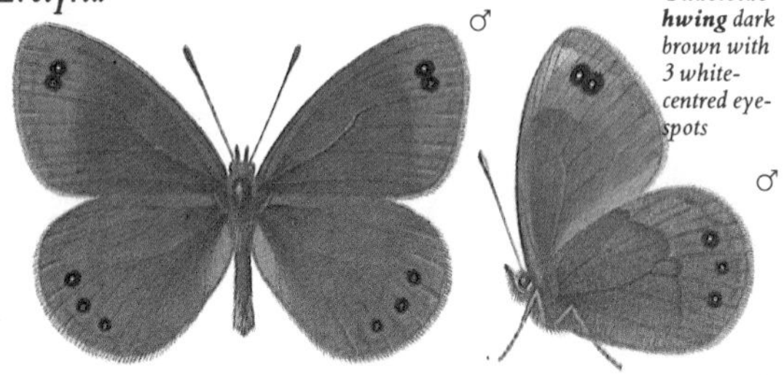
♂
Underside hwing dark brown with 3 white-centred eye-spots
♂

Very similar to *E. styx* (below); *E. styria* has a smoother underside hindwing and less red on the upperside. The underside hindwing of the female is grey-brown. *WS:* 46–52 mm; *Flight:* July–Sept; *Gen:* 1; *FP:* grasses; *D:* Austria, Switz, N Italy.

# Stygian ringlet

## E. styx

♀ is paler
♂
Underside hwing dark, often with thin white discal band
♂

Essentially an Alpine butterfly, the Stygian ringlet flies at altitudes between 600 and 1,800 m. Has only recently been regarded as a separate species from *E. styria* (above). There are several named subspecies. *WS:* 46–56 mm; *Flight:* July–Aug; *Gen:* 1; *FP:* grasses; *D:* Austria, Switz, N Italy, N Yugoslavia.

# Autumn ringlet

## E. neoridas

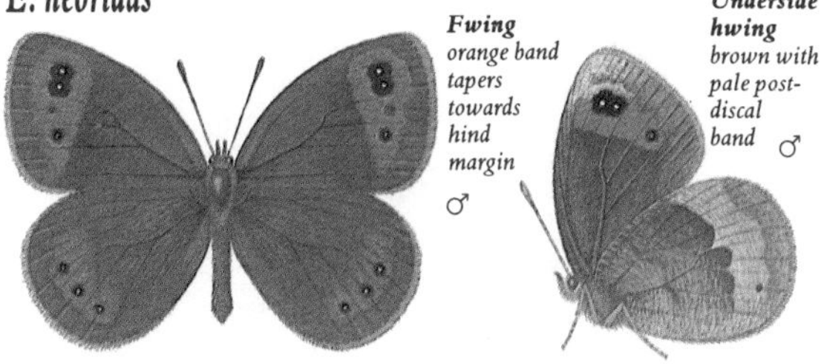
Fwing orange band tapers towards hind margin
♂
Underside hwing brown with pale post-discal band
♂

Found in mountainous areas from 600 to 1,500 m. The female is generally paler on both wing surfaces with brighter upperside markings. *WS:* 36–46 mm; *Flight:* Aug–Sept; *Gen:* 1; *FP:* unknown; *D:* Spain (E Pyrenees), S France, Italy (Alps, Apennines).

# Zapater's ringlet

## *Erebia zapateri*

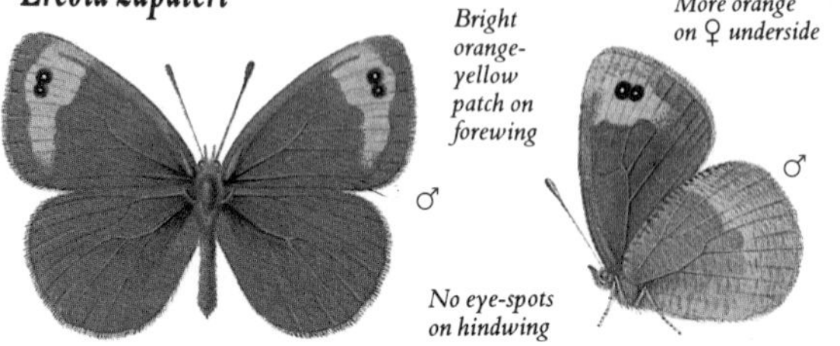
Bright orange-yellow patch on forewing
More orange on ♀ underside
♂
♂
No eye-spots on hindwing

This very local species is one of the few ringlets that are clearly recognizable in the field, on account of the bright coloration on its forewings. *WS:* 36–40 mm; *Flight:* July–Aug; *Gen:* 1; *FP:* unknown; *D:* C Spain.

# Bright-eyed ringlet

## *E. oeme*

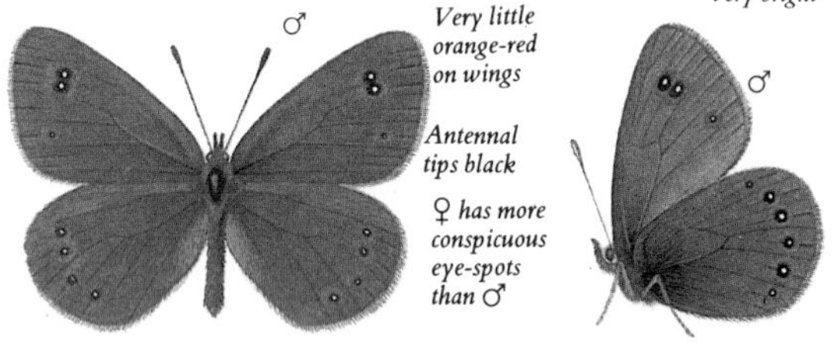
White pupils very bright
♂
Very little orange-red on wings
♂
Antennal tips black
♀ has more conspicuous eye-spots than ♂

In subspecies *lugens* the bright eye-spots are barely visible. May be found in damp meadows above 900 m. *WS:* 38–46 mm; *Flight:* June–July; *Gen:* 1; *FP:* Woodrush (*Luzula*); *D:* France, Pyrenees, Alps, Austria, Switz, Yugoslavia, Balkans, N Greece.

# Chapman's ringlet

## *E. palarica*

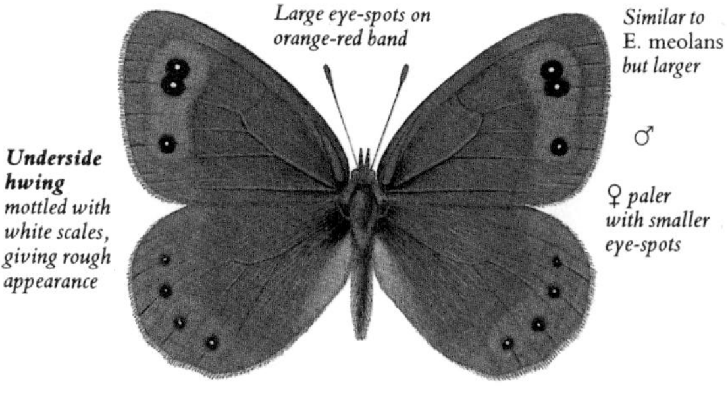
Large eye-spots on orange-red band
Similar to E. meolans but larger
Underside hwing mottled with white scales, giving rough appearance
♂
♀ paler with smaller eye-spots

The larger size and rather rough surface to the underside hindwing distinguish this butterfly from the Piedmont ringlet (p 117). Very local in rough grassland areas of Spain. *WS:* 56–60 mm; *Flight:* June–July; *Gen:* 1; *FP:* unknown; *D:* NW Spain.

# Piedmont ringlet

## *E. meolans*

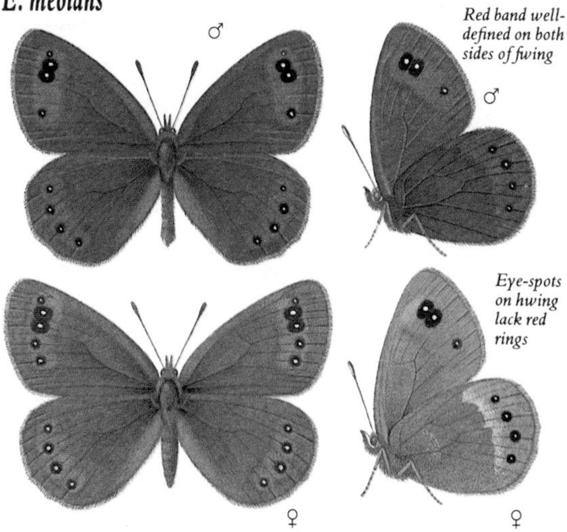
♂
*Red band well-defined on both sides of fwing*
♂
*Eye-spots on hwing lack red rings*
♀
♀

The Piedmont ringlet can be found on rocky mountain slopes from around 1,000 m up to 1,800 m. Several subspecies have been described based on variation in pattern and size; in Switzerland, subsp *valesiaca* is smaller than the specimens illustrated, with reduced red markings and vestigial eye-spots. The female, besides being paler, usually has a grey postdiscal band on the underside hindwing. *WS:* 38–54 mm; *Flight:* June–July; *Gen:* 1; *FP:* grasses; *D:* N and C Spain, C and S France, C and N Italy, Switzerland, Austria, S Germany.

# Dewy ringlet

## *E. pandrose*

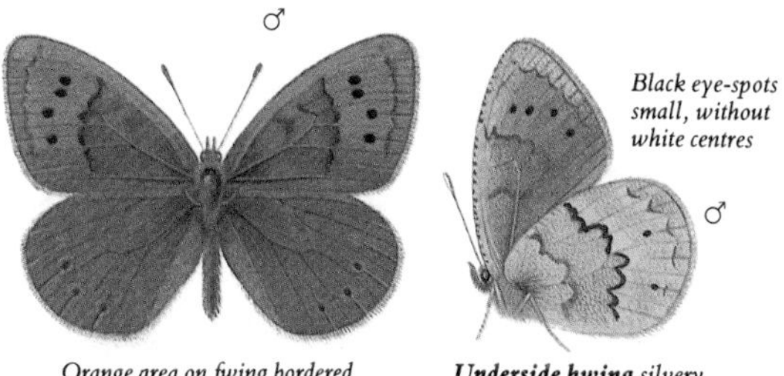
♂
*Black eye-spots small, without white centres*
♂

*Orange area on fwing bordered or crossed by dark discal line*

***Underside hwing** silvery grey with 2 wavy dark lines*

In the southern part of its range this species flies in high mountains above 1,600 m, but further north in Scandinavia it is more of a lowland insect. The female is similar to the male, except that the underside hindwing is yellowish grey. The Dewy ringlet is not as variable in pattern as some other ringlets. *WS:* 40–50 mm; *Flight:* June–Aug; *Gen:* 1; *FP:* grasses; *D:* E Pyrenees, Alps, Apennines, Balkans, Carpathians, Scand (not Denmark).

# False dewy ringlet

## *Erebia sthennyo*

♂

***Underside hwing*** *pale grey, almost unmarked*

♂

This butterfly is similar to the Dewy ringlet (p 117), but it is smaller and less widespread. Both occur in the Pyrenees above 1,800 m, but generally not in the same places. *WS:* 40–44 mm; *Flight:* June–July; *Gen:* 1; *FP:* unknown; *D:* N Spain, SW France.

# Dalmatian ringlet

## *E. phegea*

♂

***Underside hwing*** *has eye-spots all round margin*

♂

Very local in eastern Europe, the Dalmatian ringlet is distinct from other *Erebia* species. It flies over coastal cliffs and lower hill slopes in dry areas of Dalmatia. *WS:* 44–48 mm; *Flight:* May–June; *Gen:* 1; *FP:* unknown; *D:* Yugoslavia, S Russia.

# Sardinian meadow brown

## *Maniola nurag*

♂

*Prominent dark sex brand on ♂ forewing*

♀

*♀ larger, more orange in colour than ♂*

The Sardinian meadow brown is rather like a smaller, paler version of *M. jurtina hispulla* (p 119). It has a large amount of orange-yellow on both wings and occurs most frequently in the open areas of the northern part of the island. The adult females usually outlive the males. *WS:* 36–40 mm; *Flight:* June–July; *Gen:* 1; *FP:* grasses; *D:* Sardinia.

# Meadow brown

## *M. jurtina*

**Uppers** (♂) *predominantly grey-brown, with very little orange. Dark sex brand visible under cell area of forewing*

*Single black, white-centred eye-spot*

***Underside fwing** has large area of orange (both sexes)*

***Upper forewing** (♀) has extensive orange-yellow markings*

*Light and dark areas on underside hwing more clearly defined in ♀*

*Large and very brightly coloured with prominent black eye-spot on forewing*

**M. jurtina hispulla**, *a subspecies found in S Europe*

Probably one of the most common and widespread of the European butterflies, this species may be found throughout Britain and Ireland, especially in coastal areas. The extent of orange on the wings is variable and several subspecies have been described. *M. jurtina splendida*, for instance, from the west coast of Scotland, is brighter than the typical form, while the Irish subsp *iernes* has a very plain underside. The Meadow brown can be found in a number of habitats from sea-level up to 1,800 m, and is even known to occur in the centre of cities. It will fly in cloudy weather, but usually remains in a fairly restricted area. *WS:* 40–58 mm; *Flight:* June–Sept; *Gen:* 1–2; *FP:* grasses, esp Meadow grass (*Poa*); *D:* Europe (not N and C Scand).

# Dusky meadow brown

## *Hyponephele lycaon*

*Dark sex brand on ♂ fwing curves forward*
♂
**Uppers** *grey-brown with yellowish tint*

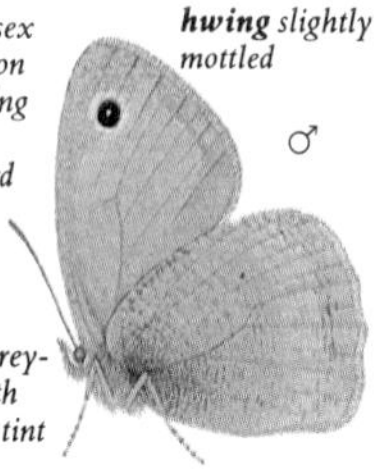
**Underside hwing** *slightly mottled*
♂

The female has a large yellow area on the upper forewing enclosing two black spots. Flies with a slow, flapping movement in dry, stony lowlands. Population has recently declined. *WS:* 40–48 mm; *Flight:* June–Aug; *Gen:* 1; *FP:* grasses, esp *Poa*; *D:* S and C Europe (not Britain, Scand, Holland, Belgium, N France).

# Oriental meadow brown

## *H. lupina*

*Larger than* H. lycaon, *with broader sex brand*
♂

**Hindwing** *margin scalloped (♂ and ♀)*
♂

Found on dry rocky hill slopes up to 1,000 m. The female has two black spots ringed in orange on the upper forewing. *WS:* 42–48 mm; *Flight:* July–Aug; *Gen:* 1; *FP:* unknown; *D:* Spain, Portugal, S France, Italy, Sicily, Yugoslavia, Greece.

# Southern gatekeeper

## *Pyronia cecilia*

*Sex brand on ♂ fwing rectangular, crossed by orange veins*
**Hwing** *lacks eye-spots on both sides*

*Markings on underside more contrasting in ♀*

Similar to the Gatekeeper (p 121) except for differences in the male sex brand and the absence of eye-spots on the underside hindwing. Flies in hot, dry, scrubby areas. *WS:* 30–32 mm; *Flight:* May–Aug; *Gen:* 2 or more; *FP:* grasses, esp *Deschampsia*; *D:* Spain, Portugal, S France, Italy, Sicily, Yugoslavia, Greece.

## Gatekeeper

### *P. tithonus*

*Fwing black eye-spot often has 2 white centres; sex brand prominent in ♂*

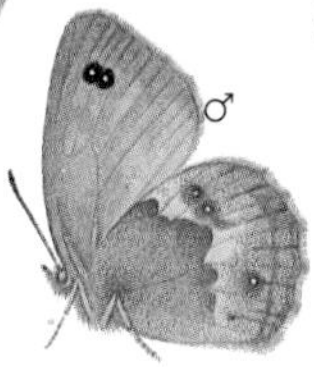

***Hindwing** has dark basal area; **underside** yellowish with 2 or 3 eye-spots*

*♀ has larger, brighter orange areas on wings and lacks sex brand*

Also popularly known as the Hedge brown, probably because of the habitat in which it is found—hedgerows, fields and wooded lanes, especially where brambles are in bloom. Locally common and widespread, but in Britain it is confined mainly to southern and central areas. *WS:* 34–38 mm; *Flight:* July–Aug; *Gen:* 1; *FP: Poa, Milium*; *D:* W, C and S Europe (not Scand, S Italy).

## Spanish gatekeeper

### *P. bathseba*

***Fwing** dark basal area obscures sex brand in ♂*

*Eye-spots on hwing ringed in yellow*

***Underside hwing** brown with narrow yellow band*

Flies in hot, dry areas up to 1,500 m. *WS:* 36–38 mm; *Flight:* Apr–Aug; *Gen:* 2 or more; *FP:* grasses; *D:* Portugal, S Spain, SW France.

## Ringlet

### *Aphantopus hyperantus*

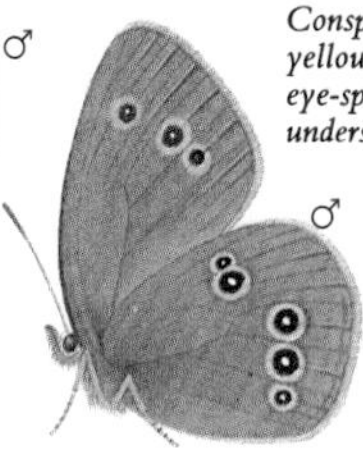

*Conspicuous, yellow-ringed eye-spots on underside*

A very dark butterfly with a variable number of obscure eye-spots on the upperside. The female is paler and has larger, more regular markings. Found in damp open woods, near hedgerows and also on sea cliffs. *WS:* 40–48 mm; *Flight:* June–Aug; *Gen:* 1; *FP:* grasses; *D:* Europe (not N Scand, S Spain, Italy).

# Large heath

## *Coenonympha tullia*

♂
♀

♂

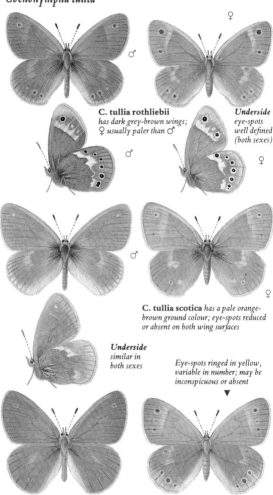

**C. tullia rothliebii** *has dark grey-brown wings; ♀ usually paler than ♂*

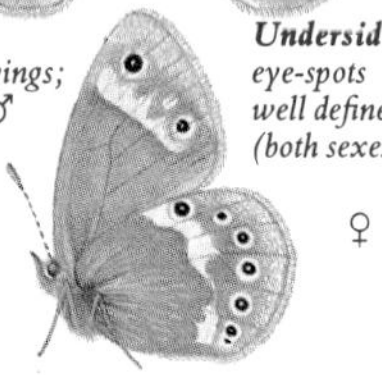
♀

***Underside*** *eye-spots well defined (both sexes)*

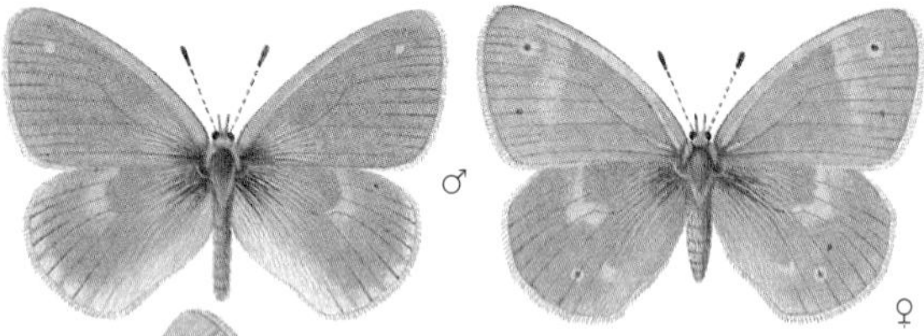
♂
♀

**C. tullia scotica** *has a pale orange-brown ground colour; eye-spots reduced or absent on both wing surfaces*

***Underside*** *similar in both sexes*

*Eye-spots ringed in yellow, variable in number; may be inconspicuous or absent*

♂ **C. tullia thimoites** *(uppersides only)* ♀

The Large heath is a northern butterfly with three subspecies in Britain: *tullia*, *rothliebii* and *scotica*. All three may vary, and intermediate forms occur between isolated populations. The species is far less widespread than in previous years and is found on damp hillsides and swampy areas of moorlands. It has a heavy, slow flight. *WS:* 30–44 mm; *Flight:* June–July; *Gen:* 1; *FP:* Beaked rush (*Rhynchospora alba*); *D:* Britain, NE France, Scand, Belgium, Switz, N Germany, Czech, Austria, Poland. ***C. rhodopensis*** (Eastern large heath) is more orange in colour and has a smaller white mark on the underside hindwing. *WS:* 32–34 mm; *Flight:* July; *Gen:* 1; *D:* C Italy, SE Europe.

# Corsican heath

## C. corinna

**Uppers** bright orange with brown marginal borders
♂
**Underside fwing** apical spot small, yellow-ringed; **hwing** has wavy yellowish band
♂

Specimens from Corsica are brighter on the underside than those found in Sardinia. The species has only been recorded from open grassy places on these two islands. *WS:* 28–30 mm; *Flight:* May–Sept; *Gen:* 2–3; *FP:* unknown; *D:* Corsica, Sardinia.
***C. elbana*** (Elban heath) is similar but has better developed eye-spots on the underside hindwing. *WS:* 24–28 mm; *Flight:* May–Sept; *Gen:* 2–3; *FP:* unknown; *D:* Elba.

# Small heath

## C. pamphilus

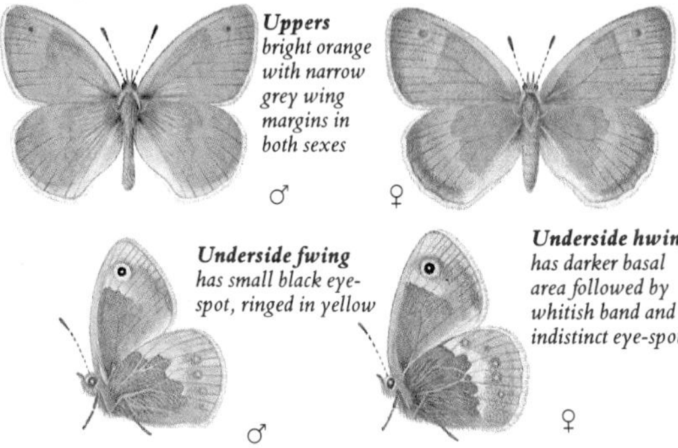
**Uppers** bright orange with narrow grey wing margins in both sexes
♂
♀
**Underside fwing** has small black eye-spot, ringed in yellow
**Underside hwing** has darker basal area followed by whitish band and indistinct eye-spots
♂
♀

A widespread and common butterfly with several subspecies. It is easily distinguished from the Large heath (p 122) by its size and dark wing borders. It will fly in both cloudy and fine weather up to 1,800 m. *WS:* 26–34 mm; *Flight:* May–Sept; *Gen:* 2 (more in south); *FP:* grasses; *D:* Europe (not N Scand).

# Alpine heath

## C. gardetta

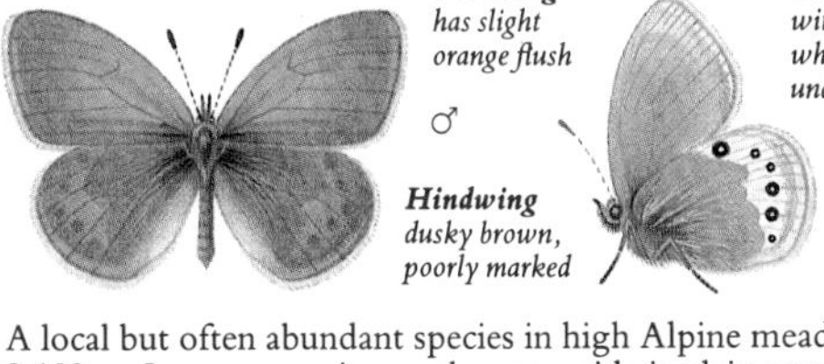
**Forewing** has slight orange flush
♂
**Hindwing** dusky brown, poorly marked
Black eye-spots without rings in white band on underside hwing
♂

A local but often abundant species in high Alpine meadows up to 2,100 m. In some specimens the upperside is plain grey and lacks any orange on the forewing. *WS:* 30–32 mm; *Flight:* July–Aug; *Gen:* 1; *FP:* unknown; *D:* Switz, Austria, S Germany, N Italy.

# Dusky heath

## *Coenonympha dorus*

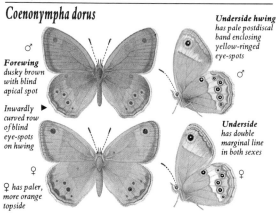

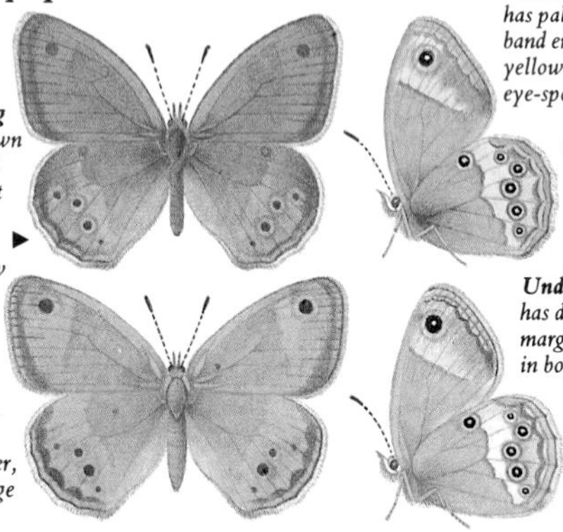
♂
***Forewing*** *dusky brown with blind apical spot*
*Inwardly curved row of blind eye-spots on hwing*
♀
*♀ has paler, more orange topside*
***Underside hwing*** *has pale postdiscal band enclosing yellow-ringed eye-spots*
♂
***Underside*** *has double marginal line in both sexes*
♀

A very variable species, often locally common in dry, rocky areas up to 1,800 m. *WS:* 28–34 mm; *Flight:* June–July; *Gen:* 1; *FP:* grasses; *D:* Spain, Portugal, S France, N and C Italy.

# Pearly heath

## *C. arcania*

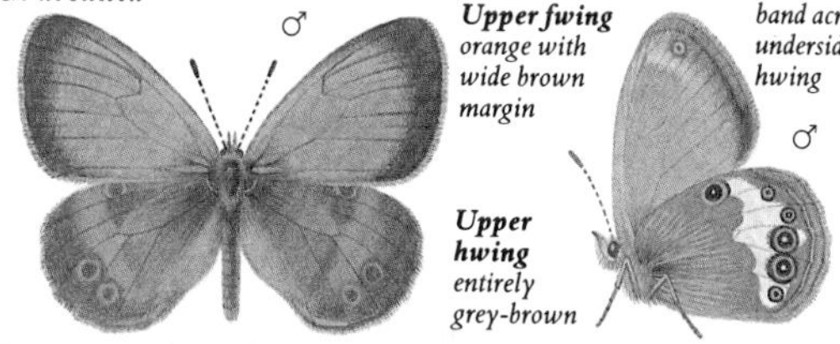
♂
***Upper fwing*** *orange with wide brown margin*
***Upper hwing*** *entirely grey-brown*
*Broad white band across underside hwing*
♂

On grassy slopes between 1,200 and 1,800 m. The females are often less common than the males. *WS:* 34–40 mm; *Flight:* June–July; *Gen:* 1; *FP:* grasses; *D:* Europe (not Britain, N Scand).
***C. darwiniana*** (Darwin's heath) is smaller, with a narrower, more even white band on the underside hindwing. Flies at 1,500 m. *WS:* 32–34 mm; *Flight:* July–Aug; *Gen:* 1; *D:* Alps.

# False ringlet

## *C. oedippus*

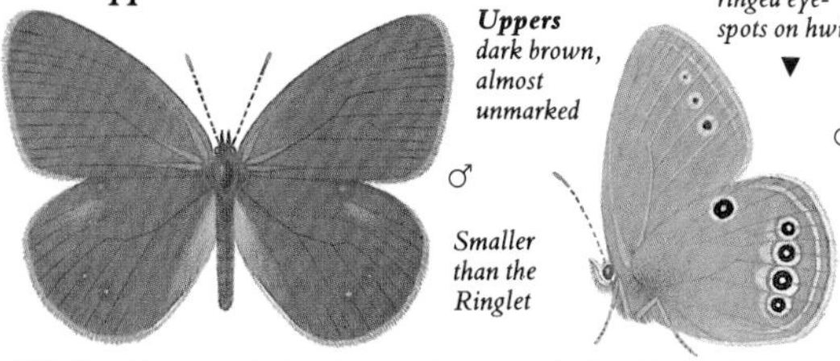
***Uppers*** *dark brown, almost unmarked*
♂
*Smaller than the Ringlet*
*Large, yellow-ringed eye-spots on hwing*
♂

*WS:* 34–42 mm; *Flight:* June–July; *Gen:* 1; *FP:* Sedge (*Carex*); *D:* SW and C France, N Italy, Belgium (rare), Austria, Hungary.

# Russian heath

## C. leander

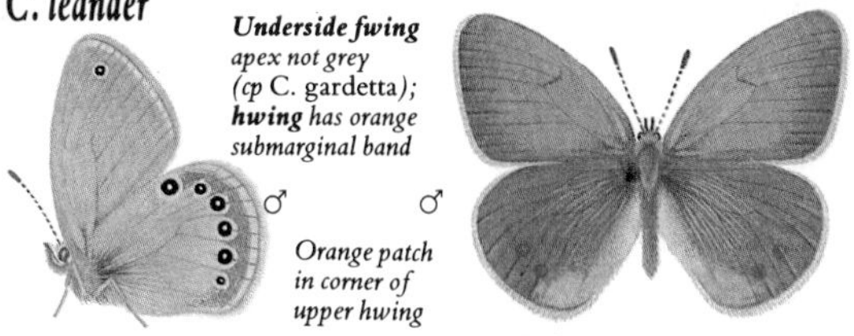
**Underside fwing** *apex not grey (cp* C. gardetta*);* **hwing** *has orange submarginal band*
♂
♂
*Orange patch in corner of upper hwing*

In the female the orange patch on the upper hindwing spreads out more and the forewings are flushed yellow-buff. It is more widespread in Asia than in Europe, and may be found on grasslands up to 1,500 m. *WS:* 32–34 mm; *Flight:* May–July; *Gen:* 1; *FP:* unknown; *D:* NE Greece, Romania, Bulgaria, S Russia.

# Scarce heath

## C. hero

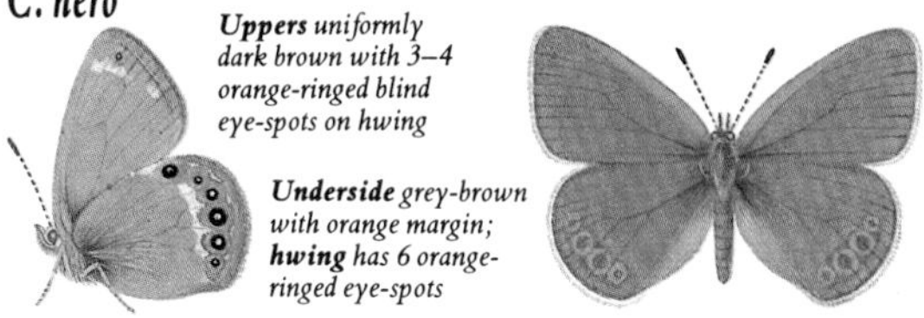
**Uppers** *uniformly dark brown with 3–4 orange-ringed blind eye-spots on hwing*
**Underside** *grey-brown with orange margin;* **hwing** *has 6 orange-ringed eye-spots*

Local and comparatively rare with widely dispersed colonies. Favours damp open terrain. *WS:* 30–34 mm; *Flight:* May–June; *Gen:* 1; *FP:* grasses (*Lolium*, *Carex*); *D:* S Scand, Belgium, NE France, Holland, Germany, Czech, Poland, Baltic states.

# Chestnut heath

## C. glycerion

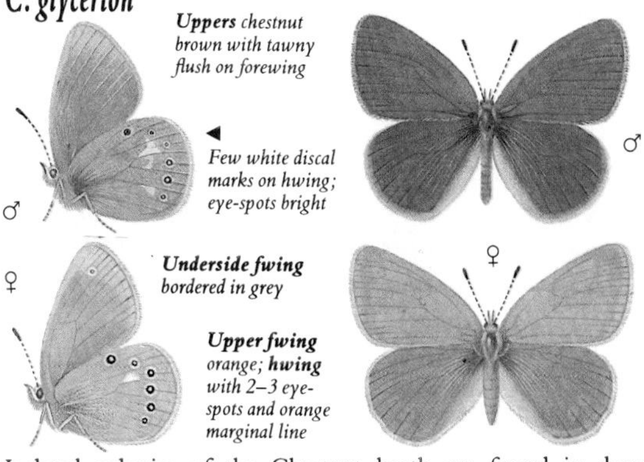
**Uppers** *chestnut brown with tawny flush on forewing*
*Few white discal marks on hwing; eye-spots bright*
♂
♂
♀
♀
**Underside fwing** *bordered in grey*
**Upper fwing** *orange;* **hwing** *with 2–3 eye-spots and orange marginal line*

Isolated colonies of the Chestnut heath are found in damp meadowland up to 1,500 m. *WS:* 32–36 mm; *Flight:* June–July; *Gen:* 1; *FP:* grasses; *D:* C and E Europe (not Britain, NW France, Scand, Spain, Portugal, Belgium, Holland, S Italy, Greece).

# Spanish heath

## *Coenonympha iphioides*

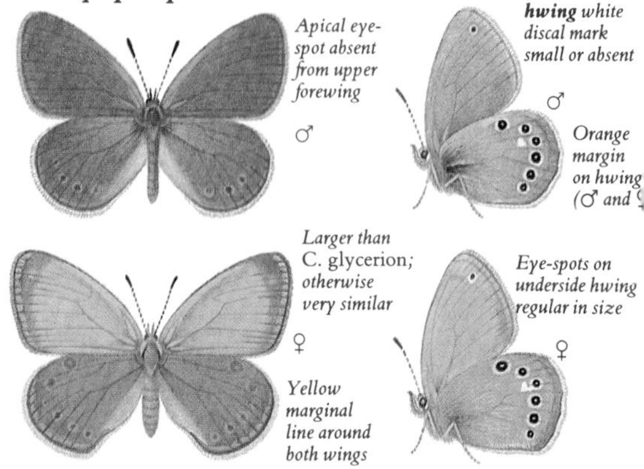

Apical eye-spot absent from upper forewing
♂
Underside hwing white discal mark small or absent
♂
Orange margin on hwing (♂ and ♀
Larger than C. glycerion; otherwise very similar
♀
Yellow marginal line around both wings
Eye-spots on underside hwing regular in size
♀


Sometimes listed as a subspecies of the Chestnut heath (p 125), a smaller butterfly with less conspicuous markings. The Spanish heath flies over grassy slopes up to 1,700 m. *WS:* 34–40 mm; *Flight:* June–July; *Gen:* 1; *FP:* unknown; *D:* N and C Spain.

# Speckled wood

## *Pararge aegeria*

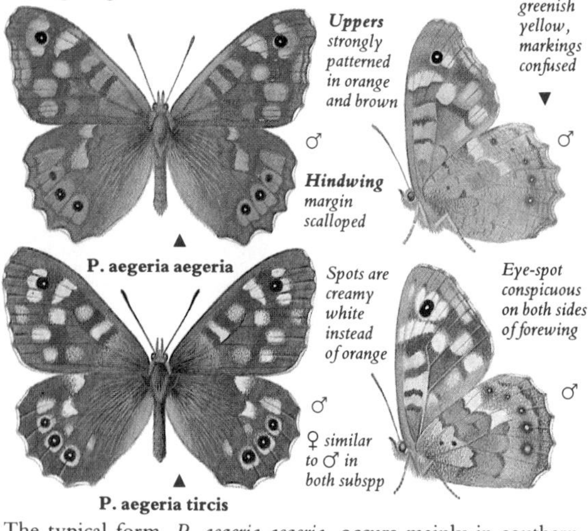

Uppers strongly patterned in orange and brown
♂
Hindwing margin scalloped
Hwing greenish yellow, markings confused
♂
P. aegeria aegeria
Spots are creamy white instead of orange
♂
♀ similar to ♂ in both subspp
Eye-spot conspicuous on both sides of forewing
♂
P. aegeria tircis


The typical form, *P. aegeria aegeria*, occurs mainly in southern Europe; further north, including Britain, it is replaced by *P. aegeria tircis*. The butterfly has a slow, fluttering flight and is commonly found in shady areas with dappled sunlight, such as woodland edges and pine forest clearings, where its spotted pattern blends in well with the surroundings. *WS:* 38–44 mm; *Flight:* Mar–Oct; *Gen:* 2 or more (1 in Scand); *FP:* grasses, esp Couch grass (*Agropyron*); *D:* Europe (not N Scand, N Scot).

# Large wall brown

## *Lasiommata maera*

♂ **Uppers** *(left) dull brown; eye-spot on fwing may have 2 white centres*

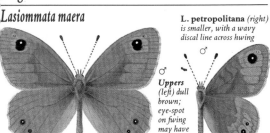

**L. petropolitana** *(right) is smaller, with a wavy discal line across hwing*

♂

Often common in forest clearings. *WS:* 44–56 mm; *Flight:* May–Sept; *Gen:* 2; *FP:* grasses, *D:* Europe (not Britain, N Scand).
***L. petropolitana*** (Northern wall brown). *WS:* 38–42 mm; *Flight:* May–Sept; *Gen:* 1–2; *FP:* grasses, esp *Festuca*; *D:* Alps, Pyrenees, Scand, Bulgaria, SE Yugoslavia, Greece.

# Wall brown

## *L. megera*

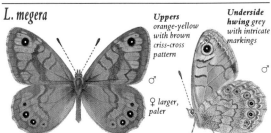

***Uppers*** *orange-yellow with brown criss-cross pattern*

♂

♀ *larger, paler*

***Underside hwing*** *grey with intricate markings*

♂

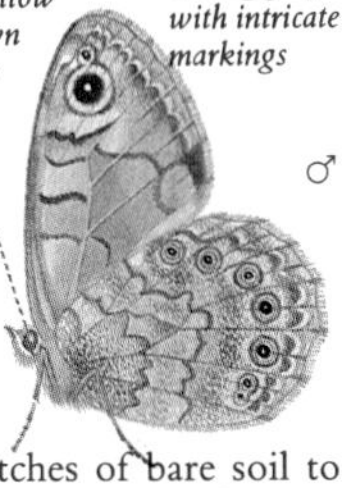

Fluttery in flight, frequently settling on patches of bare soil to bask in the sun. A widespread species, found on rough open ground and along hedgerows. *WS:* 36–50 mm; *Flight:* Mar–Sept; *Gen:* 2–3; *FP:* grasses, esp *Poa*; *D:* Europe (not N Scand, N Scot).

# Woodland brown

## *Lopinga achine*

*Ground colour greyish brown, paler on underside*

*Row of large yellow-ringed black spots on both wings*

♂

♀ *similar, often paler with slightly bigger spots*

Widely scattered colonies occur in open woodland up to 1,000 m. *WS:* 50–56 mm; *Flight:* June–July; *Gen:* 1; *FP:* grasses; *D:* France, Germany, Baltic states, S Sweden, N Italy, Yugoslavia.

# Lattice brown

## *Kirinia roxelana*

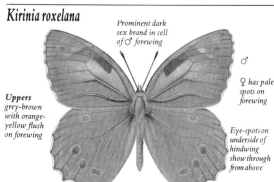

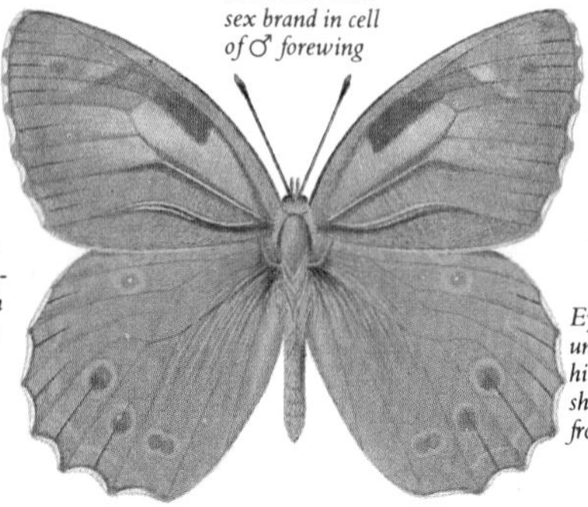
*Prominent dark sex brand in cell of ♂ forewing*
♂
*♀ has pale spots on forewing*
***Uppers** grey-brown with orange-yellow flush on forewing*
*Eye-spots on underside of hindwing show through from above*

The Lattice brown is found amongst bushes, preferring not to fly unless disturbed. *WS:* 58–62 mm; *Flight:* May–July; *Gen:* 1; *FP:* unknown; *D:* Hungary, Romania, Yugoslavia, Bulgaria, Greece. ***K. climene*** (Lesser lattice brown), a very rare species in Europe, is smaller and usually has more orange on the forewings. *WS:* 46–48 mm; *Flight:* June–July; *Gen:* 1; *FP:* unknown; *D:* SE Europe.

# **Metalmarks** Riodinidae (Nemeobiidae)

Most of the Riodinidae occur in South America and include some very colourful species. Closely related to the Blues (Lycaenidae), they are distinguished by the reduced forelegs of the male (but not female), which are useless for walking. In Europe this family is represented by one species, the Duke of Burgundy fritillary.

***Caterpillar of the Duke of Burgundy fritillary***

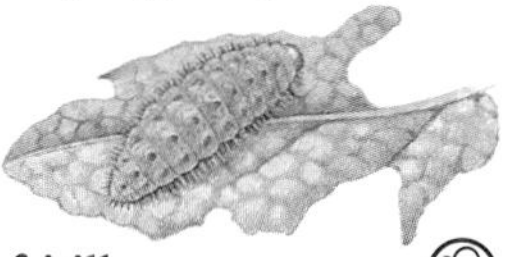
*Eggs laid on underside of cowslip leaves. Caterpillar eats most of eggshell on hatching, then continues to feed on leaf underside*
*Pale fawn woodlouse-shaped body, spotted and covered in short hairs*

# Duke of Burgundy fritillary

## *Hamearis lucina*

***Uppers** dark brown with transverse rows of orange spots; in 2nd generation these spots are smaller*
♂

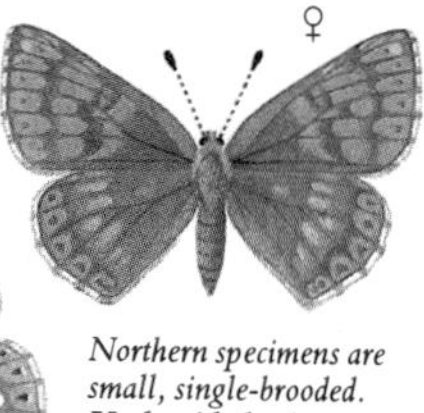
♀
*Wings of ♀ not so pointed as in ♂ and orange markings wider*

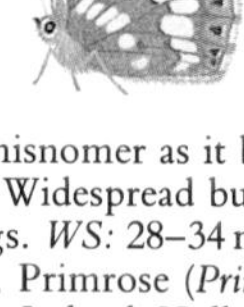
♀
*Northern specimens are small, single-brooded.* ***Underside hwing*** *has 2 rows of white spots*

The butterfly's name is a misnomer as it bears only a superficial resemblance to a fritillary. Widespread but rarely common, it is found in woodland clearings. *WS:* 28–34 mm; *Flight:* May–June, Aug; *Gen:* 2; *FP:* Cowslip, Primrose (*Primula*); *D:* Europe, incl S Sweden (not rest of Scand, Ireland, Holland, S Spain).

# Blues, Hairstreaks and Coppers Lycaenidae

This is a large family of worldwide distribution, with about 100 species in Europe and many more in the rainforests of Asia and Africa. They are normally small, metallic-coloured butterflies with marked differences between the sexes; the males are often blue or coppery, while the females are usually brown. However, both sexes have similar markings on the underside, and it is from these delicate patterns (especially on the hindwings) that the species are identified. Of the three groups into which the Lycaenidae are divided, the Blues are by far the most numerous and may be seen in abundance on chalk downs in the summer (although they are not as common as in previous years). The Hairstreaks are usually recognized by the fine hairline markings on the underside, while the Coppers are unmistakable in their brilliant coloration. Most are quick in flight and tend to settle when the sun goes in.

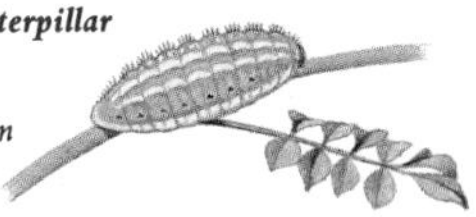
***Chalkhill blue caterpillar***
*Ants attracted to sweet secretion from honey gland*
*Feeds on vetches. Yellow stripes and black dots on green, rather slug-like body*

## Brown hairstreak

## *Thecla betulae*

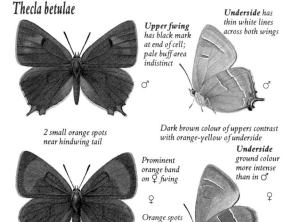

***Upper fwing*** *has black mark at end of cell; pale buff area indistinct*
♂
***Underside*** *has thin white lines across both wings*
♂

*2 small orange spots near hindwing tail*

*Dark brown colour of uppers contrast with orange-yellow of underside*

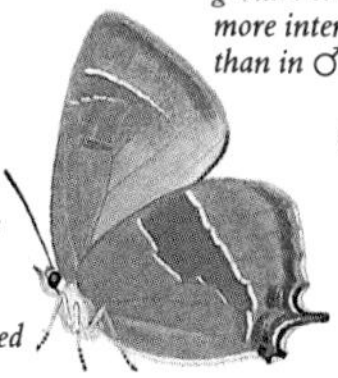
*Prominent orange band on ♀ fwing*
♀
*Orange spots near tail of upper hwing well developed*
***Underside*** *ground colour more intense than in ♂*
♀

This butterfly tends to fly in short, sharp bursts, fairly high up, and only when the sun is shining. It is mainly a woodland species, but may also fly near hedgerows and in open spaces. Its occurrence very much depends on the proximity of the food-plant, upon which the eggs are laid singly in the autumn, and remain without hatching until spring. In southern England and Wales the species is widely distributed but rather local, and is unlikely to be seen unless one purposely searches in a probable area. *WS:* 34–36 mm; *Flight:* Aug–Sept; *Gen:* 1; *FP:* Sloe (*Prunus spinosa*) and others; *D:* Europe (not Scotland, N Ireland, N Scandinavia, S Spain, S Portugal, S Italy, Mediterranean islands).

## Spanish purple hairstreak

### *Laeosopis roboris*

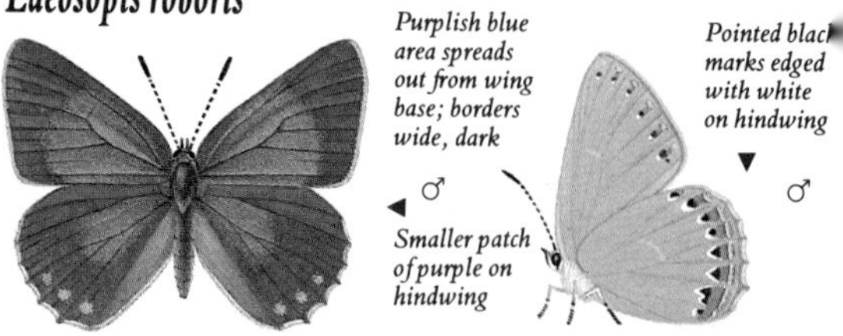
Purplish blue area spreads out from wing base; borders wide, dark
♂
Smaller patch of purple on hindwing
Pointed blac
marks edged with white on hindwing
♂

The wings of the female are more rounded and the amount of purple is restricted to the base of the forewing. Locally common where ash trees occur, up to 1,500 m. In parts of Spain it may reach pest proportions. *WS:* 24–30 mm; *Flight:* May–Aug; *Gen:* 1–2; *FP:* Ash (*Fraxinus excelsior*); *D:* SE France, Spain, Portugal.

## Purple hairstreak

### *Quercusia quercus*

**Uppers** deep purple or violet-blue, with dark borders
♂
Prominent white line on greyish background
♂
♀ is dark brown, with shiny violet area on fwing, less extensive than in ♂
♀
Orange-yellow spots near corner of hindwing
♀

The iridescent purple varies according to the way the light falls on the wings. An oakwood species, flying mainly in the tree tops; in some years it is very common. The caterpillar resembles the leaf buds on which it feeds. *WS:* 24–28 mm; *Flight:* July–Sept; *FP:* Oak (*Quercus*); *D:* Europe (local Ireland; not N Scand, N Scot).

## Sloe hairstreak ·

### *Nordmannia acaciae*

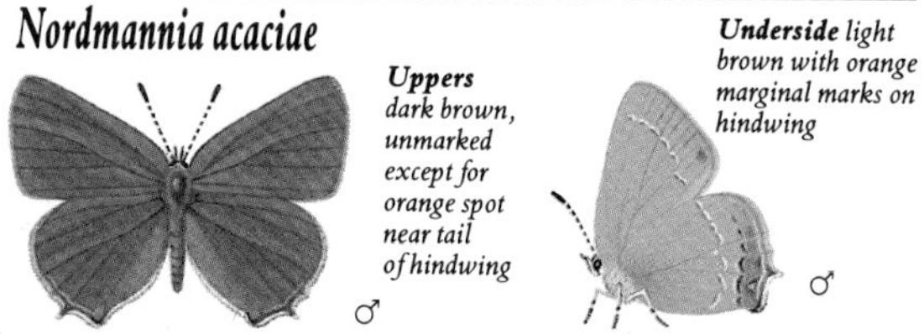
**Uppers** dark brown, unmarked except for orange spot near tail of hindwing
♂
**Underside** light brown with orange marginal marks on hindwing
♂

Found on rough ground near sloe bushes, up to 1,500 m. *WS:* 28–32 mm; *Flight:* June–July; *Gen:* 1; *FP:* Sloe (*Prunus spinosa*); *D:* Spain, France, Switz, S Germany, Italy, Balkans, Greece.

# Ilex hairstreak

## *N. ilicis*

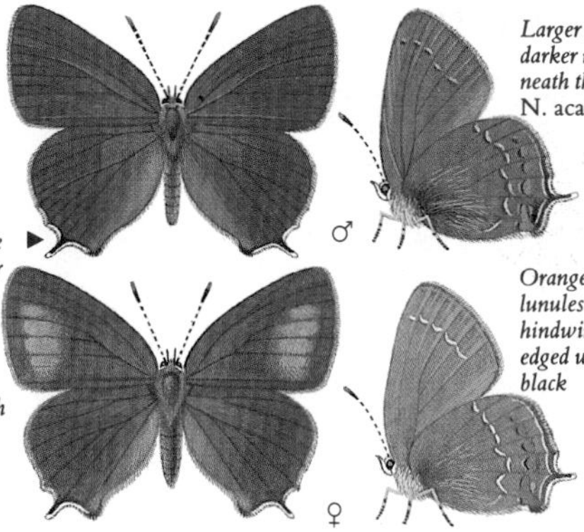
Ground colour dark brown
Small orange spot in corner of hindwing
Orange patch on ♀ fwing variable in size, sometimes absent
Larger and darker underneath than N. acaciae
Orange-red lunules on hindwing are edged with black
♂
♂
♀
♀

An active but inconspicuous butterfly, locally common on hills with small oaks. *WS:* 32–36 mm; *Flight:* June–July; *Gen:* 1; *FP:* Oak (*Quercus*); *D:* Europe (not Britain, N Scand; rare in S Spain).

# False ilex hairstreak

## *N. esculi*

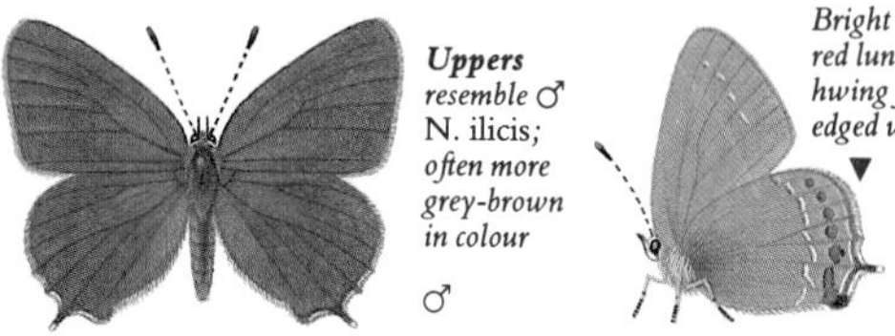
**Uppers** resemble ♂ N. ilicis; often more grey-brown in colour
Bright orange-red lunules on hwing faintly edged with black
♂
♂

The female may have an orange tinge on the upper forewing, but not as distinctive as the orange patch on the Ilex hairstreak. Found on rough hillsides with bushes. *WS:* 30–34 mm; *Flight:* June–July; *Gen:* 1; *FP:* Oak (*Quercus*); *D:* Spain, Portugal, S France.

# Provence hairstreak

## *Tomares ballus*

♂ *Light grey-brown pointed wings*  ♀ *Large areas of orange-yellow on ♀ uppers*  ♀ *Green hwing (both sexes)*

Found on rough, stony ground. *WS:* 28–30 mm; *Flight:* Jan–Apr; *Gen:* 1; *FP:* Trefoil (*Lotus*); *D:* Spain, Portugal, S France.
***T. nogelli*** (Nogel's hairstreak) is darker with grey and orange bands, edged with black dots, on the underside hindwing. *WS:* 30–32 mm; *Flight:* May–June; *FP:* Vetch (*Astragalus*); *D:* Romania.

# Blue-spot hairstreak

## *Strymonidia spini*

**Uppers** dark brown, like Ilex hairstreak; distinguished by oval patch of scales near cell of fwing (♂ sex brand)
♂
**Underside** paler than topside, with prominent thin white wavy line
♂
Orange-yellow tinge may spread over both wings
♀
Note blue spot and orange lunules near tail of hwing
♀

*f.* **vandalusica,** *a ♀ form found in Spain (uppers and unders)*

The typical female, apart from being slightly larger and more distinctly marked, is much more like the male in coloration than the form *vandalusica*. The species derives its name from the characteristic blue spot visible only on the underside of the hindwing. It is widespread in hilly, uncultivated scrubland up to 1,800 m, becoming rarer in the northern part of its range. *WS:* 28–32 mm; *Flight:* June–July; *Gen:* 1; *FP:* Buckthorn (*Rhamnus*), Sloe (*Prunus*); *D:* Europe (not Britain, Scand, Holland, Belgium).

# Black hairstreak

## *S. pruni*

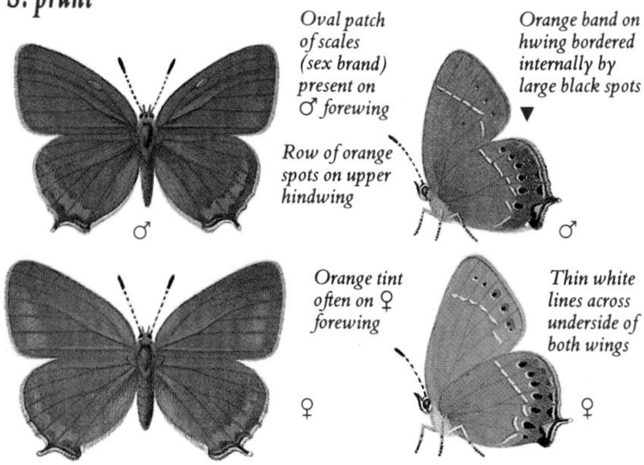
Oval patch of scales (sex brand) present on ♂ forewing
Row of orange spots on upper hindwing
♂
Orange band on hwing bordered internally by large black spots
♂
Orange tint often on ♀ forewing
♀
Thin white lines across underside of both wings
♀

The black spots which border the orange band on the underside hindwing are a characteristic feature of this butterfly. It is usually found near hedgerows and in open woodland, especially where old sloe bushes have been allowed to grow unchecked. In Britain the species is declining and is known to occur only in a few localities in the Midlands. It is more widespread (but rarely common) in central Europe. *WS:* 30–32 mm; *Flight:* June–July; *Gen:* 1; *FP:* Sloe (*Prunus*); *D:* C and E Europe, incl N Spain (not Portugal, Ireland, Norway, peninsular Italy, Holland, Belgium).

## White-letter hairstreak

### *S. w-album*

Sexes are separated by oval sex brand on ♂ forewing
♂
Ground colour dark brown; ♀ slightly paler
**Underside** thin white line forms distinct W-shape on hindwing
♂

May be confused with the Black hairstreak (p 132), but it is paler on the underside and lacks orange spots on the upper hindwing. Often near elms, feeding at bramble flowers in hedgerows. A widespread species; in Britain it is locally common in the south (incl Wales). *WS:* 30–32 mm; *Flight:* June–Aug; *FP:* Elm (*Ulmus*), Lime (*Tilia*); *D:* Europe (not Ireland, N Scand, Portugal, S Spain).

## Green hairstreak

### *Callophrys rubi*

Both wings green underneath, with incomplete row of white spots
Oval patch of scales on ♂ fwing
♂
♂
No tail on hindwing
♀ is paler brown than ♂, otherwise similar
♀
Eyes edged with white; front of head green (both sexes)
♀

The only other similar European species is *C. avis* (below). It has a short rapid flight and is well camouflaged when at rest on green leaves. Occurs in a wide range of habitats, from woodlands to moorland bogs, and has many suitable foodplants. *WS:* 26–30 mm; *Flight:* Mar–June; *Gen:* 1; *FP:* Leguminosae; *D:* Europe.

## Chapman's green hairstreak

### *C. avis*

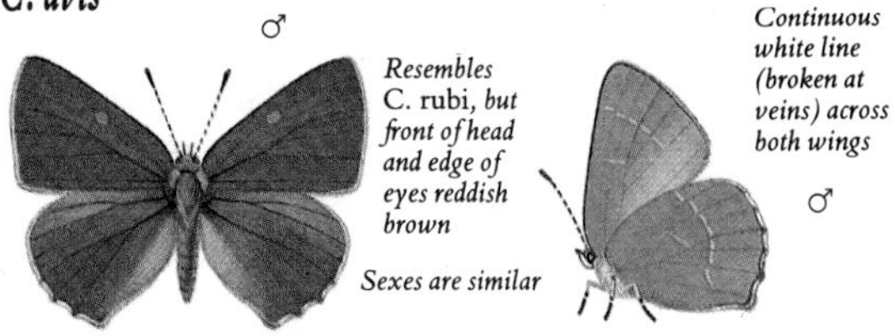
♂
Resembles C. rubi, but front of head and edge of eyes reddish brown
Sexes are similar
Continuous white line (broken at veins) across both wings
♂

Principally a North African species, its topside tends to be more red-brown than *C. rubi*. *WS:* 32–34 mm; *Flight:* Apr–May; *FP:* Strawberry tree (*Arbutus unedo*); *D:* S France, Spain, Portugal.

# Violet copper

## *Lycaena helle*

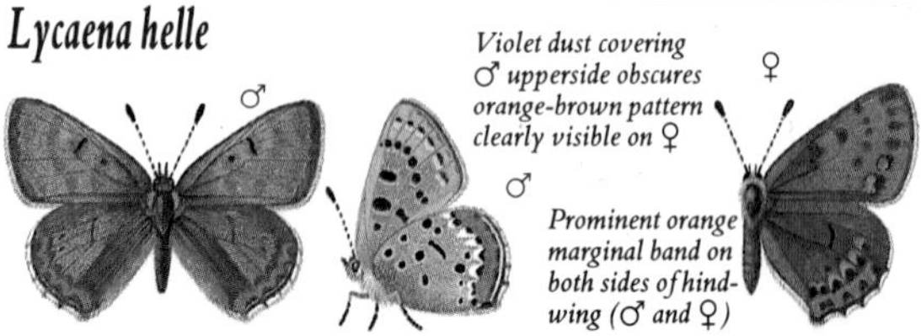
♂
Violet dust covering ♂ upperside obscures orange-brown pattern clearly visible on ♀
♀
♂
Prominent orange marginal band on both sides of hindwing (♂ and ♀)

The male is very distinctive but the female lacks the violet colour. Colonies tend to be local and isolated, in areas of wet meadowland, often near forests. *WS:* 24–28 mm; *Flight:* May–Oct; *Gen:* 1–2; *FP:* Knotgrass (*Polygonum*); *D:* Scand (not Denmark, S Sweden), Germany, France, Switz, Belgium, Poland, Czech.

# Small copper

## *L. phlaeas*

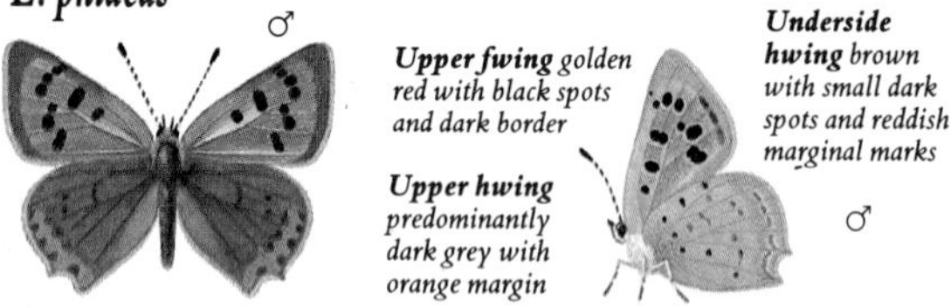
♂
**Upper fwing** golden red with black spots and dark border
**Upper hwing** predominantly dark grey with orange margin
**Underside hwing** brown with small dark spots and reddish marginal marks
♂

The female is similar but has more rounded wings. Widespread throughout Europe (except the north of Scotland), this bright little butterfly is often seen in flowery meadows. *WS:* 24–30 mm; *Flight:* Mar–Oct; *Gen:* 3; *FP:* Dock, Sorrel (*Rumex*); *D:* Europe.

# Large copper

## *L. dispar*

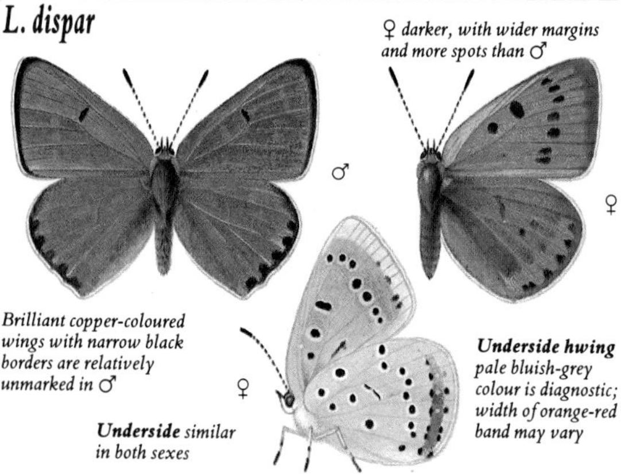
♀ darker, with wider margins and more spots than ♂
♂
♀
Brilliant copper-coloured wings with narrow black borders are relatively unmarked in ♂
♀
**Underside** similar in both sexes
**Underside hwing** pale bluish-grey colour is diagnostic; width of orange-red band may vary

Swamp drainage has been responsible for the decline of this species. The English subspecies became extinct over a century ago, and has since been replaced by the Dutch subspecies *batavus*, which was introduced into East Anglia around 1927. *WS:* 34–40 mm; *Flight:* May–June; *Gen:* 1; *FP:* Water dock (*Rumex*); *D:* England, France, Italy, Holland, Germany, Baltic states, Balkans.

# Scarce copper

## *Heodes virgaureae*

♂

*♂ has coppery wings without black spots; ♀ heavily marked, lacks lustre of ♂*

♀

▲ *Wing fringes yellowish grey*

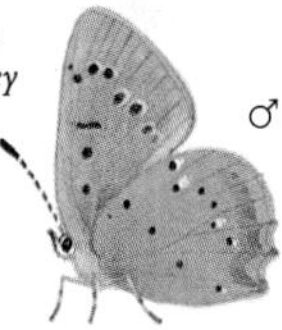

♂

***Underside** similar in both sexes*

***Underside hwing** yellow-brown with small black spots; white markings in postdiscal area are characteristic*

♀

**H. virgaureae miegii**, *a Spanish subspecies, has wider black borders than typical form*

♂

*♀ of this subsp has markings like the ♀ above, but without as much dark suffusion*

*Small black spots present on upperside*

Chiefly a central European species with colonies extending westward, the Scarce copper exhibits considerable variation over its range. It has a fast, steady flight and is locally common in flowery meadows up to 1,500 m. *WS:* 30–36 mm; *Flight:* July–Aug; *Gen:* 1; *FP:* Dock (*Rumex*); *D:* N and C Europe, incl isolated colonies in Spain and Portugal (not Britain, Holland, Belgium, N Scand).

# Sooty copper

## *H. tityrus*

***Uppers** dark grey-brown with indistinct orange marks near margin*

♂

♂

***Underside** greenish grey with small black spots and orange marginal band*

***Fwing** orange, with black spots*

***Hwing** round black marginal spots barely touch edge*

♀

♀

*Orange flush sometimes visible on fwing (♂ and ♀)*

Unlike other coppers, the male Sooty copper is not a beautiful burnished colour but more of a sooty brown. Several subspecies have been described, some of which are more orange-red on the topside. Usually in flowery meadows or in drier areas near forests, up to 2,000 m. *WS:* 28–32 mm; *Flight:* Apr–Sept; *Gen:* 2; *FP:* Dock (*Rumex*); *D:* Europe, incl S Denmark (not Britain, Scand, S Spain).

# Purple-shot copper

## *Heodes alciphron*

*Wings of ♀ broad, dark brown, with darker spots*

♂

♀

***Uppers** copper colour obscured by purple scales; spots indistinct*

*Pattern of spots well defined on underside*

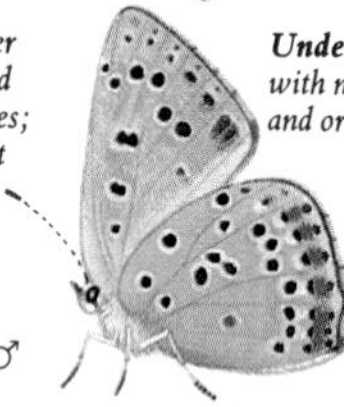

♂

***Underside** (♂ and ♀) grey with numerous black spots and orange band on hwing*

***Underside forewing** flushed with orange in ♀*

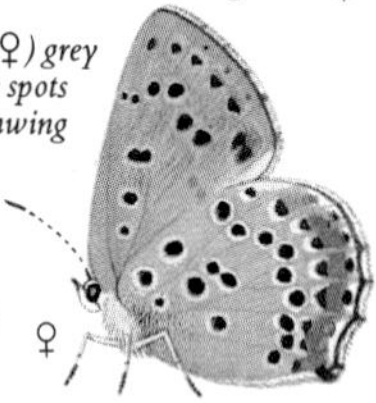

♀

**♂ H. alciphron gordius**

**♀ H. alciphron gordius**

A widespread species found in warm flowery meadows from lowlands up to 1,800 m. The row of postdiscal spots on the upper forewing of the female is uneven and this serves as a distinction from the Purple-edged copper (p 138). The amount of purple on the wings varies, as shown in subsp *gordius*, which occurs in the mountains of southern Europe. Here both sexes have more copper colour showing through on the topside and the markings are larger. *WS:* 32–36 mm; *Flight:* June–July; *Gen:* 1; *FP:* Dock (*Rumex*); *D:* Europe (not Britain, Scand, Holland, Belgium).

# Grecian copper

## *H. ottomanus*

***Uppers** gleaming golden red with wide black borders*

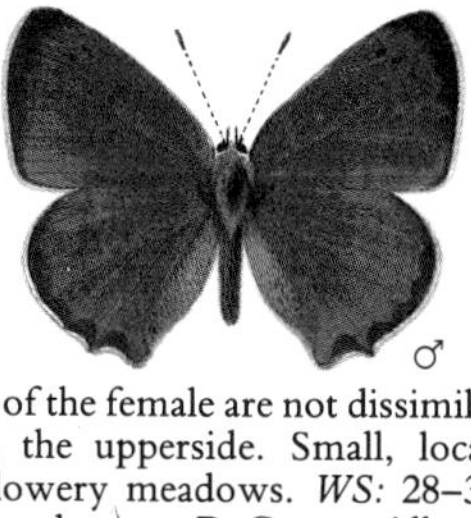

♂

*Like* H. virgaureae, *but no white spots on underside hwing; red lunules distinct*

♂

The wings of the female are not dissimilar from the Scarce copper (p 135) on the upperside. Small, local colonies are generally found in flowery meadows. *WS:* 28–30 mm; *Flight:* Mar–July; *Gen:* 2; *FP:* unknown; *D:* Greece, Albania, Yugoslavia.

# Lesser fiery copper

## *Thersamonia thersamon*

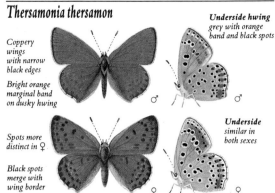

Coppery wings with narrow black edges
Bright orange marginal band on dusky hwing
♂
Underside hwing grey with orange band and black spots
♂
Spots more distinct in ♀
Black spots merge with wing border
♀
Underside similar in both sexes
♀


Specimens of the second generation often have a slight tail on the hindwing. The duskiness on the upperside tends to vary; some dark females may be confused with the Sooty copper (p 135) but are distinguished by the marginal spots on the upper hindwing which fuse with the dark border. It is more common in eastern Europe, in areas of uncultivated ground up to 1,200 m. *WS:* 28–32 mm; *Flight:* Apr–Aug; *Gen:* 2; *FP:* Dock (*Rumex*); Broom (*Sarothamnus*); *D:* Italy, Austria, Czech, Hungary, Romania, Greece, Balkans.

# Long-tailed blue

## *Lampides boeticus*

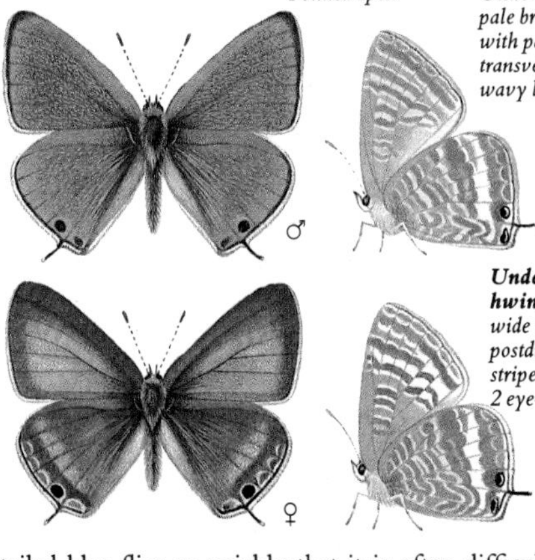

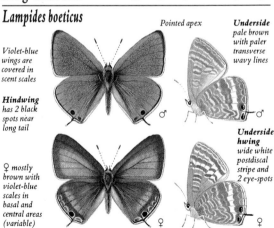

Pointed apex
Violet-blue wings are covered in scent scales
Hindwing has 2 black spots near long tail
♂
Underside pale brown with paler transverse wavy lines
♂
♀ mostly brown with violet-blue scales in basal and central areas (variable)
♀
Underside hwing wide white postdiscal stripe and 2 eye-spots
♀


The Long-tailed blue flies so quickly that it is often difficult to see. It is strongly migratory and occasionally reaches Britain from its breeding grounds in the south. Its distribution is practically worldwide, and in certain parts it is a serious crop pest, as the caterpillar actually lives inside the pods of Leguminosae. Occurs in many habitats, usually with rich vegetation, up to 2,000 m. *WS:* 30–36 mm; *Flight:* May–Sept; *Gen:* 2–3; *FP:* Leguminosae, esp *Colutea, Crotalaria*; *D:* S Europe (migrates north).

## Purple-edged copper

### *Palaeochrysophanus hippothoe*

▲

**Uppers (♂)** *dark orange-red with black borders, shot with purple, esp around fwing costa and on hwing*

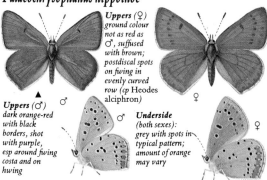

**Uppers (♀)** *ground colour not as red as ♂, suffused with brown; postdiscal spots on fwing in evenly curved row (cp* Heodes alciphron*)*

♀

♂

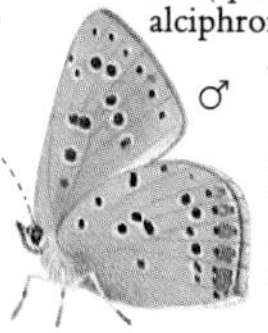

♂

**Underside** *(both sexes): grey with spots in typical pattern; amount of orange may vary*

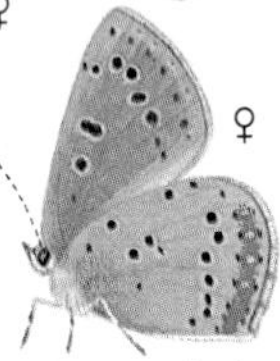

♀

The flame-red wings with gleaming purple margins are distinctive in the typical male. A variable species; the subsp *eurydame*, which occurs south of the Rhône, lacks a violet tinge and is more golden in the male, while the female is mostly brown. Widespread but local and becoming rarer, it flies in wet meadows up to 2,000 m. *WS:* 32–38 mm; *Flight:* June–July; *Gen:* 1; *FP:* Dock (*Rumex*); *D:* Europe (not Britain, S Spain, NW France, Holland).

## Fiery copper

### *Thersamonia thetis*

*Intense fiery red colour on wings; black border widest at fwing apex*

♂

**Underside hwing** *greyish with obscure yellow marginal band*

♂

The female is not so intensely coloured and has typical spot markings above. Both sexes have a thin tail on the hindwing. A rare mountain species, attracted to thyme. *WS:* 30–32 mm; *Flight:* July; *Gen:* 1; *FP:* unknown; *D:* Greece, Yugoslavia (?).

## Lang's short-tailed blue

### *Syntarucus pirithous*

♂

♂

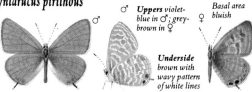

**Uppers** *violet-blue in ♂; grey-brown in ♀*

**Underside** *brown with wavy pattern of white lines*

♀

*Basal area bluish*

The variable underside pattern lacks the broad white stripe seen on the Long-tailed blue (p 137). Locally common in rough pastures near the sea. *WS:* 24–26 mm; *Flight:* Mar–Sept; *Gen:* 2–3; *FP:* Leguminosae; *D:* S Europe (all Mediterranean countries).

# Common tiger blue

## *Tarucus theophrastus*

♂

***Uppers** purplish blue with black mark in cell of forewing*

***Underside** white with black lines and spots; row of discrete postdiscal spots across both wings*

♂

♀

***Uppers** brown with white spots; pattern on underside shows through*

***Underside** markings as in ♂*

♀

The Common tiger blue occurs only locally in Europe, being more widespread in North Africa. It flies in hot, dry localities at low altitudes, often near the coast, in the vicinity of its foodplant. *WS:* 20–22 mm; *Flight:* Apr–Sept; *Gen:* 3 or more; *FP:* Jujube bush (*Ziziphus vulgaris*); *D:* S Spain.

# Little tiger blue

## *T. balkanicus*

***Uppers** purplish blue with several dark spots on forewing*

♂

***Underside** white with black spots as in* T. theophrastus*, but postdiscal spots form continuous line*

♂

***Uppers** brown with dusting of blue scales in basal area; no white spots on forewing*

♀

*Sexes are similar underneath*

♀

The distribution of this species is not well known as it has been mistaken for the Common tiger blue (above). It is distinguished by its smaller size and upperside markings. Prefers hot, dry lowlands. *WS:* 18–22 mm; *Flight:* Apr–Sept; *Gen:* 2–3; *FP:* Christ's thorn (*Paliurus spina-christi*); *D:* Greece, Yugoslavia, Bulgaria, Albania.

# African grass blue

## *Zizeeria knysna*

*Violet-blue wings with wide brown borders; ♀ brown*

♂

***Underside** grey-brown with small dark spots; ♀ similar*

♂

Two very similar subspecies of the African grass blue occur in Europe: one in Sicily and Crete, the other in isolated colonies in the Iberian peninsula. They live in damp, marshy meadows, often near streams, at low altitudes. The species is widely distributed in Africa, Asia and Australia. *WS:* 20–24 mm; *Flight:* Apr–Aug; *Gen:* 2; *FP:* Medick (*Medicago*); *D:* Spain, Portugal, Sicily, Crete.

## Short-tailed blue

### *Everes argiades*

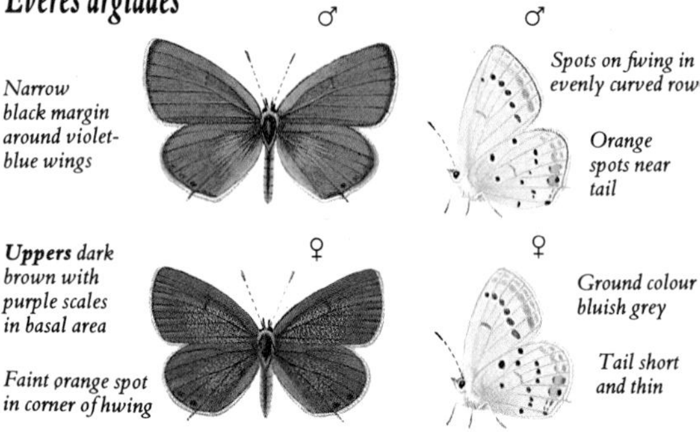
♂
♂
Narrow black margin around violet-blue wings
Spots on fwing in evenly curved row
Orange spots near tail
♀
♀
Uppers dark brown with purple scales in basal area
Faint orange spot in corner of hwing
Ground colour bluish grey
Tail short and thin

This rare migrant to Britain was once known as the "Bloxworth blue" because it was first recorded from near Bloxworth in Dorset. In southern Europe it is locally common in damp meadows up to 1,000 m. The second generation male is darker blue. *WS:* 20–30 mm; *Flight:* Apr–Sept; *Gen:* 2 or more; *FP:* Medick (*Medicago*), Trefoil (*Lotus*); *D:* Europe (not S and C Spain, Norway, Sweden; migrant to Britain, N Germany, Holland, Denmark, Finland).

## Eastern short-tailed blue

### *E. decoloratus*

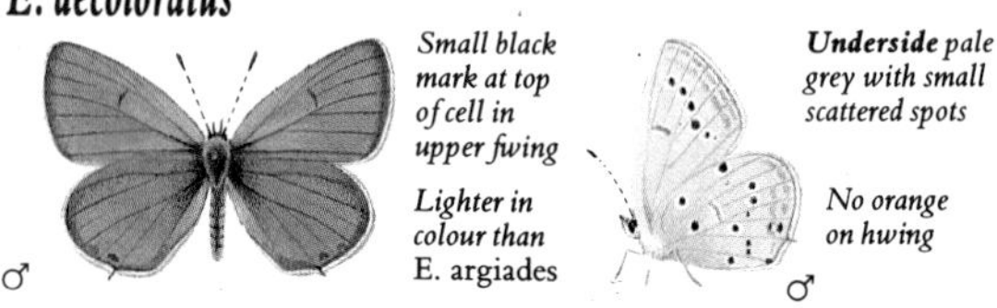
Small black mark at top of cell in upper fwing
Lighter in colour than E. argiades
Underside pale grey with small scattered spots
No orange on hwing
♂
♂

A brighter blue when it first emerges, the dark scales around the edges and along the veins becoming more noticeable with age. The topside of the female is dark brown. Flies over hill slopes up to 900 m. *WS:* 24–26 mm; *Flight:* Apr–Sept; *Gen:* 2; *FP:* Medick (*Medicago*); *D:* Austria, Romania, Bulgaria, N Greece, Albania.

## Provençal short-tailed blue

### *E. alcetas*

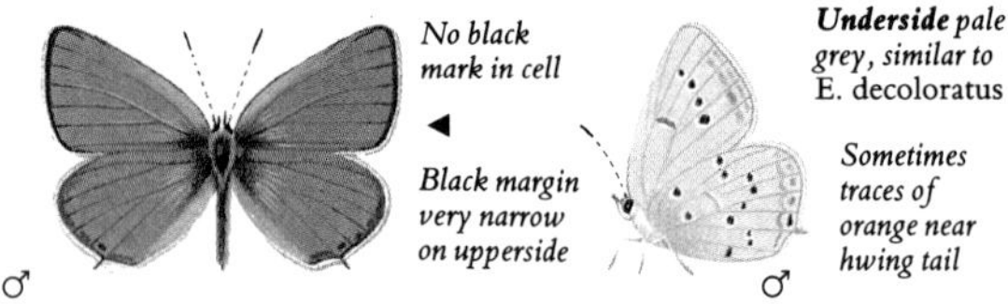
No black mark in cell
Black margin very narrow on upperside
Underside pale grey, similar to E. decoloratus
Sometimes traces of orange near hwing tail
♂
♂

Distinguished from the other short-tailed blues by the absence of orange on the underside hindwing (*E. argiades*) and the lack of any discal mark on the upper forewing (*E. decoloratus*). Occurs in isolated colonies on flowery slopes. *WS:* 26–32 mm; *Flight:* Apr–Sept; *Gen:* 2–3; *FP:* Crown vetch (*Coronilla varia*); *D:* N Spain, France, Italy, Corsica, Yugoslavia, Bulgaria, Balkans, N Greece.

# Little (or Small) blue

## *Cupido minimus*

♂
Uppers dark brown with dusting of silvery-blue scales in basal area

Underside pale grey-brown; row of spots on fwing nearly straight
♂

♀
♀ similar to ♂ but without blue scales
Note absence of tail on hwing (cp all Everes spp)

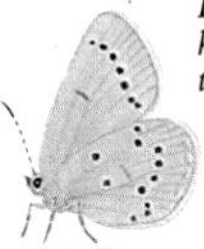
Both sexes may have a blue tinge near base
♀

A widespread grassland species, often found in limestone areas; in Britain it is very local (commoner in south). *WS:* 16–24 mm; *Flight:* Apr–Sept; *Gen:* 1–2; *FP:* Kidney vetch (*Anthyllis vulneraria*); *D:* Europe (not N Scand, S Spain).

***C. carswelli*** (Carswell's little blue) differs in having purplish scales at the wing base. *WS:* 22–24 mm; *Flight:* May; *D:* Spain.

# Osiris blue

## *C. osiris*

Uppers dark purplish blue, unmarked, with narrow black margin
♂

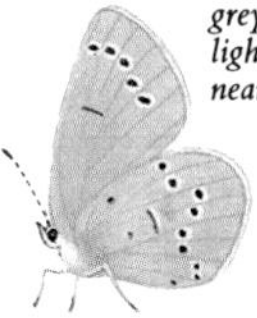
Underside pale grey-brown with light blue flush near wing base
♂

♀
♀ dark brown with slight dusting of blue scales in basal area (never in C. minimus)

Resembles C. minimus from the underside
♀

A local species, found on mountain slopes rich in flowers from 750–1,500 m. *WS:* 24–30 mm; *Flight:* May–Sept; *Gen:* 1–2; *FP:* Leguminosae, esp Sainfoin (*Onobrychis viciifolia*); *D:* N and C Spain, S France, Italy, Switzerland, SE Europe.

# Lorquin's blue

## *C. lorquinii*

♂
Ground colour violet blue
Brown borders not as wide as in Zizeeria knysna

♂

♀
No marginal marks on underside hwing

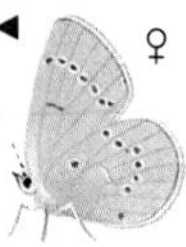
Few violet scales in basal area
♀

Flight is fluttery and often low over the ground. Very local up to 1,500 m; also occurs in North Africa. *WS:* 22–28 mm; *Flight:* May–June; *Gen:* 1; *FP:* unknown; *D:* S Spain, S Portugal.

# Holly blue

## *Celastrina argiolus*

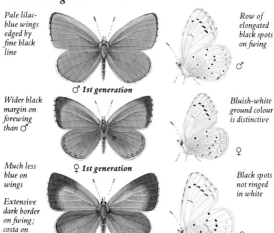

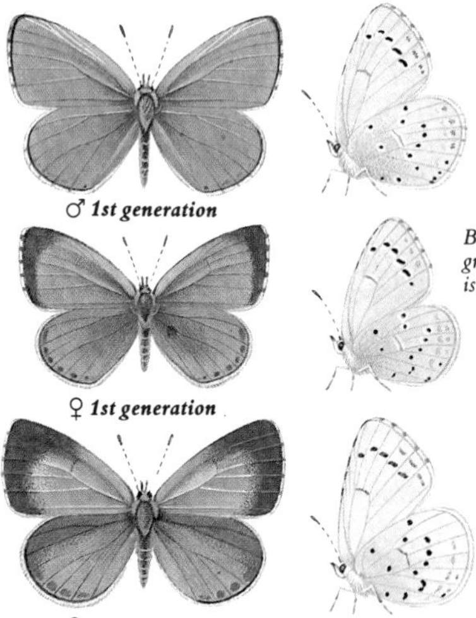
Pale lilac-blue wings edged by fine black line
Row of elongated black spots on fwing
♂
♂ 1st generation
Wider black margin on forewing than ♂
Bluish-white ground colour is distinctive
♀
♀ 1st generation
Much less blue on wings
Extensive dark border on fwing; costa on hwing dark
Black spots not ringed in white
♀
♀ 2nd generation

The Holly blue prefers wooded areas to grassland, and will visit gardens and clearings with trees and shrubs up to 1,500 m. The two generations have different foodplants: in spring the female lays her eggs on holly or dogwood, while in summer the eggs are laid on ivy. The species has increased in recent years in southern and central England, but is rare in Ireland, *WS:* 26–34 mm; *Flight:* Mar–Apr, July–Aug; *Gen:* 2; *FP:* Holly (*Ilex*), Dogwood (*Cornus*), Ivy (*Hedera*); *D:* Europe (not Scotland, NW Scand).

# Black-eyed blue

## *Glaucopsyche melanops*

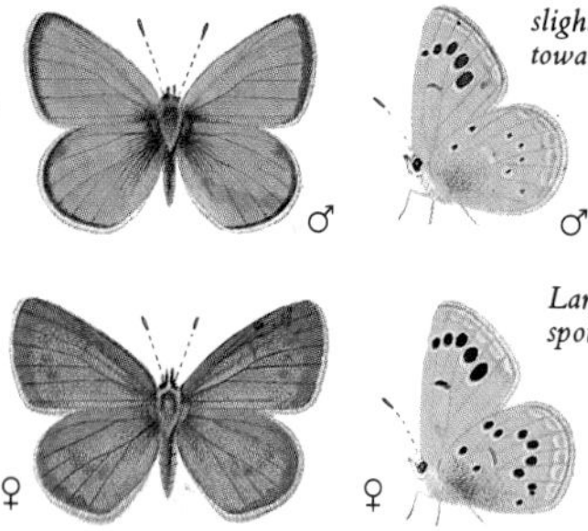
Uppers pale purplish blue with narrow brown margin
Underside brownish grey, slightly darker towards base
Uppers similar to, but smaller than, G. alexis
♂
Marginal markings faint
♂
Large oval black spots on forewing
Purplish-blue area much reduced; wings heavily suffused with dark scales
♀
♀
Spots on hindwing bigger in ♀

Distinguished from the Green-underside blue (p 143) by the detail on its underside. There are two subspecies in Europe: subsp *algirica* (not shown) also occurs in North Africa. Flies in heathy, open woods up to 900 m. *WS:* 22–32 mm; *Flight:* Mar–May; *Gen:* 1; *FP:* Leguminosae, esp Greenweed (*Genista*), Leopardsbane (*Doronicum*); *D:* Spain, S France, N Italy.

# Green-underside blue

## G. alexis

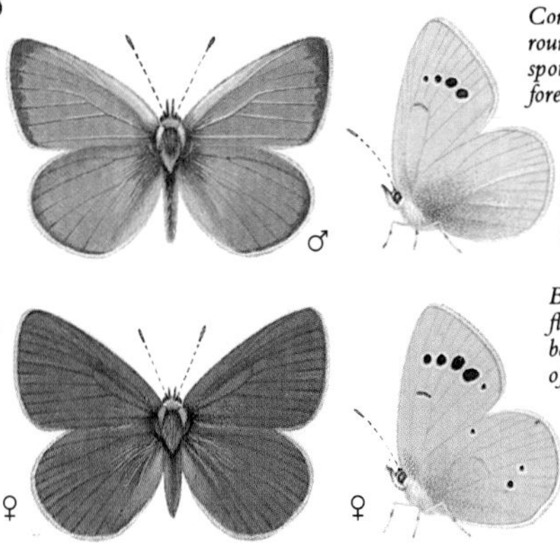
Unmarked, pale purplish-blue wings with brown borders
♂
Conspicuous round black spots on forewing
♂
Paler than G. melanops
Uppers dark brown with faint blue tinge near base (variable)
♀
♀
Blue-green flush in basal area of hwing
No marks near margin

A widespread species found in sunny open areas near trees up to 1,200 m. The spots on the underside vary, but the blue-green base and absence of any marginal marks are distinctive. *WS:* 26–36 mm; *Flight:* Apr–June; *Gen:* 1; *FP:* Leguminosae, incl Broom (*Cytisus*); *D:* Europe (not Britain, Portugal, SW Spain, N Scand).

# Odd-spot blue

## Turanana panagaea

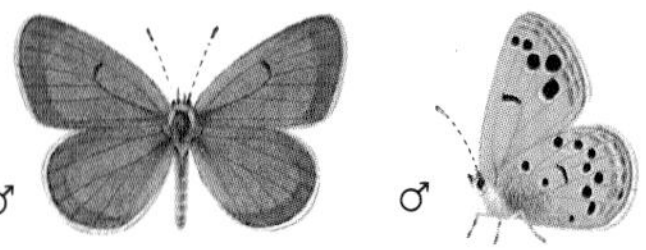
Black mark at top of cell in fwing; dark brown margins quite broad
♂
♂
Large spot on fwing out of sequence with other marginal spots (hence the name "odd spot")

Local in mountainous areas between 900 and 2,100 m. Little is known about this species. *WS:* 20–22 mm; *Flight:* May–July; *Gen:* 1; *FP:* unknown; *D:* Greece (Mt Chelmos, Taygetos mts).

# Scarce large blue

## Maculinea telejus

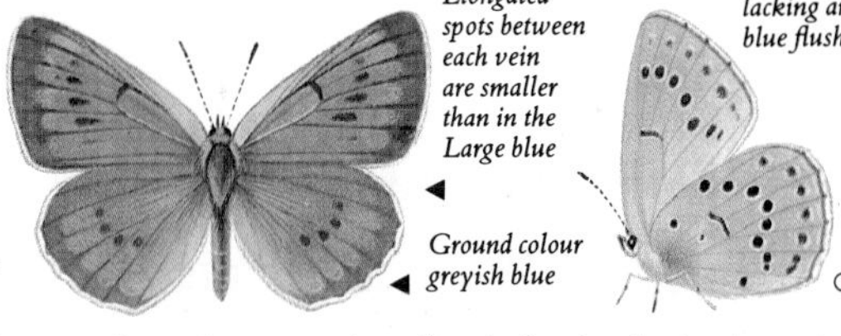
Elongated spots between each vein are smaller than in the Large blue
Ground colour greyish blue
♂
Pale brown, lacking any blue flush
♂

This rare butterfly occurs in a few isolated colonies in central Europe, generally in wet meadows up to 2,000 m. The female is similar but has wider dark margins and larger spots. The caterpillar lives with ants (see *M. arion*, p 144). *WS:* 32–36 mm; *Flight:* July; *Gen:* 1; *FP:* Great burnet (*Sanguisorba*); *D:* France, Holland, Switz, S Germany, N Italy, Austria, Hungary.

# Large blue

## *Maculinea arion*

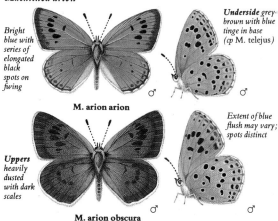

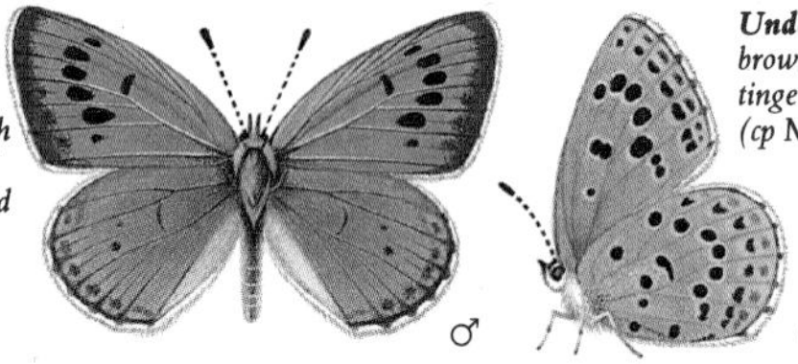
*Bright blue with series of elongated black spots on fwing*
***Underside** grey-brown with blue tinge in base (cp* M. telejus*)*
♂
♂

**M. arion arion**

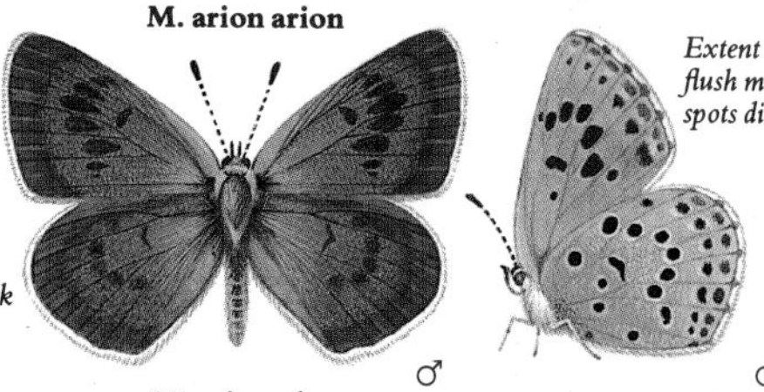
*Extent of blue flush may vary; spots distinct*
***Uppers** heavily dusted with dark scales*
♂
♂

**M. arion obscura**

The Large blue has been declared "probably extinct" in Britain after the failure of all the eggs in 1979 from the last-known colony in Devon. The butterfly has a most remarkable life cycle, and its dependence on a certain species of ant (*Myrmica*), combined with changing environmental conditions, have been largely responsible for its extinction. The eggs are laid on thyme, on which the caterpillars feed during their first few weeks of life. The caterpillars later wander off alone and are "discovered" by ants which are attracted by the sweet secretions of the caterpillar. The ants carry the caterpillar to their nest, where they proceed to "milk" it, and in turn the caterpillar becomes carnivorous, feeding on young ant larvae. Here the caterpillar hibernates until spring, when it pupates and emerges from the nest as an adult.

Various subspecies exist on the mainland of Europe, and these are found on heaths and grassland, often near the coast, from sea level up to 1,800 m. *WS:* 32–40 mm; *Flight:* June–July; *Gen:* 1; *FP:* Wild thyme (*Thymus serpyllum*); *D:* Europe (not Norway, S Spain, Portugal, all Mediterranean islands except Corsica).

# Dusky large blue

## *M. nausithous*

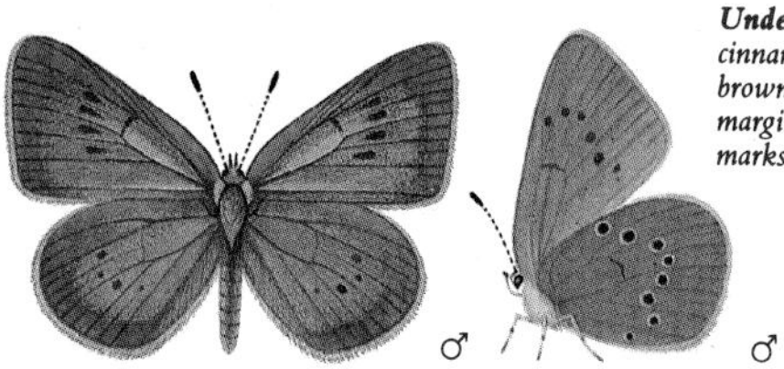
*Ground colour darker, more purplish than* M. telejus
***Underside** cinnamon brown; no marginal marks*
♂
♂

The female is dark brown with an occasional blue tinge in the base. Very local in swampy lowlands, often near lakes. The caterpillar is associated with ants (see *M. arion*). *WS:* 34–36 mm; *Flight:* July; *Gen:* 1; *FP:* Great burnet (*Sanguisorba*) ; *D:* N Spain, France, Switz, Austria, Germany, Hungary, Holland (?), N Italy (?)

# Alcon blue

## M. alcon

**Uppers** *pale lilac-blue, not marked, with thin dark brown border*

♂

*No blue-green dust on hwing*

♂

**Underside** *(both sexes) light brown with black spots ringed in white*

*Dark spots sometimes present on upper fwing*

♀

*♀ is predominantly dark brown, with violet-blue suffusion in basal area*

*The typical form (♂ and ♀ above) is commoner in Germany, NE France, Belgium and the Balkans*

♂

**M. alcon rebeli** (right)

***Uppers** more vivid. **Underside** may have blue-green tinge in base of hindwing*

*May be found in the Pyrenees, Massif Central and Apennines*

The typical form is found in wet lowland meadows, but subsp *rebeli* prefers dry, sandy areas up to 1,800 m. The caterpillar lives with ants. *WS:* 34–38 mm; *Flight:* June–July; *Gen:* 1; *FP:* Gentian (*Gentiana*); *D:* Europe (not Britain, Norway, Portugal).

# Baton blue

## Pseudophilotes baton

*Chequered fringes*

♂

**Uppers** *light blue with black discal mark on both wings*

♂

♀

*Amount of purple may vary*

♀

**Underside hwing** *has orange marginal lunules*

***Panoptes blue*, P. panoptes** *(upper and under)*

*More purplish in colour*

♂

*No orange lunules on underside hwing; black spots clear, well-formed*

♂

***P. baton.*** Widespread in central Europe, occurring in flowery meadows up to 2,200 m. Caterpillar is associated with ants. *WS:* 20–24 mm; *Flight:* Apr–Sept; *Gen:* 2; *FP:* Thyme (*Thymus*); *D:* Europe, incl S Finland (not Scand, Britain, S Spain, Holland).

***P. panoptes.*** Indistinguishable in the field. *WS:* 18–22 mm; *Flight:* Apr–May, July; *Gen:* 2; *FP:* Thyme; *D:* Spain, Portugal.

# False baton blue

## *Pseudophilotes abencerragus*

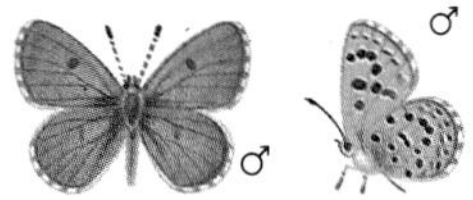
**Uppers** suffused with dark scales; basal area blue
Chequered fringes
♂
♂
**Underside** greyish brown with distinct black spots, ringed in white

Some specimens closely resemble the Panoptes blue (p 145), but they are usually a darker, more metallic blue. In rough, heather-clad areas at 700–1,200 m. *WS:* 18–22 mm; *Flight:* Apr–May; *Gen:* 1; *FP:* unknown; *D:* S and C Spain, Portugal.

# Bavius blue

## *P. bavius*

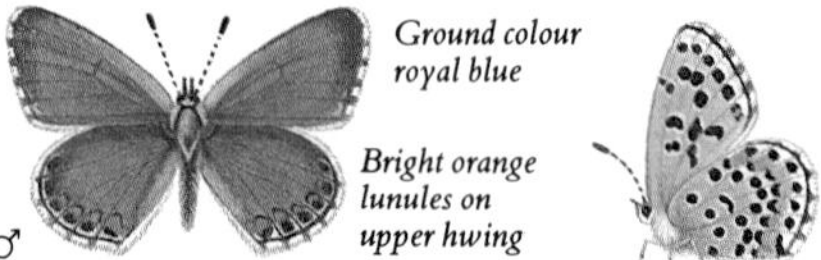
Ground colour royal blue
Bright orange lunules on upper hwing
♂
**Underside** grey with black spots; wide orange ban on hindwing
♂

The specimen illustrated is subsp *hungaricus*; other subspecies occur in N Africa. The female is mostly black above, with blue in the base. In rough pastures to 900 m. *WS:* 24–30 mm; *Flight:* May–Aug; *Gen:* 2; *FP: Salvia argentea; D:* Romania, Greece.

# Iolas blue

## *Iolana iolas*

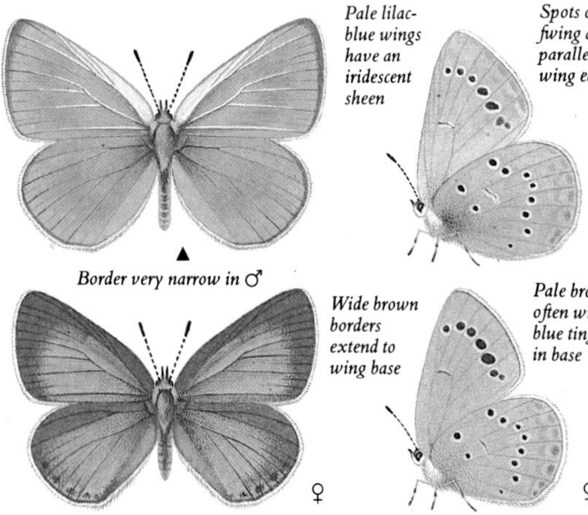
Pale lilac-blue wings have an iridescent sheen
Spots on fwing are parallel to wing edge
♂
Border very narrow in ♂
Wide brown borders extend to wing base
Pale brown often with blue tinge in base
♀
♀

A large, bright butterfly that lives in uncultivated areas, often on rocky mountain slopes, up to 2,000 m. The marginal spots on the underside are very faint. The caterpillar lives inside the pods of Bladder senna. *WS:* 36–42 mm; *Flight:* May–June, Aug–Sept; *Gen:* 1–2; *FP:* Bladder senna (*Colutea arborescens*); *D:* Spain, S France, Switz, Italy, Austria, Hungary, Czech, Romania, Greece.

# Grass jewel

## *Freyeria trochylus*

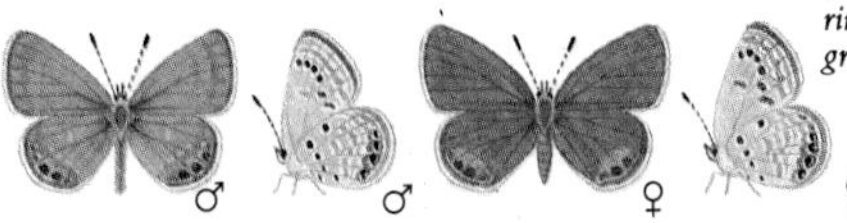
Orange lunules on hwing
♂
♂
♀
♀
Spots on hindwing ringed in green

The European range of the Grass jewel is confined mainly to Greece and the outlying islands, but in Africa and Asia it is far more widespread. The black marginal spots on the underside hindwing gleam rather like jewels when basking in the sun. It flies close to the ground in stony areas with sparse vegetation up to 600 m. *WS:* 16–18 mm; *Flight:* Mar–Sept; *Gen:* 3 or more; *FP:* Heliotrope (*Heliotropium*); *D:* Greece, Crete, Turkey.

# Chequered blue

## *Scolitantides orion*

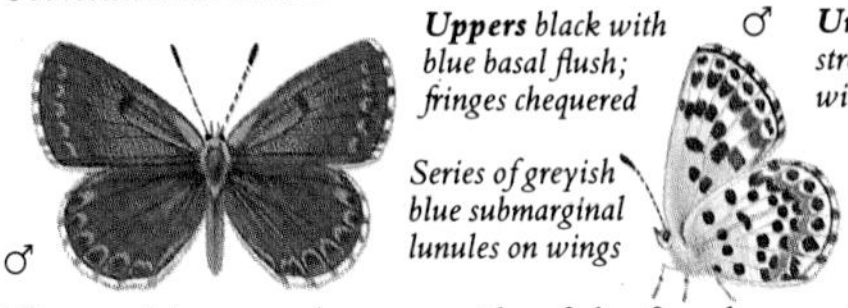
♂
**Uppers** black with blue basal flush; fringes chequered
Series of greyish blue submarginal lunules on wings
♂
**Underside** whitish, strongly patterned with black spots
Orange band on hindwing

The markings on the upperside of the female are often obscured by dark scales but the underside is similar to the male. The subspecies found in southern Europe (*lariana*) is darker, with hardly any blue on the wing. Occurs in small, isolated colonies on rocky ground up to 900 m. *WS:* 26–32 mm; *Flight:* June–July; *Gen:* 1; *FP:* Stonecrop (*Sedum*); *D:* S Scand (not Denmark), E Spain, S and C France, Switz, N Italy, Balkans, Romania, Greece.

# Zephyr blue

## *Plebejus pylaon*

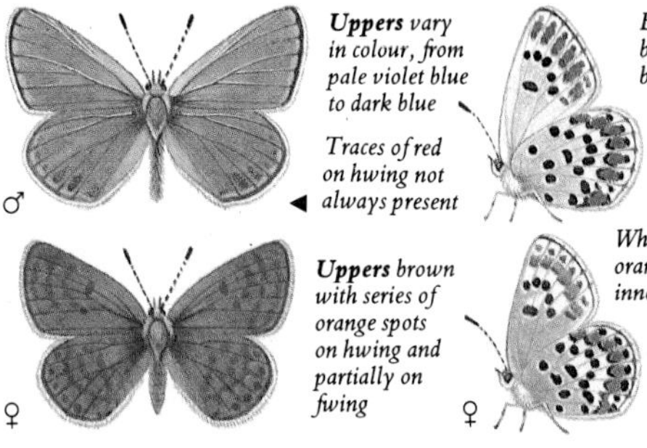
♂
**Uppers** vary in colour, from pale violet blue to dark blue
Traces of red on hwing not always present
Bright orange band across both wings
♂
♀
**Uppers** brown with series of orange spots on hwing and partially on fwing
♀
White area between orange lunules and inner black spots
Black marginal spots lack green centres (cp P. argus)

The various subspecies that have been described differ mainly in shade of blue (male) and presence of orange marginal spots (female) on the upperside. Widely separated colonies occur on grassy slopes from sea level to 1,500 m. *WS:* 28–34 mm; *Flight:* May–July; *Gen:* 1; *FP:* Milk vetch (*Astragalus*); *D:* Spain, N Italy, Switzerland, Bulgaria, Hungary, Albania, Romania, Greece.

# Silver-studded blue

## *Plebejus argus*

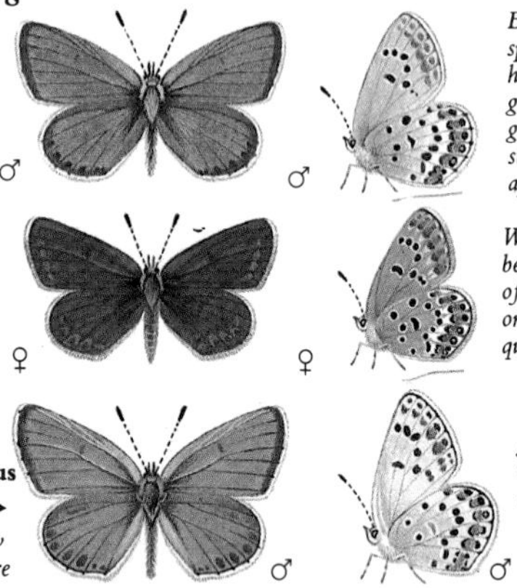
**Uppers** *purplish blue, slightly darker than* P. pylaon ♂
♂
*Black marginal spots on hwing have tiny blue-green centres giving "silver-studded" appearance*
♀ *dark brown with orange lunules (may be absent)* ♀
♀
*White band between 2 rows of black spots on hindwing quite prominent*
**P. argus hypochionus** *from Spain* ▶
*Border narrow where spots are well defined*
♂
**Underside** *greyish white, tinged blue in basal area*
♂

The Silver-studded blue is easily confused with Idas blue and Reverdin's blue, but closer examination will show that it has slightly wider black margins on the upperside. The most reliable character, however, is on the male foreleg, which has a spine on the tibia in the Silver-studded blue, but not in the others. Essentially a heathland butterfly, it will also occur on chalk grassland, and many subspecies have been described. In Britain, where it breeds mainly in the south, one subspecies from Wales (*caernensis*) is smaller and has a different foodplant (Rock rose). *WS:* 24–34 mm; *Flight:* May–Aug; *Gen:* 1–2; *FP:* Gorse (*Ulex*), Broom (*Cytisus*); *D:* Europe (not N Scand, Ireland, Scotland).

# Idas blue

## *Lycaeides idas*

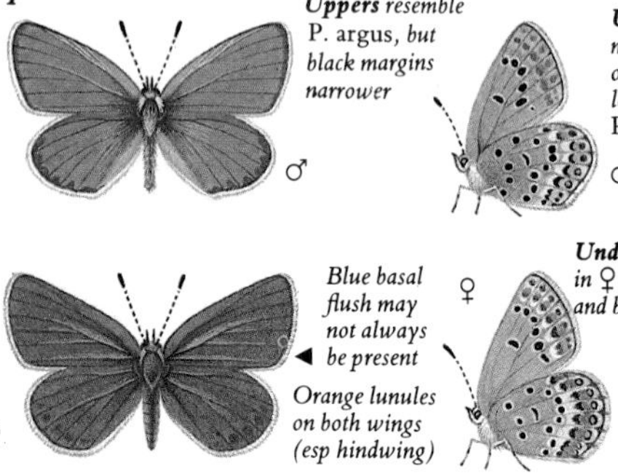
**Uppers** *resemble* P. argus, *but black margins narrower*
♂
**Underside** (♂) *more brownish, orange lunules less clear, than* P. argus
♂
*Blue basal flush may not always* ◀ *be present*
*Orange lunules on both wings (esp hindwing)*
♀
♀
**Underside** *markings in ♀ often larger and brighter than ♂*
*Marginal spots have blue-green centres*

The Idas blue has many subspecies based on differences in size, colour and pattern distributed throughout most of Europe. It may be common on rough ground up to 1,200 m, and is extremely difficult to separate from the Silver-studded blue where the two species fly together. The caterpillar overwinters in an ants' nest. *WS:* 28–34 mm; *Flight:* June–Aug; *Gen:* 2 (1 in N); *FP:* Leguminosae; *D:* Europe (not Britain, Sicily; local in Spain).

# Reverdin's blue

## *L. argyrognomon*

*Clear violet-blue wings, unmarked; resembles* L. idas *but larger*

♂

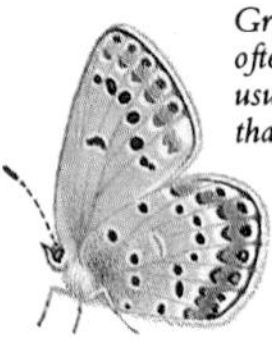

*Ground colour often whitish, usually paler than* L. idas

♂

*Orange lunules absent from fwing in this specimen*

♀

***Hwing*** *black V-shaped spots on inside of orange band gently curved*

♀

The black V-shaped spots on the underside hindwing are more curving in this species than the acutely angled spots of the Idas blue (p 148), but this character is not always easy to see. In rough areas to 1,000 m. *WS:* 28–34 mm; *Flight:* May–Aug; *Gen:* 2; *FP:* Crown vetch (*Coronilla*); *D:* France, C Germany, S Norway, S Sweden, Switz, Austria, Hungary, Romania, Italy, Greece.

# Cranberry blue

## *Vacciniina optilete*

♂

***Uppers*** *deep violet blue with narrow margin*

*♀ dark brown with variable violet tinge*

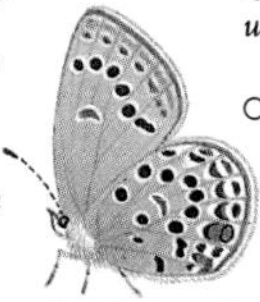

***Underside*** *grey with distinct spots*

♂

*Note red spot with blue scales*

Usually found in the vicinity of its foodplant in marshy and boggy areas on mountain slopes from lowlands to 2,000 m. A local species which is becoming increasingly rare as its habitat diminishes. Smaller specimens with less conspicuous markings occur at higher altitudes. *WS:* 24–30 mm; *Flight:* July; *Gen:* 1; *FP:* Cranberry (*Vaccinium oxycoccus*); *D:* Scand, Baltic states, Holland, Germany, Czechoslovakia, Switz, Yugoslavia.

# Cretan argus

## *Kretania psylorita*

***Uppers*** *brown, small orange spots sometimes absent*

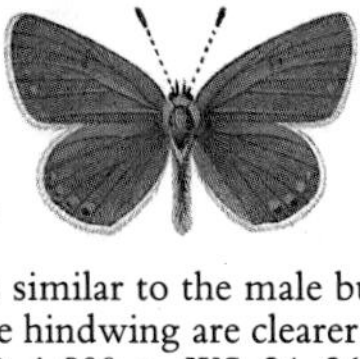

♂

***Underside*** *pale brown with small faint markings*

♂

The female is similar to the male but the marginal spots on both surfaces of the hindwing are clearer. Known only from Mt Ida in Crete at 1,600–1,800 m. *WS:* 24–26 mm; *Flight:* June; *Gen:* 1; *FP:* Milk vetch (*Astragalus*); *D:* Crete.

# Geranium argus

## *Eumedonia eumedon*

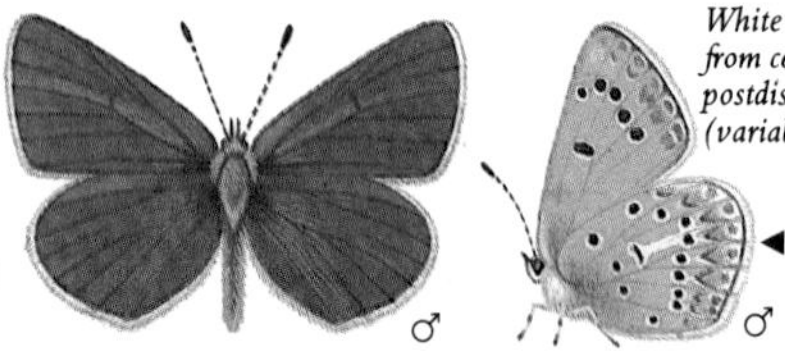
**Uppers** dark brown, unmarked
♀ bigger, with indistinct orange spots on hindwing
White streak from cell to postdiscal spc (variable)
♂
♂

Flies in mountainous areas up to 2,400 m. *WS:* 28–32 mm; *Flight:* June–July; *Gen:* 1; *FP:* Cranesbill (*Geranium*); *D:* Spain, France, Italy, Austria, Germany, Poland, Balkans, Scand (not Denmark).

# Silvery argus

## *Pseudaricia nicias*

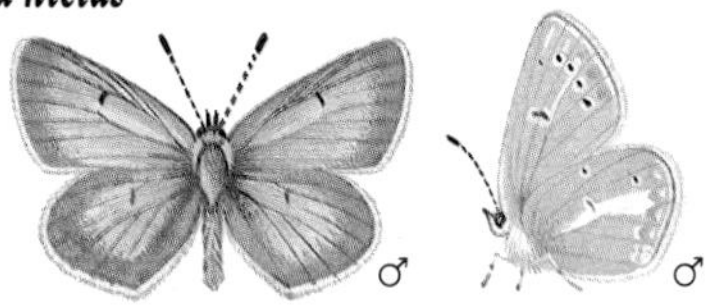
**Uppers** aquamarine with wide brown borders (narrower in northern race)
**Underside** pale grey-brown with small spots; white streak across hwing
♂
♂

The female is brown on the topside with pale brown fringes. On mountains at 800–1,500 m. *WS:* 22–26 mm; *Flight:* July; *Gen:* 1; *FP:* Cranesbill (*Geranium*); *D:* Finland, Sweden, Alps, Pyrenees.

# Blue argus

## *Aricia anteros*

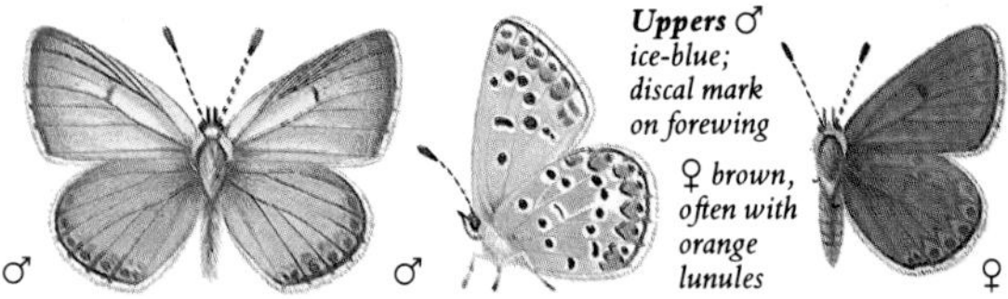
**Uppers** ♂ ice-blue; discal mark on forewing
♀ brown, often with orange lunules
♂
♂
♀

A local species, found on flowery mountain slopes at 900–1,500 m. *WS:* 30–32 mm; *Flight:* June–July; *Gen:* 1; *FP:* unknown; *D:* Bulgaria, Yugoslavia, Greece.

# Spanish argus

## *A. morronensis*

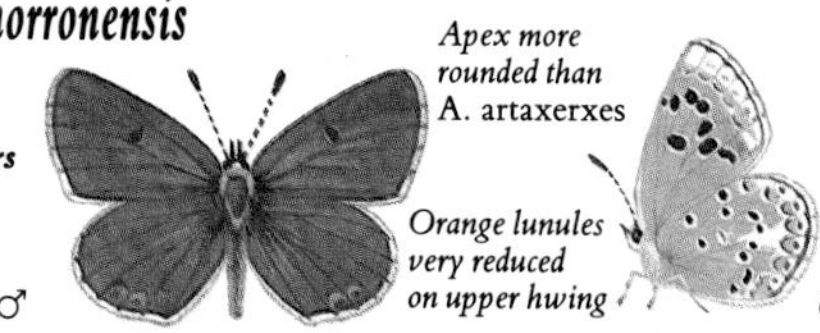
**Uppers** dark brown
Apex more rounded than A. artaxerxes
Orange lunules very reduced on upper hwing
**Underside** orange spots on both wings faint
♂
♂

Differs from the Mountain argus (p 151) in the reduced number of orange lunules on the upperside, and their faintness on the underside. Isolated colonies occur at 900–2,000 m. *WS:* 26–30 mm; *Flight:* July–Aug; *Gen:* 1; *FP:* unknown; *D:* C Spain.

# Brown argus

## A. agestis

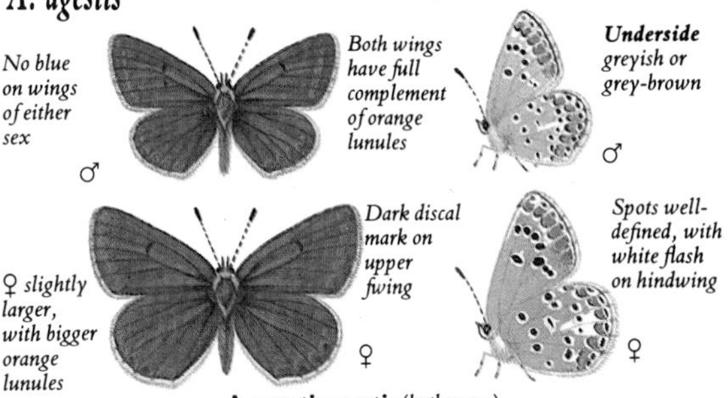
No blue on wings of either sex
♂
Both wings have full complement of orange lunules
**Underside** greyish or grey-brown
♂
♀ slightly larger, with bigger orange lunules
Dark discal mark on upper fwing
♀
Spots well-defined, with white flash on hindwing
♀

**A. agestis agestis** (*both sexes*)

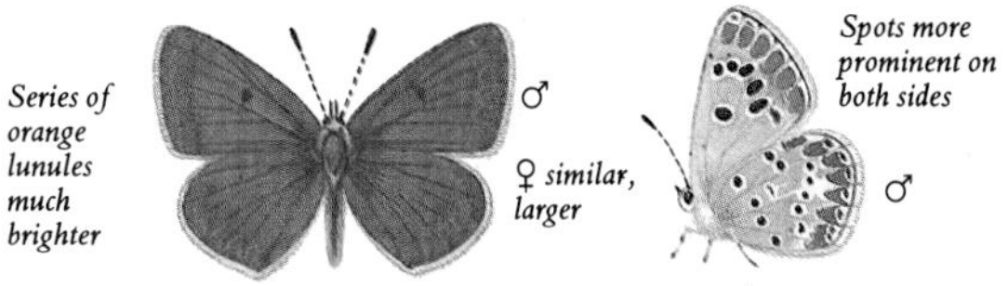
Series of orange lunules much brighter
♂
♀ similar, larger
Spots more prominent on both sides
♂

**A. agestis cramera** from Spain and Portugal

A widespread and common species found throughout most of western and central Europe, including England and Wales. In northern England and Scotland it is replaced by the Mountain (or Scotch) argus, which until 1967 was considered to be a subspecies of *agestis*. The two species are distinguished by the presence of a white discal spot on both sides of the forewing of the Mountain argus, which also has fewer orange marginal spots. The Brown argus is very active in sunny weather, and flies rapidly over heathland and rough grassy areas up to 900 m. It also occurs in sandy coastal regions. In southern Europe there are usually three generations, but further north only two are produced. Overwinters as a caterpillar. *WS:* 22–28 mm; *Flight:* Apr–Aug; *Gen:* 3; *FP:* Rock rose (*Helianthemum*), Storksbill (*Erodium*); *D:* Europe (not Ireland, Scotland, Norway, Finland, Sweden – except S).

# Mountain (or Scotch) argus

## A. artaxerxes

White spot on forewing diagnostic
♂
♂

♂ **A. artaxerxes allous**

The white markings on both wing surfaces are not constant and several subspecies have been described (e.g. *allous*) which are more like the Brown argus. Generally the orange lunules are fewer in the Mountain argus and the black spots on the underside are absent or vestigial. The females tend to be slightly larger with better developed orange spots. In Scotland and northern England it is locally common on moorlands. *WS:* 22–32 mm; *Flight:* June–Aug; *Gen:* 1; *FP:* Rock rose (*Helianthemum*); *D:* Scotland, N England, Scand, Spain, France, Italy, Switz, Austria, E Europe.

# Glandon blue

## *Agriades glandon*

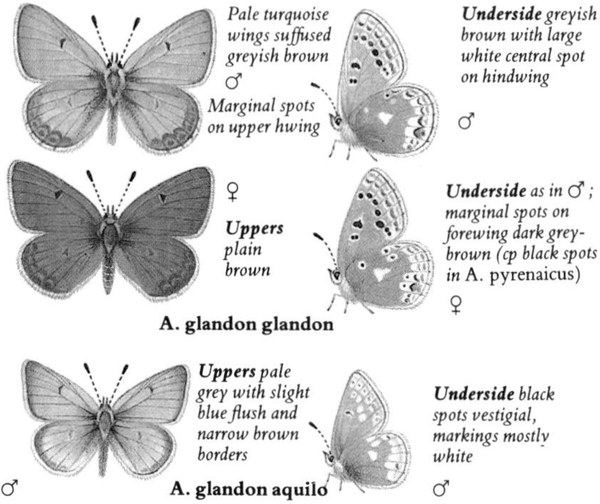
Pale turquoise wings suffused greyish brown
♂
Marginal spots on upper hwing
**Underside** greyish brown with large white central spot on hindwing
♂
♀
**Uppers** plain brown
**Underside** as in ♂; marginal spots on forewing dark grey-brown (cp black spots in A. pyrenaicus)
♀
A. glandon glandon
**Uppers** pale grey with slight blue flush and narrow brown borders
**Underside** black spots vestigial, markings mostly white
♂
A. glandon aquilo
♂

The Glandon blue is very variable and has several subspecies in different parts of Europe. Many lack black spots on the underside hindwing and the white markings may join to form long stripes (as in subsp *aquilo*). Until recently *A. glandon aquilo* was regarded as a distinct species, with a different foodplant (Alpine milk vetch) and a range restricted to the lowlands of Arctic Norway. Other subspecies occur in mountainous areas up to 2,400 m. *WS:* 20–30 mm; *Flight:* June–Aug; *Gen:* 1; *FP:* Primulaceae, esp *Soldanella; D:* Spain (Sierra Nevada, Pyrenees), Alps, N Scand.

# Gavarnie blue

## *A. pyrenaicus*

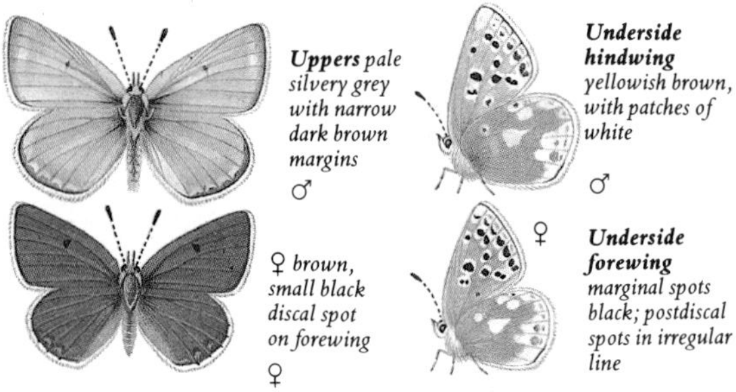
**Uppers** pale silvery grey with narrow dark brown margins
♂
**Underside hindwing** yellowish brown, with patches of white
♂
♀
♀ brown, small black discal spot on forewing
♀
**Underside forewing** marginal spots black; postdiscal spots in irregular line

Resembles the Glandon blue, and is distinguished in the male by its pale silvery topside with narrow dark margins. The female is identified by the black marginal spots on the underside forewing (present in both sexes). There are several subspecies which occur in widely separated colonies on mountains above 1,500 m. *WS:* 22–28 mm; *Flight:* July; *Gen:* 1; *FP:* Androsace (*Androsace villosa*); *D:* Spain (Pyrenees, Cantabrians), Yugoslavia, Turkey.

# Alpine argus

## *Abulina orbitulus*

*Gleaming sapphire-blue wings with narrow black borders*

♂

♂

***Underside*** *marginal spots obscure;* ***fwing*** *spots reduced, or absent*

*White marks lack black centres*

There are two distinct populations of this species in Europe: the southern race lives in Alpine meadows above 1,700 m, while the northern race flies at 900–1,200 m. The female is mainly brown, often tinged blue at the wing base. *WS:* 24–28 mm; *Flight:* July–Aug; *Gen:* 1; *FP:* Milk vetch (*Astragalus alpinus, A. frigidus*); *D:* Alps, C Norway, C Sweden.

# Mazarine blue

## *Cyaniris semiargus*

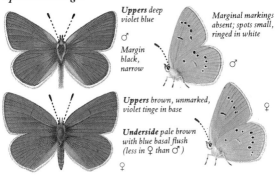

***Uppers*** *deep violet blue*

♂

*Margin black, narrow*

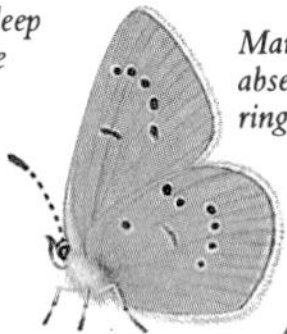

*Marginal markings absent; spots small, ringed in white*

♂

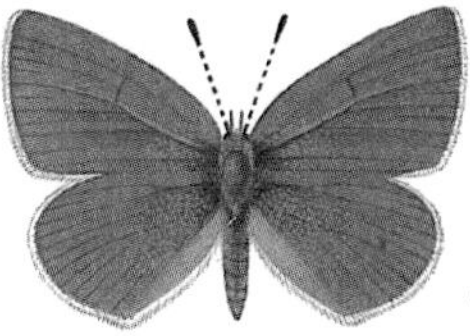

***Uppers*** *brown, unmarked, violet tinge in base*

***Underside*** *pale brown with blue basal flush (less in ♀ than ♂)*

♀

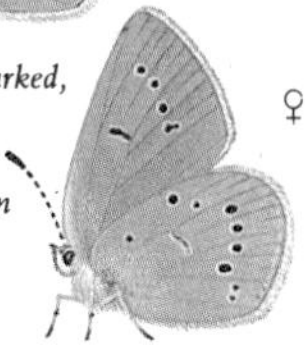

♀

The Mazarine blue has a slow, almost clumsy, flight, usually low over the ground. Found in rough, flowery meadows, often near coasts, up to 1,800 m. A rare migrant to Britain, but widespread on the mainland of Europe. Groups of males may occasionally be seen feeding at damp patches on paths. *WS:* 28–34 mm; *Flight:* June–Aug; *Gen:* 1; *FP:* Clover (*Trifolium*), Kidney vetch (*Anthyllis*); *D:* Europe (not N Scand; migrant to Britain).

# Greek mazarine blue

## *C. helena*

***Uppers*** *deep violet-blue, like* C. semiargus *but smaller*

♂

***Underside*** *pale brown with orange lunules on hindwing*

♂

A very local and uncommon species that is sometimes ranked as a subspecies of the Mazarine blue. The distinctive orange lunules on the underside hindwing may be faintly visible on the upper surface. On mountains at 1,200–1,500 m. *WS:* 26–28 mm; *Flight:* June–July; *Gen:* 1; *FP:* Clover (*Trifolium*); *D:* N Greece.

# Damon blue

## *Agrodiaetus damon*

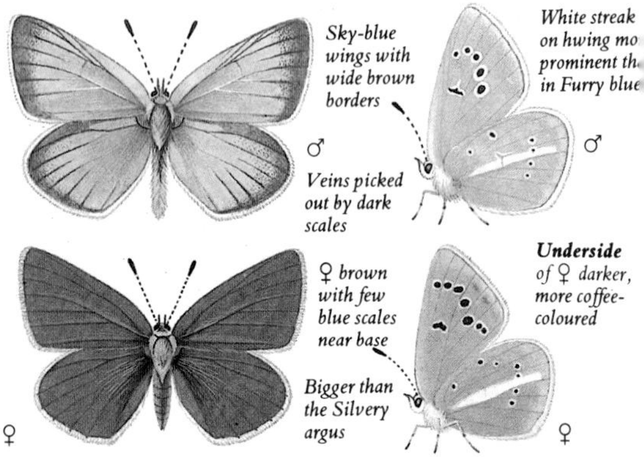
Sky-blue wings with wide brown borders
♂
Veins picked out by dark scales
White streak on hwing mo
prominent th
in Furry blue
♂
♀ brown with few blue scales near base
Bigger than the Silvery argus
♀
Underside of ♀ darker, more coffee-coloured
♀

The Damon blue occurs in scattered colonies on grassy slopes up to 2,200 m. The caterpillars are attended by ants (see Large blue, p 144). *WS:* 30–34 mm; *Flight:* July–Aug; *Gen:* 1; *FP:* Sainfoin (*Onobrychis*); *D:* Spain, France, Italy, Germany, Balkans, Greece.

# Furry blue

## *A. dolus*

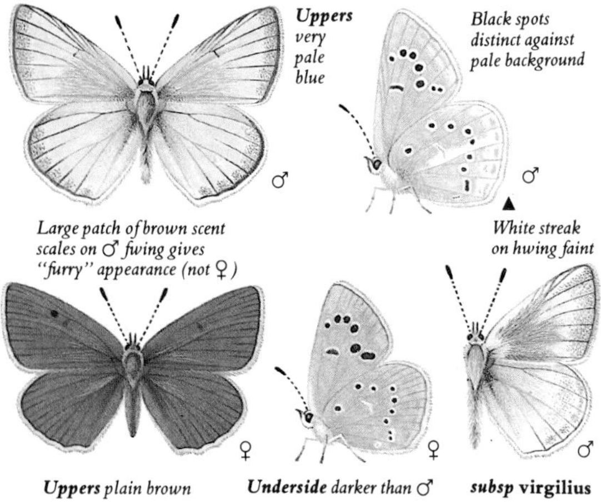
Uppers very pale blue
♂
Black spots distinct against pale background
♂
Large patch of brown scent scales on ♂ fwing gives "furry" appearance (not ♀)
White streak on hwing faint
♀
♀
♂
Uppers plain brown
Underside darker than ♂
subsp virgilius

Many species of *Agrodiaetus* are difficult to distinguish, and the Furry blue, with its various subspecies, is no exception. *A. dolus virgilius*, from Italy, is more greyish white with dark veins and a slight blue basal flush. The white streak on the underside may be absent in some specimens. *WS:* 32–38 mm; *Flight:* July–Aug; *Gen:* 1; *FP:* Sainfoin (*Onobrychis*); *D:* N Spain, S France, C Italy. ***A. ainsae*** (Forster's furry blue) is similar but smaller. *WS:* 30–32 mm; *Flight, Gen, FP:* as for *A. dolus; D:* N Spain.

## Anomalous blue

### *A. admetus*

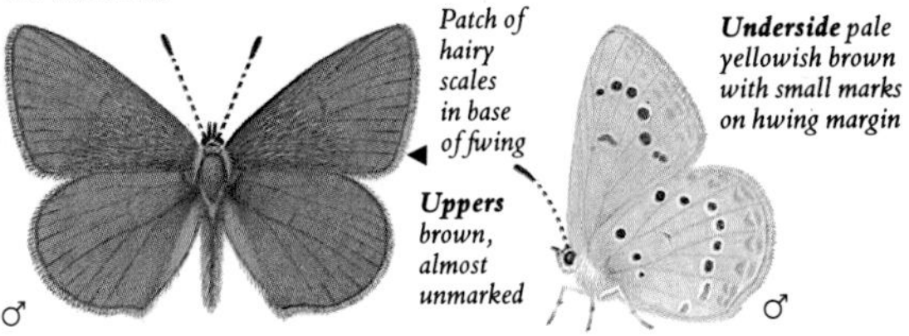
Patch of hairy scales in base of fwing
Underside pale yellowish brown with small marks on hwing margin
Uppers brown, almost unmarked
♂
♂

Isolated colonies occur in rocky areas, often at low altitudes. *WS:* 30–38 mm; *Flight:* June–July; *Gen:* 1; *FP:* Sainfoin (*Onobrychis*); *D:* Romania, Czech, Hungary, Bulgaria, Yugoslavia, Greece.

## Oberthur's anomalous blue

### *A. fabressei*

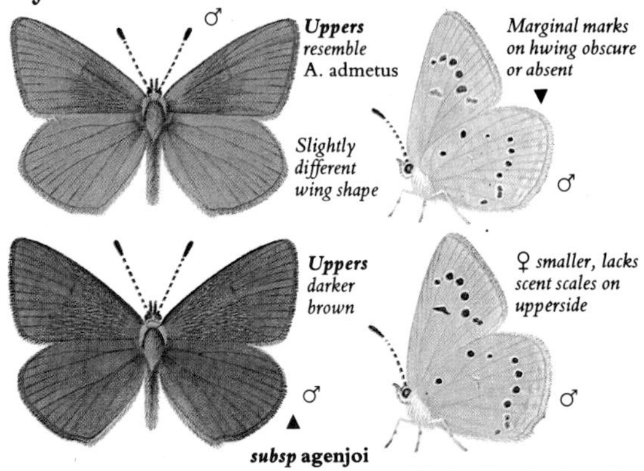
♂
Uppers resemble A. admetus
Marginal marks on hwing obscure or absent
Slightly different wing shape
♂
Uppers darker brown
♀ smaller, lacks scent scales on upperside
♂
♂
subsp agenjoi

Both subspecies occur in Spain in small, local colonies; the nominate subspecies (top) prefers hot mountainous areas, while *A. fabressei agenjoi* flies in grassy lowlands. *WS:* 30–36 mm; *Flight:* June–Aug; *Gen:* 1; *FP:* unknown; *D:* Spain.

## Ripart's anomalous blue

### *A. ripartii*

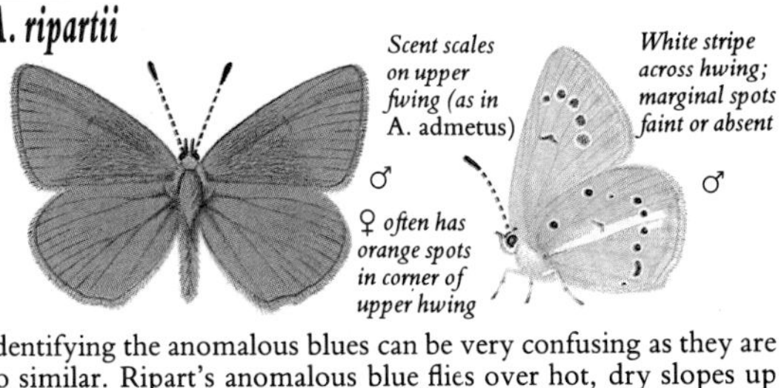
Scent scales on upper fwing (as in A. admetus)
White stripe across hwing; marginal spots faint or absent
♂
♂
♀ often has orange spots in corner of upper hwing

Identifying the anomalous blues can be very confusing as they are so similar. Ripart's anomalous blue flies over hot, dry slopes up to 900 m. *WS:* 28–34 mm; *Flight:* July–Aug; *Gen:* 1; *FP:* Sainfoin (*Onobrychis*); *D:* N Spain, S France, Italy, Bulgaria, Yugoslavia.

# Escher's blue

## *Agrodiaetus escheri*

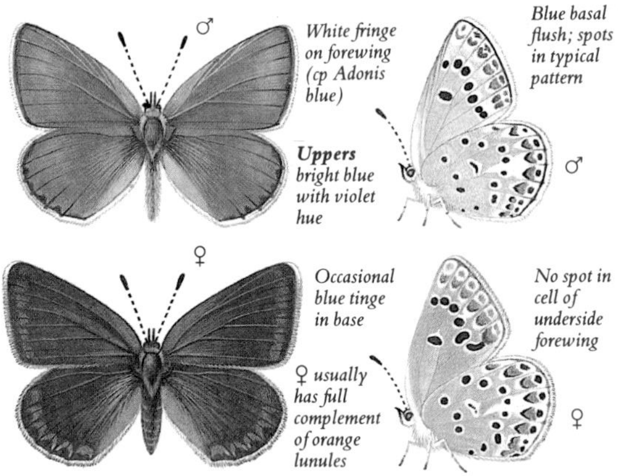

♂
*White fringe on forewing (cp Adonis blue)*
*Blue basal flush; spots in typical pattern*
***Uppers** bright blue with violet hue*
♂
♀
*Occasional blue tinge in base*
*No spot in cell of underside forewing*
*♀ usually has full complement of orange lunules*
♀


A bright butterfly with many subspecies which vary from deep sky-blue to pale silvery blue; may be confused with Adonis blue (p 160). Occurs locally on stony slopes up to 2,000 m. *WS:* 34–40 mm; *Flight:* June–July; *Gen:* 1; *FP:* Milk vetch (*Astragalus*); *D:* Spain, Portugal, France, Switz, Italy, Yugoslavia, Greece.

# Chelmos blue

## *A. iphigenia*

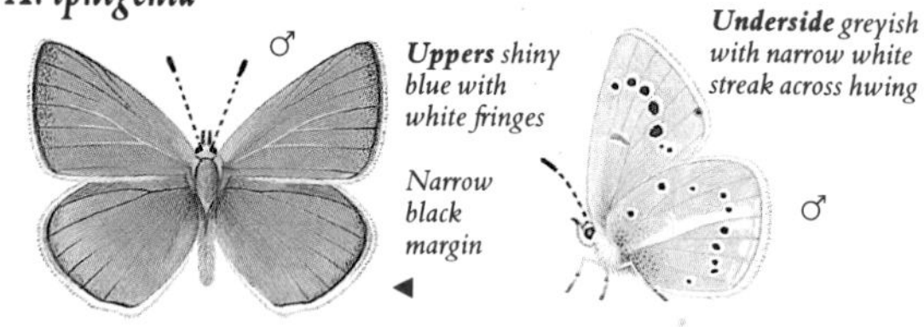

♂
***Uppers** shiny blue with white fringes*
***Underside** greyish with narrow white streak across hwing*
*Narrow black margin*
♂


The female is plain brown on the upperside. Known only from Mt Chelmos, on rough slopes at 500–1,500 m. *WS:* 28–32 mm; *Flight:* July; *Gen:* 1; *FP:* unknown; *D:* S Greece.

# Chapman's blue

## *A. thersites*

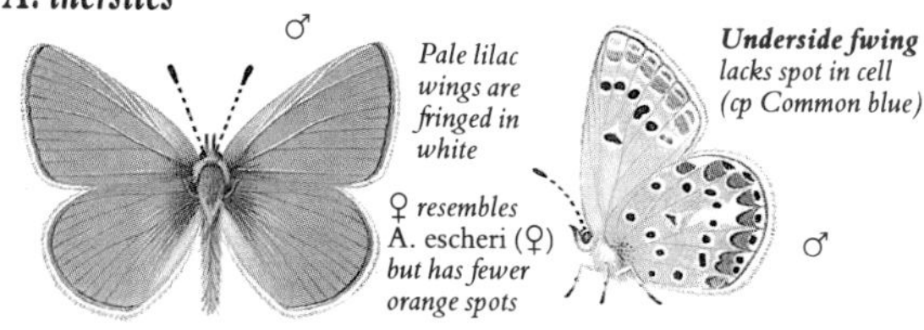

♂
*Pale lilac wings are fringed in white*
***Underside fwing** lacks spot in cell (cp Common blue)*
*♀ resembles* A. escheri (♀) *but has fewer orange spots*
♂


Widespread but local; in meadows to 1,500 m. Easily mistaken for the Common blue (p 161). *WS:* 26–32 mm; *Flight:* May–Sept; *Gen:* 2–3; *FP:* Sainfoin (*Onobrychis*); *D:* S Europe (to 50° N).

## Grecian anomalous blue

### *A. aroaniensis*

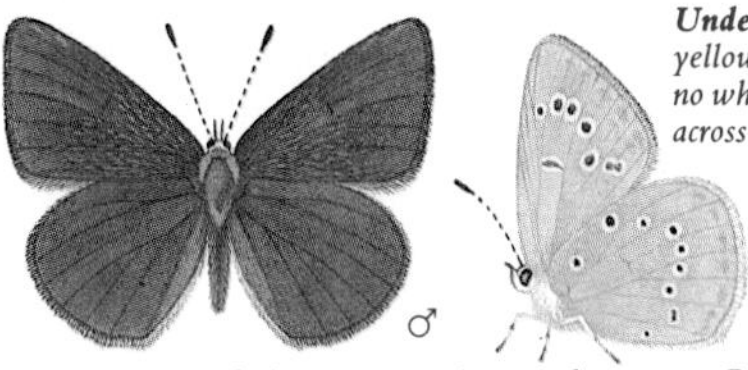
**Uppers** *dark brown, similar to* A. fabressei agenjoi
**Underside** *pale yellowish brown; no white stripe across hindwing*
♂
♂

The exact distribution of this species is not known. Occurs at 700–1,800 m. *WS:* 28–32 mm; *Flight:* July–Aug; *Gen:* 1; *FP:* unknown; *D:* Greece, N Italy (subsp *humedasae*).

## Chestnut anomalous blue

### *A. pelopi*

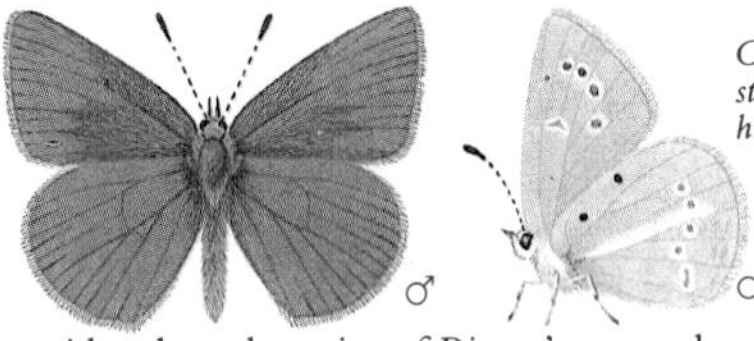
**Uppers** *brown, virtually unmarked*
*Clear white stripe across hindwing*
♂
♂

Formerly considered a subspecies of Ripart's anomalous blue (p 155). Flies over stony hill slopes. *WS:* 30–34 mm; *Flight:* July–Aug; *Gen:* 1; *FP:* probably Sainfoin (*Onobrychis*); *D:* Greece.

## Pontic blue

### *A. coelestinus*

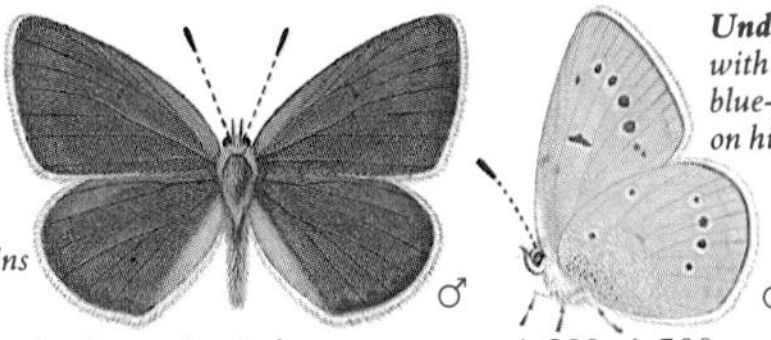
**Uppers** *deep blue with wide black margins*
**Underside** *grey, with extensive blue-green flush on hindwing*
♂
♂

Known only from the Peloponnesus at 1,200–1,500 m. *WS:* 22–26 mm; *Flight:* June; *Gen:* 1; *FP:* Vetch (*Vicia*); *D:* Greece.

## Higgins anomalous blue

### *A. nephophiptamenos*

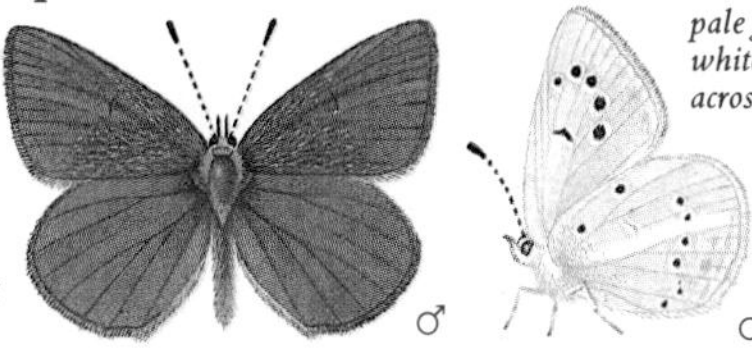
*Dark brown wings have a yellowish sheen*
*Active in low cloud and mist*
**Underside** *very pale grey, with white streak across hindwing*
*Occurs at 1,600–2,000 m*
♂
♂

*WS:* 28–34 mm; *Flight:* July; *Gen:* 1; *FP:* unknown; *D:* N Greece.

# Amanda's blue

## *Agrodiaetus amanda*

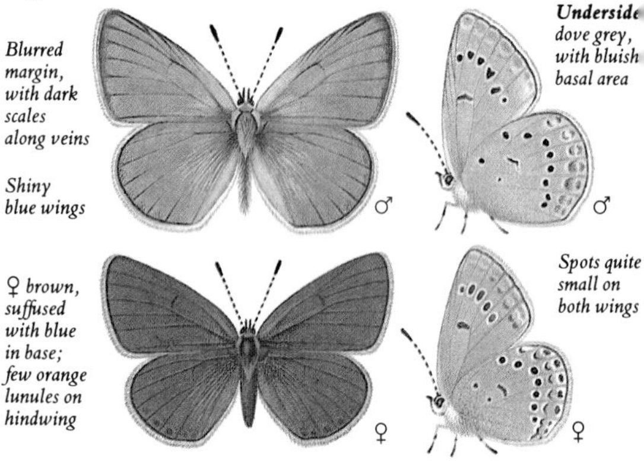

**Underside** dove grey, with bluish basal area
Blurred margin, with dark scales along veins
Shiny blue wings
♂
♂
Spots quite small on both wings
♀ brown, suffused with blue in base; few orange lunules on hindwing
♀
♀


Once fairly common, Amanda's blue is now quite rare. Females from Scandinavia often have more blue on their wings. On moors and boggy hillsides up to 1,500 m. *WS:* 32–38 mm; *Flight:* June–July; *Gen:* 1; *FP:* Tufted vetch (*Vicia cracca*); *D:* Europe (not Britain, Norway, N Sweden, N and W France, Holland, Belgium).

# Turquoise blue

## *Plebicula dorylas*

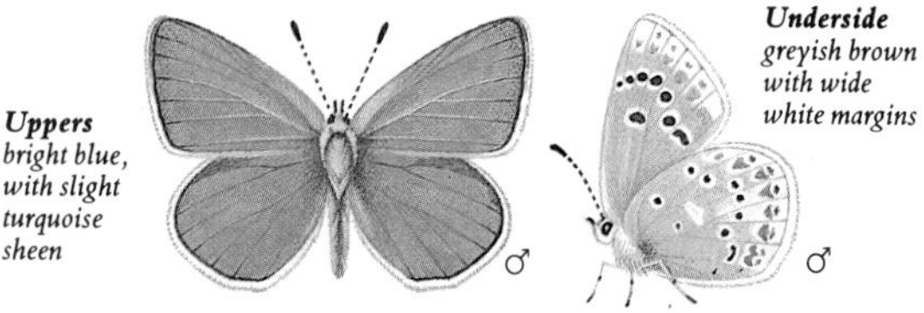

**Underside** greyish brown with wide white margins
**Uppers** bright blue, with slight turquoise sheen
♂
♂


Local in pastures and sandy areas at 900–1,500 m. *WS:* 30–34 mm; *Flight:* May–Sept; *Gen:* 2; *FP:* Leguminosae; *D:* S, C Europe. **P. golgus** (Nevada blue) is smaller and deeper in colour. *WS:* 26–30 mm; *Flight:* July; *Gen:* 1; *FP:* unknown; *D:* Spain.

# Mother-of-pearl blue

## *P. nivescens*

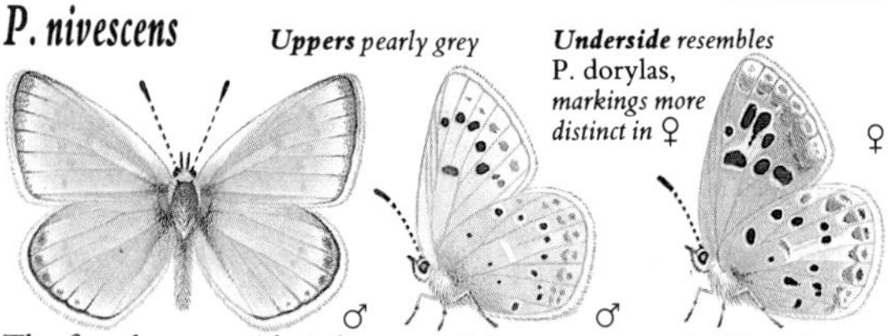

**Uppers** pearly grey
**Underside** resembles P. dorylas, markings more distinct in ♀
♀
♂
♂


The female upperside is brown with orange marginal lunules on both wings. A local species found on mountains from 900 to 1,800 m. *WS:* 30–36 mm; *Flight:* June–July; *Gen:* 1; *FP:* unknown; *D:* Spain.

# Meleager's blue

## *Meleageria daphnis*

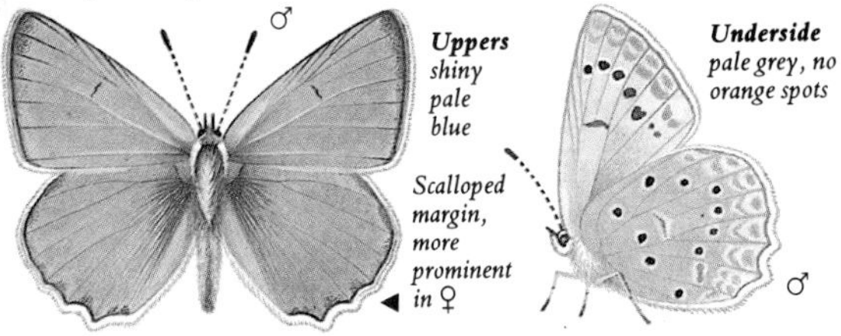
♂
**Uppers** shiny pale blue
Scalloped margin, more prominent in ♀
**Underside** pale grey, no orange spots
♂

Widespread but local on dry hill slopes up to 1,500 m. *WS:* 36–38 mm; *Flight:* June–July; *Gen:* 1; *FP:* Milk vetch (*Astragalus*); *D:* NE Spain, S France, Italy, Sicily, Switzerland, E Europe.

# Chalk-hill blue

## *Lysandra coridon*

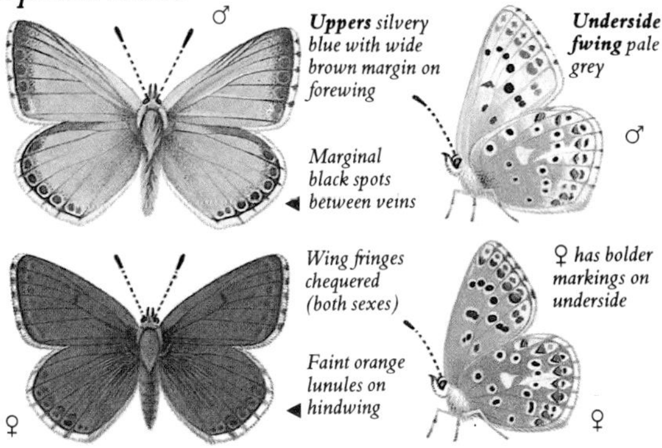
♂
**Uppers** silvery blue with wide brown margin on forewing
Marginal black spots between veins
**Underside fwing** pale grey
♂
Wing fringes chequered (both sexes)
Faint orange lunules on hindwing
♀ has bolder markings on underside
♀
♀

The blue colour is variable and many varieties have been named. In Britain it used to be found in large numbers in the south, but it is now less common. The caterpillar is often attended by ants. *WS:* 30–36 mm; *Flight:* July–Aug; *Gen:* 1; *FP:* Horseshoe vetch (*Hippocrepis comosa*); *D:* Europe (not Scand, S Spain, Portugal).

# Provence chalk-hill blue

## *L. hispana*

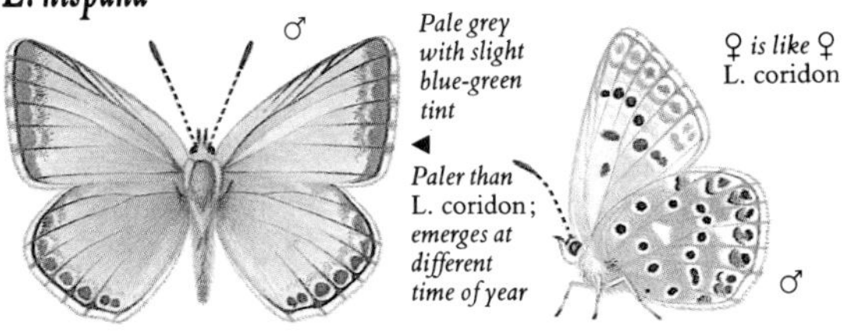
♂
Pale grey with slight blue-green tint
Paler than L. coridon; emerges at different time of year
♀ is like ♀ L. coridon
♂

On grassy slopes not above 900 m. *WS:* 32–36 mm; *Flight:* Apr–May, Sept; *Gen:* 2; *FP:* unknown; *D:* NE Spain, S France, N Italy.

## Spanish chalk-hill blue

### *Lysandra albicans*

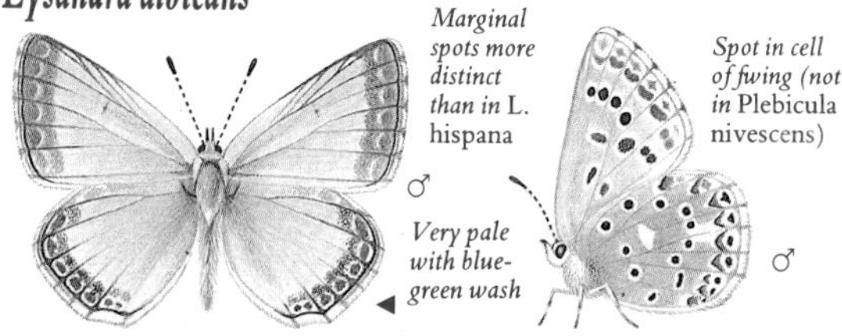
Marginal spots more distinct than in L. hispana
Spot in cell of fwing (not in Plebicula nivescens)
♂
Very pale with blue-green wash
♂

On sunny slopes from 900 to 1,500 m; specimens from lower altitudes are often paler than those which fly higher up. The female is brown with orange marginal spots on both wings. *WS:* 36–42 mm; *Flight:* June–Aug; *Gen:* 1; *FP:* unknown; *D:* Spain (not W).

## Adonis blue

### *L. bellargus*

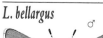

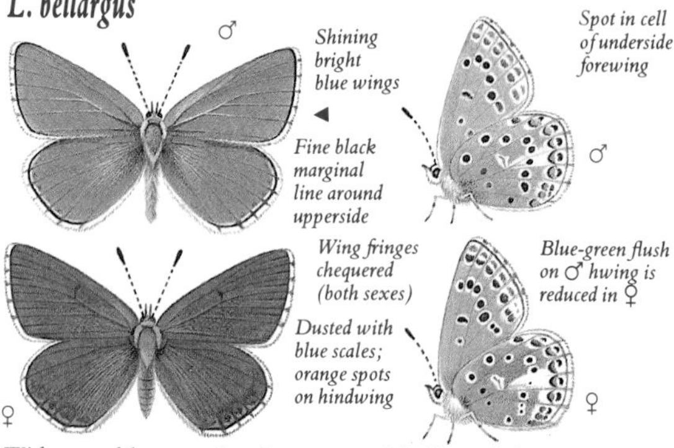
♂
Shining bright blue wings
Spot in cell of underside forewing
Fine black marginal line around upperside
♂
Wing fringes chequered (both sexes)
Blue-green flush on ♂ hwing is reduced in ♀
Dusted with blue scales; orange spots on hindwing
♀
♀

Widespread but restricted to areas of chalky soil (to 2,000 m); in Britain, small colonies of the Adonis blue occur very locally in the south. May be mistaken for the Common blue (p 161) in the field, but the shiny blue colour of the male is distinctive. The caterpillar is active at night and visited by ants. *WS:* 28–34 mm; *Flight:* May–June, Aug–Sept; *Gen:* 2; *FP:* Horseshoe vetch (*Hippocrepis comosa*); *D:* Europe (not Ireland, Scotland, Scand).

## Macedonian blue

### *L. philippi*

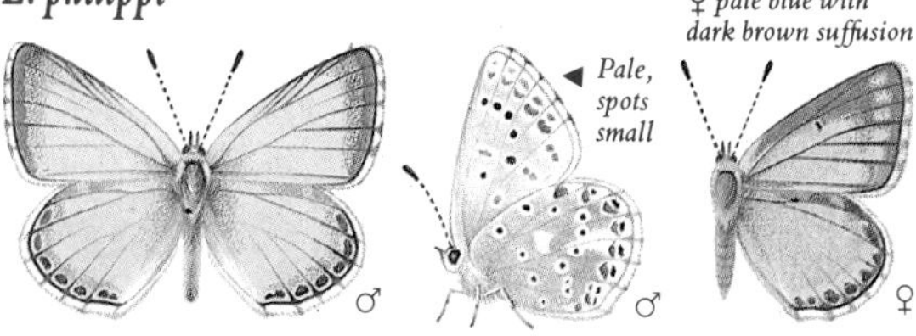
♀ pale blue with dark brown suffusion
Pale, spots small
♂
♂
♀

Not a great deal of information is available on this species. Flies up to and above the tree line at 700–1,000 m. *WS:* 30–38 mm; *Flight:* July; *Gen:* 1; *FP:* unknown; *D:* NE Greece.

# Eugene's blue

## Polyommatus menelaos

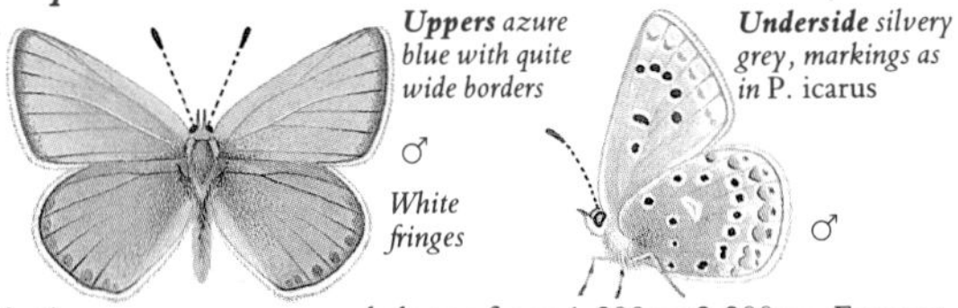
**Uppers** azure blue with quite wide borders
♂
White fringes
**Underside** silvery grey, markings as in P. icarus
♂

Active over scree-covered slopes from 1,200 to 2,200 m. Formerly considered a subspecies of the Eros blue. *WS:* 27–34 mm; *Flight:* June–July; *FP:* Milk vetch (*Astragalus*); *D:* S Greece.

# Common blue

## P. icarus

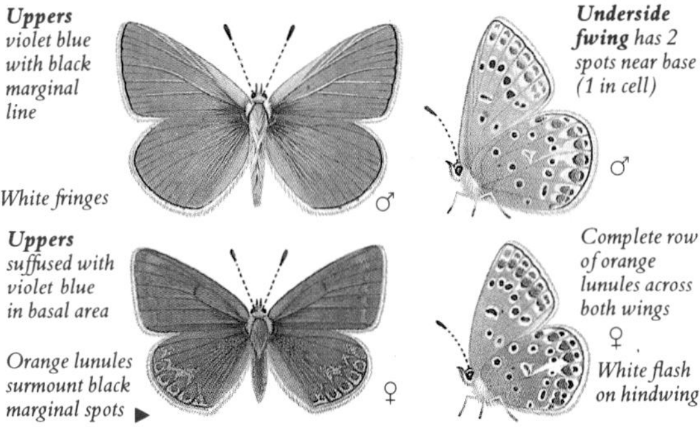
**Uppers** violet blue with black marginal line
White fringes
♂
**Underside fwing** has 2 spots near base (1 in cell)
♂
**Uppers** suffused with violet blue in basal area
Orange lunules surmount black marginal spots
♀
Complete row of orange lunules across both wings
♀
White flash on hindwing

One of the commonest and most widespread of butterflies, found in most open grassy places from sea level up to 1,800 m, including urban parks and gardens. The butterfly is prone to variation and individuals may be found which have slightly different markings on the underside. Specimens from late broods also tend to be smaller and paler. The caterpillar feeds on the underside of leaves. *WS:* 28–36 mm; *Flight:* Apr–Sept; *Gen:* 3 (1 in N); *FP:* Leguminosae, esp Clover (*Trifolium*); *D:* Europe.

# Eros blue

## P. eros

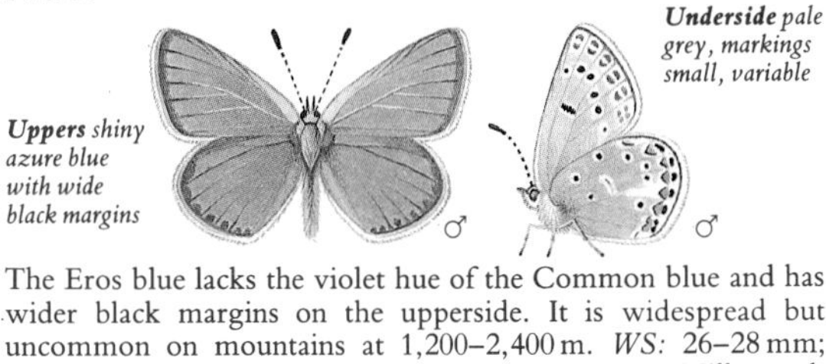
**Underside** pale grey, markings small, variable
**Uppers** shiny azure blue with wide black margins
♂
♂

The Eros blue lacks the violet hue of the Common blue and has wider black margins on the upperside. It is widespread but uncommon on mountains at 1,200–2,400 m. *WS:* 26–28 mm; *Flight:* July–Aug; *Gen:* 1; *FP:* Leguminosae, esp Milk vetch (*Astragalus*); *D:* Pyrenees, Alps, Apennines, Balkans.

# False eros blue

## *Polyommatus eroides*

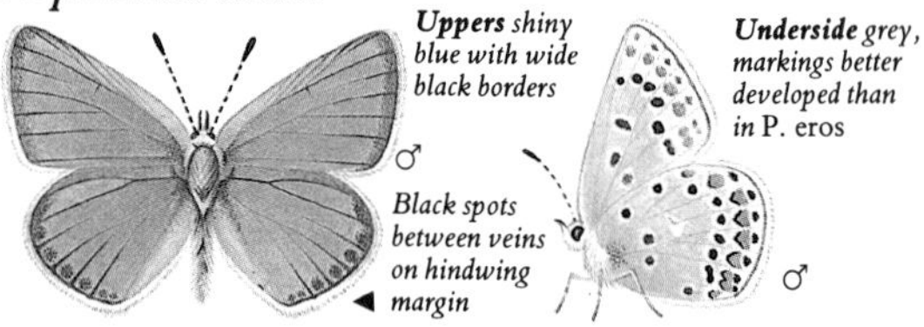
***Uppers*** *shiny blue with wide black borders*
♂
*Black spots between veins on hindwing margin*
***Underside*** *grey, markings better developed than in* P. eros
♂

The upperside of the female is grey-brown with variable orange markings and usually lacks any blue scales. This species is very local and occurs on mountain slopes from 1,200 to 1,800 m. *WS:* 30–36 mm; *Flight:* June–July; *Gen:* 1; *FP:* unknown; *D:* E Germany, Czechoslovakia, Albania, Bulgaria, N Greece.

# Day-flying moths

While most moths fly by night, there are many species which are active during the day. In fact, in Britain there are probably more day-flying moths than there are butterflies. The structure of a moth is not that different from a butterfly, but it may vary quite considerably, as shown in the selection below. Moths tend to have thin or feathery (pectinate) antennae, never clubbed ones as in butterflies, although in the burnet moths they are slightly thickened towards the apex. They also have a linkage between the fore- and hindwings, and the wing venation is different. Many day-flying moths are brightly coloured, and while most moths will fly in the day if disturbed, those shown here (with the exception of the restless Cinnabar) actively seek the sunshine.

**Six-spot burnet**
***Zygaena filipendulae***

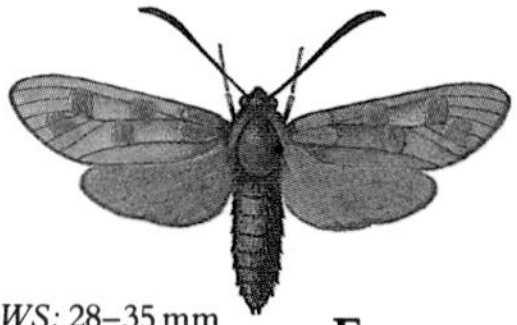

*WS:* 28–35 mm

**Netted mountain moth**
***Semiothisa carbonaria***

*WS:* 20–21 mm

**Emperor moth**
***Saturnia pavonia***

*WS:* 50–80 mm

**Orange underwing**
*Archiearis parthenias*

*WS:* 33–35 mm

**Burnet companion**
*Euclida glyphica*

*WS:* 26–31 mm

**Beautiful yellow underwing**
*Anarta myrtilli*

*WS:* 22–25 mm

**Hummingbird hawk-moth**
*Macroglossum stellatarum*

*WS:* 45–51 mm

**Frosted yellow**
*Isturgia limbaria*
*WS:* 23–26 mm

**Syntomid moth**
*Syntomis phegea*

*WS:* 28–38 mm

**Latticed heath**
*Semiothisa clathrata*

*WS:* 22–26 mm

**Chimney sweeper**
*Odezia atrata*

*WS:* 23–26 mm

**Kentish glory**
*Endromis versicolora*

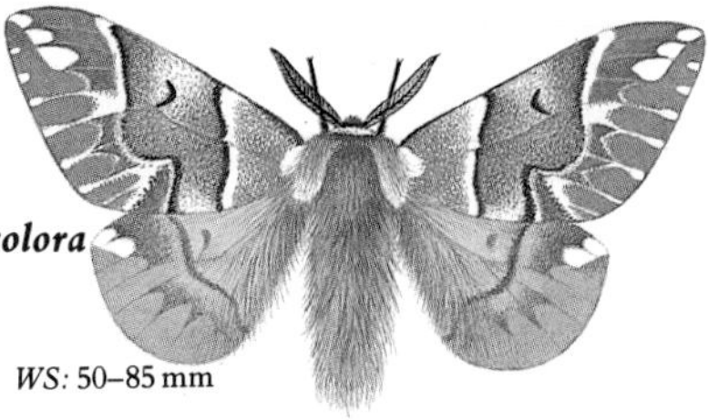

*WS:* 50–85 mm

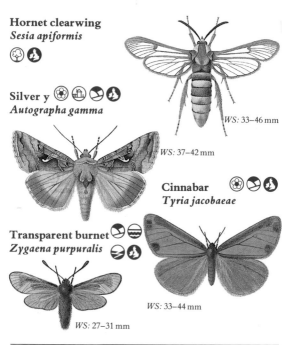

**Hornet clearwing**
***Sesia apiformis***

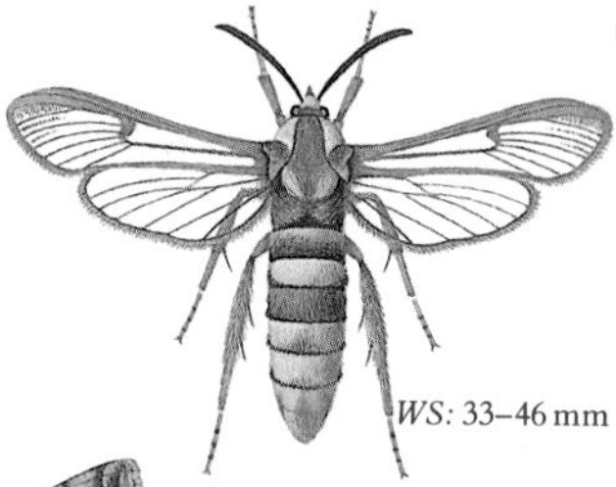

*WS:* 33–46 mm

**Silver y**
***Autographa gamma***

*WS:* 37–42 mm

**Cinnabar**
***Tyria jacobaeae***

*WS:* 33–44 mm

**Transparent burnet**
***Zygaena purpuralis***

*WS:* 27–31 mm

---

# References


*A Field Guide to the Butterflies of Britain and Europe* L. G. Higgins and N. D. Riley, Collins, London, 1980

*British Butterflies, A Field Guide* Robert Goodden, David and Charles, Newton Abbot, 1978

*The Classification of European Butterflies* L. G. Higgins, Collins, London, 1975

*South's British Butterflies* T. G. Howarth, Warne, London, 1973

*Butterflies in Colour* L. Lyneborg, Blandford Press, London, 1974

*Butterfly Watching* Paul Whalley, Severn House, London, 1980

*Hamlyn Nature Guide, Butterflies* Paul Whalley, Hamlyn, London, 1979

*The Observer's Book of Caterpillars* David J. Carter, Warne, London, 1979

*Wild Flowers of Britain and Northern Europe* R. G. Fitter, A. Fitter and M. Blamey, Collins, London, 1974

*The Concise Flowers of Europe* Oleg Polunin, Warne, London, 1979


# Acknowledgements


The author would like to express his thanks to Richard Lewington not only for his beautiful illustrations, but also for his assistance in selecting specimens. He would also like to thank the following people and organizations for their help:

Dr L. G. Higgins and the late Mr N. D. Riley, for advice on the systematic arrangement of European butterflies;

Dr John Brown, for advice and loan of specimens;

Dr Paul Freeman and the Trustees of the British Museum (Natural History) for loan of specimens (from which the majority of species were illustrated);

Mr C. A. Sizer and Mr B. R. Baker of the Reading Museum and Art Gallery, for advice and loan of specimens;

Michele Staple and Hazel West of Mitchell Beazley, for patient co-operation during the preparation of this book.

# Index

There is still some disagreement amongst specialists about the correct generic position of some of the European butterflies. The most recently accepted combinations of generic and specific names are used in this index.